What advance readers are saying about
Just Between You and Me

DEANE CAMERON, President and CEO, The Corporation of Massey Hall and Roy Thomson Hall, former President, EMI Music Canada, Member of the Order of Canada

"Wow, what a book! So honest, lots of detail, and a great read. Myles Goodwyn is a powerful songwriter, singer, and musician. He is a respected survivor of the turbulent music industry, while being a loved and admired Canadian. He is a wonderful man with a generous heart and impressive soul. He embraces the truths of life. I know so very many artists and musicians from around the globe who respect Myles and list him as an influence in their music careers. Myles, I salute you, thank you, and will forever admire your talents as an artist and a man!"

FRANK DAVIES, President, Let Me Be Frank Inc., founder of the Canadian Songwriters Hall of Fame

"As one of Canada's foremost rock songwriters of the past forty-plus years, Myles Goodwyn clearly demonstrates a unique talent for writing undeniable hooks and timely and accessible lyrics, and the wherewithal to make some great records with his Juno Hall of Fame band April Wine."

PAUL DEAN, lead guitarist for LOVERBOY

"Born in 1946, I have two years on Myles. I swear, so much of this could be my story, too. So many parallels, the same memories, only the names have changed. This book is a great trigger, a catalyst. It brought so much of my life back to me, stuff that otherwise probably would've been gone forever. Thanks, Myles!"

BARRY STOCK, lead guitarist for THREE DAYS GRACE

"Prior to my success with Three Days Grace, I was offered the position of guitar tech with April Wine, and I was thrilled, to say the least, as I had grown up a huge fan. Through those years I became great friends with Myles, and I have always felt blessed to hear his stories. In these pages, Myles talks about his childhood, his struggles, and the history of one of the greatest Canadian rock bands, April Wine. This is a fantastic read!"

JEFF STINCO, Juno Award–winning recording artist, guitarist for SIMPLE PLAN

"Myles Goodwyn's great songs and punishing guitar assault on the radio forged my musical tastes as I was growing up, and yet, there's always been an aura of mystery around April Wine. This is a great story filled with colourful anecdotes on how it was to be a successful Canadian musician in the '70s and early '80s, and how it is today."

ROBB REINER, drummer for ANVIL, subject of the documentary *Anvil!*, named by *The Times* (UK) as "possibly the greatest film yet made about rock 'n' roll"

"The iconic, real rock voice of legendary Canadian hard music band April Wine, songwriter Myles Goodwyn has always had the magic with his songs, in my humble view, creating a legacy of timeless, unforgettable music that remains relevant to this day forward. Finally, the whole story (and what a story!) detailing what really happened. Thank you for all the amazing music, my friend."

KIM MITCHELL, singer/songwriter, performer, and radio personality

"Being onstage is the easy part. If you dare, let Myles walk ya through the rest."

JIM HENMAN, singer, songwriter, and original member of APRIL WINE

"After a friendship of more than five decades, I thought I knew Myles Goodwyn. That is, until I read *Just Between You and Me*. The up-close-and-personal writing style of his memoir make it an easy, entertaining, and revealing read."

SASS JORDAN, Juno Award–winning singer and performer

"Myles is a bona fide enigma—part guitar god and part tender balladeer and a true titan of Canadian rock. In this fascinating glimpse into his private world, Myles cracks open his heart to reveal the man behind the myth and the stories behind the songs that were such a big part of my musical coming of age."

GIL MOORE, drummer for TRIUMPH and owner of Metalworks Studios

"Myles Goodwyn is unequivocally Canada's greatest rock 'n' roll songwriter. He's written more hits than anybody, and as Yogi Berra once famously said, 'You could look it up!' There's a great human story off the stage as well, and this book chronicles Myles' personal journey as only he can. This is the inside story of the life Myles sang about in 'Rock 'n' Roll Is a Vicious Game' (my personal favourite song). The many gold and platinum awards for his chart-topping success with April Wine are a testament to Myles' talent. This book is a testament to his humanity. Enjoy!"

SAM ROBERTS, Juno Award–winning singer/songwriter

"An inspiring and all too close-to-the-bone read for anyone who's ever played, or dreams of playing, in a rock 'n' roll band. All of the beauty and all of the demons."

BRUCE GUTHRO, award-winning Canadian singer/song-writer, singer for RUNRIG

"What a wonderful read. Myles walked me back through much of my own past telling his unique and fascinating life story. April Wine was a very big part of the soundtrack to my young life. It was fascinating to experience and truly feel a common bond throughout this book with a man I've always looked up to. My only issue is I can't read the cover without singing the title!"

IAN THOMAS, Juno Award–winning recording artist

"A candid look behind the curtain of one of Canada's most popular bands."

BILL HENDERSON, singer and founding member of CHILLIWACK and Member of the Order of Canada

"*Just Between You and Me* reflects the changed reality for Canadian classic rock bands. Now quite secure in their twilight years, they are experiencing a wonderful camaraderie as they continue gigging across the country and exchanging stories of the gritty reality of the first decades of their careers, which were absorbed in tumultuous and intense competition with each other. With strings, frets, talent, and wits they carved out places for themselves in the music industry. Lovely in yer face storytelling, Myles!"

LEE AARON, rock and jazz recording artist

"Myles Goodwyn has written a book that captures the '70s and '80s scene and all its excesses with vivid realism, as well as delving into his personal tribulations with great candor. He documents his journey from small-town kid to rock star to recovery with honesty and gratitude. For fans of April Wine this book is a must-read!"

JACK DE KEYZER, Juno Award–winning blues guitarist and singer

"Myles Goodwyn has walked the walk and rocked the rock world. He now talks the talk, in this no-holds-barred, quintessential Canadian rock star memoir."

MATT ANDERSEN, Juno Award–nominated blues singer/ songwriter

"Goodwyn is the perfect example of the 'triple threat': great lyrics, killer guitar, and the voice to drive it all home. He continues to give us songs that we will be singing along to for years to come and riffs that will make us crank our stereos to 10."

MARK BRADAC, guitarist for TEAZE

"A must-read from the heavyweight champ of Canadian rock! As a producer, Myles singlehandedly delivered Teaze's finest moments."

GARY YATES, award-winning director of the film *High Life*

"You know the music behind the man, now meet the man behind the music. Myles' saga from childhood to rock star—with all the trappings of sex, drugs, money, triumph, and heartbreak—captivates from page one."

PAUL BRONFMAN, Chairman/CEO of Comweb Corp. and William F. White International Inc. and Chairman of Pinewood Toronto Studios Inc.

"I met Myles at nineteen years old when I worked an April Wine tour in 1976. Right away, I felt his warmth and generosity towards the crew and the people around him. Throughout the years he has not lost his sense of humanity and compassion, his natural positive energy, and his engaging enthusiasm. I truly love the man. His memoir is wonderful and a must-read for all fans of Myles and his band, April Wine."

RICK BRONSON, comedian and TV host

"Although most may know Moe (my Jewish name for Myles) as a skilled musician, singer, songwriter, and producer, to me Myles is my comedy muse. Whenever I'm in need of a laugh, one visit or call to my buddy is all it takes. He can riff comedy with the best of them and can light up a room without ever picking up a guitar."

PAUL SANDERSON, Entertainment Lawyer, Sanderson Law

"Straight to the point and straight from the heart, that's Myles Goodwyn. This book gives you an insight into his life, the life of a Canadian rock legend who has had one hell of a ride, one heck of a life, and who is still rocking. Myles is the real deal."

GEORGE ELMES, Booking Agent, The Feldman Agency

"A great read! I have known Myles and have been the band's booking agent for over 40 years, yet I still found many new things of interest. Myles gives a straight-up account, the good and the bad, and doesn't shy away from the tough topics. Well done, Myles! This is a must-read."

ROBERT HENMAN, author of *The Child as Quest* and *Behind the Altar*

"*Just Between You and Me* reveals the genesis of the artistic temperament of a particular Canadian rock musician, Myles Goodwyn, and his influence not only on a rock 'n' roll band called April Wine but on the overall Canadian scene of popular music. More importantly, it reveals the difficulties and struggles of that band to break into the international scene. This book is a very good contribution to the history of rock 'n' roll's emergence into the Canadian culture."

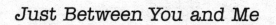

Just Between You and Me

"Just Between You and Me"

Myles Goodwyn

A Memoir

Harper
Collins

Published by HarperCollins Publishers Ltd

First edition

All photos provided courtesy of the author.

HarperCollins books may be purchased for educational, business,
or sales promotional use through our Special Markets Department.

HarperCollins Publishers Ltd
2 Bloor Street East, 20th Floor
Toronto, Ontario, Canada
M4W 1A8

www.harpercollins.ca

Library and Archives Canada Cataloguing in Publication
information is available upon request

ISBN 978-1-44344-670-9

Printed and bound in the United States of America
RRD 9 8 7 6 5 4 3 2 1

Dedicated with unconditional love to my three children,
Amber, Aaron, and Cary,
and to the enduring memory of my mother and father,
Roberta Anne and Francis Robie Goodwin

Contents

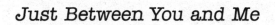

Just Between You and Me

Prologue

On the morning of November 28, 2008, I awoke from a restless sleep feeling terrible. I was nauseous and extremely weak. Truth be told—and that is the point of this publication—I was used to feeling dreadful and enervated on many a morning, but through sheer willpower I was usually all right with enough resolve to carry on.

I had gone to bed somewhat intoxicated the night before. I say somewhat; others might and did say, as it turned out, that I probably went to bed three sheets to the wind and feeling no pain. Well, folks, I was in pain that morning and I was having a rough time, and it was soon to get much rougher. Things were bad. I just had no idea how bad.

Was it Dean Martin who said, "I feel sorry for people who don't drink, because when they wake up in the morning, that's as good as they're going to feel all day"?

I limped to the kitchen for a quick coffee, which I carefully carried back upstairs so I could get showered and dressed. But first I made an effort to make sure I wasn't forgetting anything before I left for the airport. I never liked to pack the night before a trip; I still don't. I prefer to throw it all together last minute, although I will have a casual look-see the night before to make certain I'll be able to put my hands on what I need quickly when I do pack, and that's about it, folks. This lack of preparation usually works.

If I do forget something, aside from essential things like my ID, my driver's licence, and my personal deck of cards—that deck would include mostly various credit cards—then I'd just buy what I needed at the next town. No biggie.

This particular morning I had a very hard time coping with everything. I kept telling myself to keep going. *You can do it, Goody!*

I left the bathroom after my shower to go back into the bedroom to dress, only I didn't quite make it. I was violently sick. I threw up all the cookies and much more. My body was expelling poison. Nasty business.

I took deep breaths and steadied myself with both hands against the wall. My vision was blurred. This was serious. As serious as Jerry Mercer, the hefty then-drummer for April Wine, also known for his brutish appetite, at an all-you-can-eat buffet. Yes, *that* serious!

That morning I ploughed on, tenacious in my determination to get to the airport on time and fly to Halifax, Nova Scotia, where, along with other members of April Wine, past and present, I was going to receive a lovely award from local radio station Q104 FM. I somehow managed to pack and be ready when friend and bandmate Brian Greenway arrived to take us both to Montreal's Pierre Elliott Trudeau International Airport.

"Good morning, Brian," I managed weakly as I slipped into his car that morning.

"Good morning," he replied innocently.

We left for the airport.

The drive from my home to the airport takes about thirty-five minutes, door to door. About twenty minutes into the drive I asked Brian to pull over. I felt like I was going to be sick again.

We got off Highway 40 west at the exit for Sainte-Anne-de-Bellevue, Quebec, which is about forty kilometres west of Montreal. I stood off to the right of the car. I crouched down and tried to throw up, but despite feeling sick, I could not. I stood up. And then . . . nothingness.

Brian Greenway:

Myles got out and bent over trying to vomit but nothing was coming up. After about a minute of this I saw him stand up, and then he passed out and fell over backwards, striking his head very hard on the concrete sidewalk. I jumped out and rushed over to find him with his eyes semi-open but unconscious with his lips trembling.

I called his name a few times with no response. I lifted his head to get it off the snow and slush on the sidewalk, and that's when I saw the blood flowing from the wound in his head. I gently put his head back down, not wanting to move him further in case he had suffered a neck injury in the fall, and called 911.

By this time a trucker, who was stopped in the rest area, was running over to help. People in passing cars, who had seen him fall, were also stopping to help. I gave 911 the coordinates as to where we were. By this time, I had help on the scene from a female passerby who thankfully was a nurse named Natalie, who was also in agreement not to move Myles, who was conscious by this time and wanting to get up. He was confused and asking what had happened and where I was. I was getting a blanket and umbrella from the car to shelter him with.

Within six minutes two police cars from the Quebec Provincial Police arrived, assessed the situation, and called the ambulance. Minutes later, the fire department arrived and took over the scene, still not moving Myles. He wanted to get up and was very cold but was not allowed to move by the first responders. He wanted to know where I was, and I called out that I was here and with him.

I called Breen [LeBoeuf, bass player for April Wine at the time] and told him the situation as I knew it and advised him not to get on the flight and that I would keep him in the loop.

After about ten to fifteen minutes—it may have been less or more; there was so much going on to remember—the ambulance arrived. After a few minutes' examination, they put Myles on a back board and stretcher and then into the ambulance but did not depart to the hospital. I waited outside the vehicle, and after a few minutes, one of the ambulance techs came out to talk to me. He asked me how long we had been partying for.

I replied, "What?"

He said that Myles was very, very intoxicated. I knew Myles had been battling alcohol for some time, but I had little idea he had been drinking again in the last year. The police at this point were very interested to talk to me again to see if I was driving drunk. Of course, I had not been, but they had to check.

I was allowed into the ambulance. Myles was awake and coherent. The ambulance techs at this point were aware of just who Myles was. I don't know what they thought but, then again, they are professionals and have seen just about everything in their job.

We stayed at the roadside for at least twenty-five minutes before I was notified they were going to transport him to the Lakeshore General Hospital some fifteen minutes away.

I had gone into Myles' bag to see if there was a phone number for Lisa, Myles' wife at the time, who was in Florida. I found a cell number for her and was going to call her from the hospital, but Lisa called as I was following the ambulance to the hospital. I informed her as to what I knew and told her I would keep her updated.

About forty-five minutes had gone by since Myles had collapsed, and I had parked and entered emergency at the Lakeshore General Hospital. Breen had also just arrived from the airport.

At the hospital, Breen and I were allowed to be at bedside in the emergency ward with Myles, who was very awake and aware, while we waited for the doctor to come. We half-heartedly joked with him, and Myles was exclaiming that "he really blew it this time." What were we to say? This was neither the time nor the place to make any sort of judgmental remarks. I still was making calls to Steff Pilon [April Wine's road manager] and George Elmes [April Wine's booking agent] explaining what was happening and that getting to Halifax for the Q104 awards was out of the question.

There was an orderly in emergency named David who recognized Myles and Breen and me as being with April Wine. David made sure that Myles was comfortable and provided him with whatever he could to keep him comfortable until the doctor examined him.

Tests were done and results were given as quickly as can be done in a large hospital. The doctor told me that Myles was a very lucky man to have come to the hospital when he did. He had lost a very large amount of blood and was bleeding internally. Not from the fall, but from severe alcohol distress. Had he not come to the hospital he would have died from loss of blood within the next twenty-four hours. Wow, indeed! I was starting to see that more than the show was going to be cancelled. I could see months of recuperation ahead, and it occurred to me that the band might be over. What a bizarre way to end it. Not something I would have thought of, but then life is full of surprises.

Myles was apologetic to Breen and me for "letting us down." We told him that whatever he had to do, we'd be behind him.

More tests were done and the doctor conferred with Myles in private. A few hours had passed by now. It was almost noon.

Myles had collapsed at about 8:15 a.m. At about 1:00 p.m. the doctor informed us that Myles was being transferred to Montreal General downtown, as the type of treatment he needed was more available there.

I went home and continued to work with George and Steff on the phone to control the situation. It found its way into the news nationally the next day through the hospital or someone involved in the event. I drafted a release for our website, as many questions were being asked by fans. Other than visiting Myles the next day at the hospital, that was my involvement on that day.

Breen LeBoeuf:
I followed the ambulance on the trip from Lakeshore Hospital to Montreal General. I had a fair idea of what was coming. The physical and psychological distress that had come to a head this day spoke volumes to me. I was about to celebrate eighteen years of sobriety on the 12th of December. Without suffering the same type of physical damage that had floored Myles, I had hit bottom in my own way years before.

The emergency ward at the older downtown hospital was a lot smaller and overcrowded. Myles was eventually admitted and assigned a bed. I spent my time with him when the staff would allow. Sometimes it was so nuts in there that there was no place for me to stand.

Myles was being sedated and so was in and out of conscious-ness. When he would come around, he would try to understand his condition. Early on he tried to joke a bit, but he was so weak and sedated that he had a hard time keeping me in his field of vision. He was often thirsty. His mood was changing with the medica-tion. Occasionally, they would wheel him out for testing at some other location in the hospital. As the day wore on, he became more and more disenchanted with what was happening to him. He was being poked and prodded and was not happy with the situation.

Information came in dribs and drabs. I spent a great deal of the time in a small "family room." When fresh staff would come on, I would have to explain that I was not family but was in touch with his wife who was visiting in Florida. Most of what I learned of Myles' condition came from him. He would relay to me what the doctors and nurses were telling him.

He was bleeding from the esophagus. His liver was likely affected, hopefully not severely enough to stop it from doing its job. Myles was in bad shape and not out of the woods.

When I left the hospital mid-evening, Myles was sleeping. I drove home to Trois-Rivières for a good night's sleep and returned to the hospital shortly after noon on Saturday.

Other than Brian's dropping by to visit during the afternoon, Saturday was more of the same. The bleeding seemed to be under control, but Myles was still being sedated and hydrated. They were giving him a cocktail of medications to control the bleeding, avert infection, and help with any alcohol withdrawal symptoms. There was probably more that I've since forgotten.

The day seemed to last forever. I stayed until late evening and then went to crash at a friend's place.

Sunday around ten o'clock I returned to the hospital only to *find someone else parked where Myles had been the night before. After checking with several people, I finally learned that he had checked himself out and taken a cab home shortly after dawn. I freaked. A vivid image came to mind: Myles alone at home, breaking open a private stash and drinking until the bleeding resumed. I raced (literally) to his house, afraid of what I might find. On the way, I called Brian to meet me there.*

Myles was asleep upstairs in his bed when we arrived. I checked his breathing: slow and regular. I asked Brian to help me search for hidden alcohol. We went down to the studio, thinking this was his lair, so logically, if he wanted to imbibe without the family knowing, this would be the place for him to hide the juice.

We found nothing. I have to admit, we didn't search very thoroughly. There were simply too many places to hide a bottle. The main floor was not, in my way of thinking, a logical place for him to conceal booze. I checked the bar, finding liqueurs and cognac, no vodka, his drink of choice.

We decided there was no point in the two of us waiting for Myles to wake so Brian went home. I went upstairs and sat for a while outside his bedroom door, wanting to stay within earshot should he get into trouble. After a bit, I went downstairs and called my older, wiser brother for advice. He told me I was a fool to be there alone, that this situation called for a team of two.

Before I could get more organized, Myles came down. He seemed somewhat less drugged, more coherent, and still very agitated. He explained to me how he had to escape from that dreadful hospital, that the staff had been abusive, that he was not getting the rest he could at home.

I asked him if he had been drinking, and he admitted having taken a last drink upon arriving. The heel of a bottle he had hidden; nothing more, he assured me. He showed me the empty. He swore there were no others.

I tried to convince him that he was gambling with his life, that he needed medical supervision in the worst way, and that we had to get him to the hospital immediately.

He bargained with me. It was classic. He would call his doctor buddy and ask him what he should do. I held the cards, knowing any doctor would back me on this call. And that's how it played out. Dr. Stan told him to get his ass to the hospital post-haste.

Before we left for the hospital, Lisa and Cary [Myles' youngest son] came in from Florida. Myles and Lisa spent an intense half hour discussing how they felt and what was to be done immediately and in the near future. Then Myles and I left.

We returned to Lakeshore emergency. After a reasonably short wait—a little over an hour—we were told by the male nurse working admissions that Myles could not stay, that he would have to return to the Montreal General since they had his charts. I couldn't believe it. We were heading out of the parking lot when Lisa managed to reach me on my cell to tell me to get back in there with Myles, that the specialist wanted him admitted. That was a close one, since Myles had no intention of returning to the General.

Once he was settled into the emergency ward and waiting for the doc to come by, I slipped out for a wedge of pizza that the male nurse had ordered for me.

When I returned to Myles' bedside, he was sitting up, excited to tell me that he was being released and that he could go home. The doctor had come by and taken a look at him. He had also asked him a few questions. Myles then made the error of letting slip that he had told the doctor his last drink was on Friday.

I made an excuse and slipped away to find the male nurse. I told him that Myles had been drinking alcohol that very day, that I had only his word that it was "just one drink," that he could be in real danger.

I returned to Myles' bedside. He was sure he would be going home, right up to the point where the male nurse came over and told him he was staying since he'd recently ingested alcohol and needed supervision.

When we were alone, Myles asked me if I'd squealed on him, and I answered something like "You betcha." I was in the deep stuff. I left for home on a sour note.

I will explain later, in my own words, what happened to me that caused the events that Brian and Breen describe here. It's painful to remember these events, let alone retell and therefore relive that part of my past, but I am determined to tell it like it was and how it is today and the in-between.

When I was finally able to come home from the hospital and rehab after my brush with death, I was still weak and worn down, and it showed. I remember looking at myself in the mirror and not recognizing the person looking back. It really scared me, folks. Would I ever see the Myles Goodwyn who had existed only a few months before, or was it too late?

So here it is, the story of a boy from Nova Scotia who, through hard work and steadfast determination, found success as a founding member and leader of one of the most popular bands in Canadian music history.

I'm telling my story here, the truth and nothing but the truth as I know it, warts and all.

PART ONE

The Early Years

1

—

didn't cry, I remember that.

I remember my dad and my brothers, Barry and Allan, all crying. We were standing at the foot of our driveway on a sunny summer day in June 1959. We were all holding each other, pressed together, clinging, sobbing. All but me, that is.

I stared up at the sky and far, far away. I know I felt confusion and guilt that I wasn't crying at the news that our mother was dead. I just didn't know why not. I was eleven years old, and I was in shock.

I have never been able to remember my mother, except for the memory of a woman with her head bandaged being at my grandmother's house. At least I *think* it was my grandmother's house in Dartmouth, Nova Scotia.

As I watched her slowly move about, I must have felt unable to go to her, to embrace her, to comfort her. I regret that very much because it might have also brought me comfort and closure. That might have made a huge psychological difference in my ability to cope with her passing.

I was told later that the first signs that there was something amiss with my mother's health was a numbness around her face, the same sensation you get when the effects of the Novocain start to wear off after going to the dentist to have a cavity filled or a tooth pulled. They told her the cause was probably the sun in her eyes and that she should wear sunglasses. In the end, the doctors suspected it was something else, and eventually they found a brain tumour, which they removed. Unfortunately, they didn't get all of the cancer, which she found out around Christmas 1958. In January 1959, she went back for another operation that was delayed for three weeks because she had developed a bad cold. They operated on her in February of that year, and on that same day, the doctors told the family she had only three months to live. Sadly, their prediction came true. She died on May 16, 1959.

My aunt Lola and uncle Bob say that their dad, my grandfather, believed in premonitions. He got up early the morning my mom died, and like he always did, he lit a fire in the wood stove. He told them he had a dream, and in that dream Mom came to the back door all dressed in white and she said, "Dad, I've come home!" It wasn't very long after that they got the call that she had died.

My mother is dead and everything I experienced with her up until this time has been forgotten, at least to my conscious self. Everything. All the birthday parties, the Christmases, the first days back to school, the last days of school, and the first days of summer vacation. Being picked up, being put down at night, repeating the Lord's Prayer together at bedtime, as I'm sure we did because she and my father were religious in an old-fashioned, nice, simple kind of way.

Forgotten are the times I collected stuff with her, stuff that falls from trees and stuff that falls out of the sky, like me, when

I'd fall and skin my knees and she would kiss them better. Her being there for everything during the first ten years of my life, all gone. Erased. Unbelievable. (The fucking mind is a fucking complicated piece of grey fucking matter. You can quote me.)

My poor mother was only twenty-eight years young, and it turned my dad into an old man way before his time.

We were now a family torn apart.

My father turned to drinking. I turned to music. One of my brothers, Barry, the second down from me in age, was a lot bigger than my youngest brother, Allan, and me. He was tough and he took this emotional trauma out with his fists. He was known locally as a fighter. He would fight with anybody. He was angry. Allan was quiet as a church mouse. He never had much to say. To this day, he is still very quiet. He has never really changed in that regard, as far as I can tell, and he's the one who easily tears up with any talk of our mother.

We boys did not attend our mother's funeral.

Our father, or those close to him during this heartbreaking time, felt we were better off if we didn't know about it, and so we were handed off to somebody who took us to a park that day, in downtown Dartmouth.

I have pictures of us at the park, my two brothers and me. I was ten, Barry was eight, and Allan six, and the pictures taken that day show us happy, smiling as if we were having a great old time. We look like we didn't have a care in the world, even though our dear mother was being buried that very same day.

I guess back then *they* thought it was better if we were "protected" from the solemn affair of placing our mother in a coffin and lowering her into the cold, thankless ground, forever. They were just trying to protect us from the pain and the sorrow of being witness, I realize that. Of course, we know better these days. We understand now that we all need closure, even kids. For children, honesty and openness are essential in order for them to accept life's terms and move on. But my brothers and I never had that opportunity; we were robbed. Too bad. The consequences of their "thoughtfulness" back then would leave emotional scars forever.

As far as me being told of my mother's demise, the days and nights immediately following and the subsequent funeral, which, as I said, I did not attend, sadly, is about all I remember of those sorrowful few weeks in June 1959.

She was buried in Fall River, Nova Scotia, in a double-sized lot. There was room for two gravesites there. My dad built a white picket fence around the entire double lot so nobody could walk over her grave. It was the only grave that had a white picket fence in that cemetery, and he built it all himself. I used to go with him when he cared for it.

I didn't go for many years after I moved out of the Maritimes, and eventually, he never went either because he moved to another part of the province. Maybe he felt at a point in his life where he just had to get away from all that because the memories were slowly killing him.

I went back some years later and the fence was falling apart and rotting. It had been a long time since my dad had moved out of the area, and the grave was just left the way it was, no longer tended. The gravesite has since been cleaned and there are no rotting pieces of a white picket fence left anymore. In 2014, my brother Allan and I moved Dad's remains from where he had been buried in Hopewell, Nova Scotia, in 1993, to the double gravesite in Fall River next to our mother.

Six months after our mother passed on, we had our first Christmas without her. My poor dad was devastated and trying to cope with giving his boys their first merry Christmas without their mom. Here was a man ravaged with grief, sitting with his three orphaned boys at a table in a plain private dining room in some hotel in Dartmouth, sharing with us boys a special Christmas supper. How terrible that day must have been for him.

For me it was just odd. I don't remember being sad as much as feeling respectful to Dad and his effort to be there for us. Here we were in a restaurant having a traditional Christmas meal in this small, drab dining room, the quiet closeness making the event even more noticeably absurd. There was no attempt at gaiety, no laughter or cheerful conversation. How could there be? It was an awkward, melancholy time. There was no merriment to be found on that doleful day fifty-seven years ago.

But all things pass.

That Christmas we received gifts from the good people of Waverley, Nova Scotia. Some gifts were new and others second-hand. There were toys and practical things, like footwear and clothing. Folks helped their neighbours back then. It was a small town, and when my dad became a widower with three young boys to care for, it was a concern to many in the community. Their thoughts and prayers were with us.

My father was employed, of course, but everyone knew he made a modest wage and could use the help, although I'm very sure he never asked for a lick. He was a strong and proud man, our father. Nonetheless, their gifts were appreciated, their kindness a blessing.

Life went on, and of course, we all survived the hard times.

There are many long-term effects on children when one

parent dies young and the rest of the family is left to carry on. What the effects are depends of course on many circumstances. In our family's case, the effects were not always clear or immediate. In my case, I believe the consequences were more obvious straightaway.

I became a loner, but then again, so did everybody else in the house. Dad became a quiet, distant man who eventually got the reputation of being tough, guarded, and hard to befriend. He was liked and respected, I think, but he had no real friends that I know of. No one came to our house for social visits, anyway, and he never went out with the boys as far as I know. He was a rock back then, an island. Many years later he would eventually open up to people and become more social and, I hope, found some kind of peace before the end of his days. I never spent much time with Dad as an adult, and it's one of those things you wish with all your heart that you could change, but alas, it's too late.

We were all, each of us, handling life differently at the time. Never did we seek out each other's company for comfort, advice, or love. We were four males living under the same roof and yet we never really communicated with each other, and that was what we needed more than anything. But we didn't know how, I guess, and sadly, we never did learn how.

We became a dysfunctional family, to say the least.

Our home in Waverley, the house where my mother lived and died during a period of a few short years, was named Halfway to Heaven. A home could never be more incorrectly named. The inspiration for the name came from the fact that it was physically situated high on a hill overlooking Lake William. The name suggests peace and serenity. Ironically, life there was anything but.

2

have never taken much time to research my family's history, but as the idea of writing my memoir slowly unfolded, I thought I might take a brief look back to get some idea of where my family came from—where I came from.

It seems in the mid-1600s, some of the Goodwin clan left Suffolk County, England, for the colonies and settled in the Massachusetts area. Apparently, some of my relatives may have distinguished themselves by graduating from Harvard, Yale, and other institutions regarded with some distinction by some people. When the Colonials decided to break with Britain, the Loyalists, those wishing to remain under the security of Britain, decided around 1765 to head north to places like Nova Scotia. Some of the Goodwin clan went along. They settled in a small village on the southern tip of Nova Scotia known as Argyle. One hundred years later, some of the Goodwins moved to the Magdalen Islands in the Gulf of Saint Lawrence.

The islands were mainly French, and fishing was one of the main ways of subsistence. My grandparents were both born there. My grandfather lived in his birthplace of East Cape until 1923, at which time he purchased land in Grosse Isle and moved his house there. My father, Frank Robie—Bud to his close friends—was born there on April 2, 1928.

My grandfather had a sawmill and sawed wood for people from driftwood off the beach. Back in those days, a lot of pulp wood washed ashore on the beaches of the Magdalen Islands, having been swept off the decks of the ships that were carrying the wood overseas. Also, booms broke loose in the rivers in storms in northern New Brunswick and the Gaspe, drifted down to the islands, and came ashore along the many beaches.

My grandfather also had a fox farm, which was actually his father's. After his father died in 1940, my grandfather sold it along with the rest of his property, and the family moved to Tufts Cove, Nova Scotia, where he worked as a carpenter. The house on the islands was remodelled by the new owner, and I'm told it's still standing.

Beginning in the mid-1920s, my grandfather, Francis Goodwin, had begun building small fishing boats, although one vessel that he built, the *Francis Robie*, was much larger, a 28.3-ton vessel registered out of Charlottetown, Prince Edward Island. Why did he name it after my father? I'm not sure. He had another son, Ray. Perhaps my father helped him build it. The ship was sold off the island and went missing off the coast of Nova Scotia with four crew members on November 11, 1946. It is perhaps this trade, which my grandfather worked at, that influenced my father as he spent much of his spare time working with wood by building houses. The family moved a second time in 1940, this time to Caribou, Nova Scotia, near Pictou, which has been a ship-building town for more than two hundred years. I'm told my grandfather took up subsistence farming.

It was in Caribou that my mom and dad met and married

before moving to Woodstock, New Brunswick, where I was born. When my grandparents, Nan and Bomps, moved to Brantford, Ontario, our family made the move as well, and we all ended up living in a couple of old houses on King Street in that city. Bomps went back to working at carpentry for a company called Kromar Construction, a job he held for many years. Aunt Agnes was a dining room hostess at a new hotel called the Graham Bell. My father, my uncle Ray, and my aunt Viv all worked at Brantford Cordage, a rope manufacturing plant. It has been said that if the wind was right, you could smell them coming home from work. Hemp oil stinks really bad. Nan wouldn't let them in the house until they took off their work clothes. But it paid the bills.

Eventually, we all moved back east. Nan and Bomps would later return to Ontario a number of times. Bomps, who was staying in Hamilton, Ontario, with Aunt Agnes at one point, died from gangrene. In 1980, our beloved Nan, who was living with Aunt Viv in Brantford, died of a heart attack. When my mother died it was Nan who cooked the meals, washed the clothes, and generally did things that typically, back then, a mother would do. Nan was a saint. She was the old-fashioned, salt-of-the-earth kind of person who only did the right thing, ever, and never complained or asked for a thing for herself. May she rest in eternal peace.

My mother's maiden name was Turple. The first Turples recorded in Canada came to Halifax with the German Protestant settlers from Prussia around 1750. Johann Gottfried Torple (Torple was obviously anglicized to Turple), a school teacher, arrived with his wife Sophia and their three or four sons from which, it is believed, all the Turples in Nova Scotia are descended. They lived in a district west of Halifax at the head of the

Northwest Arm, an inlet that is part of Halifax Harbour, known as Dutch Village, a name erroneously given to the district by non-German locals who undoubtedly meant Deutsch Village.

The community was also known as Armdale. During the time the Torples were settling in the area, there were a number of attacks by the Mi'kmaq people on the British blockhouses at Armdale, the first in 1751 and the second in 1753, during the conflict between the British and the French for control of Nova Scotia known during this period as Father Le Loutre's War.

As the schoolmaster, Johann Torple was revered by the settlers. Reverend Weldon Mosher, the curate of St. George's Anglican Church in Halifax, wrote, "Little did these German settlers who came to Halifax shortly after the founding of the city realize the part which they and their descendants would play in making history for Nova Scotia, in general, and Halifax, in particular . . . The history and growth of education in the city cannot be complete without the reference to those early pioneers, including Johann Gottfried Torple, who came as a Schoolmaster for the settlement in June of the year 1750. The religious life of the city still bears their stamp."

Johann and Sophia Torple's great grandsons moved from Clam Bay, northeast of Halifax on Nova Scotia's Eastern Shore, to Pictou County, situated in the northern part of Nova Scotia along the Northumberland Strait, in the early 1900s to follow fishing. They made their living off the sea much as my grandfather who built boats did.

Pictou County encompasses the towns of New Glasgow, Pictou, Stellarton, and Caribou, a place made remarkable for me by the fact that my parents, Frank Robie Goodwin and Roberta Anne Turple, met there. On November 4, 1947, they were married in Pictou. My mother, Roberta Anne—Bertie to her friends and family—was born in Central Caribou on November 9, 1931. I still have relatives there today on both sides of the family.

My mother met my father after his family arrived in Central Caribou from the Magdalen Islands. Apparently, there was competition between my mother and a girl named Kathleen Banks for my father's attention. I've been told by members of my mother's family that the song "I'll Take You Home Again, Kathleen" was one my father dared not sing or even hum around my mother.

Shortly after my parents' marriage, they moved to Woodstock, New Brunswick, an industrial town offering a varied source of industrial occupations. My father, who would put his hand to many things over the years ahead, most likely had pre-arranged a job in some Woodstock industry.

On June 23, 1948, I was born, registered at birth as Miles Francis Goodwin. The three of us did not remain in Woodstock for long. In 1949, we moved to Brantford, Ontario, where my brother Barry was born on September 2, 1950. My father's parents also moved to Brantford around that same time. Again, we did not stay long, moving to Tufts Cove, Nova Scotia, in 1952.

Tufts Cove is an urban neighbourhood in Dartmouth, Nova Scotia, situated on the eastern shore of Halifax Harbour in the North End of Dartmouth. The area was named after the Tufts family who, as United Empire Loyalists, left the American Revolution in Massachusetts and settled on the land in 1776.

Just as my grandparents had followed us to Brantford sometime in the late 1940s, they again followed us—or we followed them—to settle in Tufts Cove. My father began work with a cordage (rope) company and later would work for Naval Research

Establishment on Windmill Road just a few blocks outside the eastern-most boundary of Tufts Cove. During the summer of 1952, my mother had been ill with jaundice, and her sister, Aunt Marjorie Shaw, took care of Barry and me at that time. Our brother, Allan, was born in Tufts Cove on December 11, 1952.

My earliest memories are of living in Tufts Cove.

I was quite young when we lived there, and I remember very little about the area. The picture in my mind is of a place consisting of dirt roads that frequently turned to mud on rainy days, of rickety picket fences and small, box-shaped houses. (Many of these houses were later purchased and torn down in 1964 to make way for the Tufts Cove Generating Station.) We were situated close to the harbour and we could see it, at least in part, from where we lived. We could hear the sounds of busy naval activity echoing off the surrounding hills, an industry that added the pungent scent of gas and oil to the fresh, salty essence of the ocean breeze carrying the fragrance of seaweed, kelp, and so much more. And there was the constant loud and annoying screaming of seagulls, guilty as sin the lot of them, considered by many to be responsible for almost every petty crime perpetrated in the area.

I remember that not too far from our small house in Tufts Cove there was a corner store peddling last-minute items and inexpensive sundries that included candy. From time to time I was allowed to visit the corner store, and someone would walk me there, all the while holding my small, restless hand in theirs, on an exciting quest for penny candy and such. Typically, the walk from our front door on the road that leads to all things sweet and tasty took about ten minutes. The same trip home could easily take an hour as I slowly enjoyed some candy or perhaps a chocolate bar. That's a nice memory. There are just some things you shouldn't hurry.

The grade school I attended at the time was quite large and constructed of red brick. It was partly surrounded by woods. I recall catching a fish or two in a small lake somewhere off in those woods behind the school. The lake, I assume, is still there, unless it was filled in over the years.

Albro Lake was home to a variety of fish including rainbow trout and brook trout. One day, my father took me fishing in that magical spot. I was so excited when I finally got a fish on the hook that, as it neared the surface, I gave a tug on the line with such force that the fish ended up in a tree behind us. My father had to climb up and retrieve it. It was an embarrassing but exciting experience, destined for future retellings. As I recall, we caught a few more fish and then dad built a small fire so we could have pan-fried trout for lunch. He had come prepared.

When I was five I was in line with the other kids waiting my turn to get the Salk polio vaccine injection, which had just been developed and was being offered to schoolkids as part of a mass immunization campaign, when the kids ahead of me freaked out. It was a perverse twist on the domino effect. As you heard those in front of you crying, you'd start whimpering, and with each footstep closer to the origin of all this apparent pain and suffering, the howls would begin in earnest. With some, it was full-out, ear-shattering, take-your-breath-away screaming.

When it came time for my injection, I had *real* reason to raise a ruckus—the needle broke off in my arm! They immediately pulled it out with a pair of pliers and gave me a second shot while I howled in fear and pain. Some years later, the memory of that day would come back to me in Technicolor.

I really don't remember all that much more about our stay in Tufts Cove—and notice I use the word "stay." Doesn't sound like a place we called home, does it? Rather just a town passed through on the way to somewhere that matters.

I do recall that a lot of us were living together in that small space. The house was definitely too small for two adults and three children. One day, I remember being excited because we were told we were moving to the country where there would be woods and lots and lots of space for us three brothers to run and explore, and we would have our own lake to swim in.

In 1955, we moved into a modest-sized house on a hill overlooking Lake William in Waverley, a small rural village about twelve kilometres outside of Dartmouth, Nova Scotia. By modest, I mean a petite fixer-upper requiring lots of TLC. The fixing up never stopped during all the years I lived there. But it was beautiful nonetheless.

At our doorstep, we had the clear, clean waters of Lake William, which is about five kilometres in length with a winding road following its shoreline, surrounded by natural hardwood forests. It was a great place for a kid to grow up, especially in the summers. I learned how to swim and actually became quite good at it.

Fishing was my passion, perhaps because of those experiences catching trout with my dad a few years earlier in Tufts Cove. Back then, you ate what you caught. Today so many lakes and rivers are polluted and the catch inedible. But back in the day, the water was clear, clean, and drinkable. Beautiful wooded hills rise from Lake William's shores, and it was there that I spent my time as a kid exploring and playing. The summers were the best, with so much for kids to do to keep busy right up until it was time for bed. We spent all our time outside in the fresh air, living life to the max. Even rainy days were wonderful. Life in the country was good.

During the winter months, the lake was great for some serious ice skating. Lake William froze solid from one beautiful end to the other, and where the ice was not covered in snow or the snow was not too deep, the skating was spectacular. With a lake this large, it was a real thrill. Hockey rinks were made by plowing away the snow in the shape of a rink and then flooding the cleared area with lake water to a depth of several inches. If necessary, we cut a hole in the ice and pumped water into the area, where it would freeze to form the makeshift rink and become just as smooth as the real thing.

We made spectacular bonfires on the frozen lake. Believe me, there were a lot of romantic goings-on in the glow of those warm fires. Innocent, beautiful, and unforgettable. To this day, I have memories of the lovely young ladies dressed in winter attire, a pair of skates—always white—a winter coat with a fur collar, a scarf, and usually furry ear muffs or a warm sensible hat and a wraparound scarf. They were cute as heck.

What my father bought on Waverley Road—from a man named Mr. Bean—was not much more than a two-bedroom shack. The property was about three acres in all, and my dad named it Halfway to Heaven because it was situated high on a hill. The road that ran past the house was Waverley Road. It ran from Waverley to Dartmouth, and it was, and still is, a winding, narrow two-laner that was actually quite dangerous if the speed limit was not respected. Many a car went off the road during the years that I lived there. Over the years, I was often the first at an accident after a car left the road and ended up at the bottom of an embankment across from where we lived, which gave me recurring bad dreams.

Still, I loved the place. We had no one living in front of, behind, or on either side of us. We were surrounded on three sides by woods, and the front of the property overlooked the beautiful lake. Today, it's all quite different, with neighbours on three sides.

But back then, it was sweet. Wildlife was always right outside or near the house, with partridge, pheasant, and even deer in the backyard. The one and only deer I ever shot was a few hundred yards from the house. For this young man, it was the ultimate adventure living where we were surrounded by wildlife. I soon took to wearing a Davy Crockett raccoon hat. In my wonderfully active imagination, I was a mixture of Davy Crockett, "the King of the Wild Frontier," Jim Bowie, and Huck Finn. Oh, yeah, and Miles Francis Goodwin. (I would change the spelling of my name to Myles Goodwyn within a few short years.)

I was so into loving the country life that I became almost obsessed with a lifestyle that had me hunting or fishing almost every day. If I wasn't in school, I was in the woods. My main form of hunting was with traps: rabbit snares.

Every day, I'd get into my "frontier" clothing with my trusty knife strapped on my side. After that first year, I carried a .22 single-shot rifle. Later, that rifle was replaced by a single-shot ten-gauge shotgun. I shot that large doe with the shotgun. When my dad heard that I shot a deer, he arrived home that day with a beautiful hunting knife as a gift. I carried that knife Dad gave me all the time. Not only was he proud of me for the kill, but it meant food for the family. There would be lots of deer meat over the coming winter months, and that was a real blessing.

That was an exciting day for me and a great memory still. Shooting my first (and last) deer was great, but making my dad happy and proud, and being able to bring to our kitchen table food other than fish or rabbit was the best part.

That was an exciting day and a great memory. I no longer hunt, but back then I loved the adventure and the challenges involved in hunting deep in the woods behind our house.

There had to be at least fifty traps spread out through the woods, covering approximately a two-mile route. I'd check every one, every day. I knew where they all were, and if I found a rabbit in a snare, I'd untangle the wire, which wasn't always easy to do as it was often tight around the animal's neck and frozen in ice and snow. I would take off my gloves to allow me to work the snare wire off in order to claim the rabbit, often in temperatures well below freezing.

One day an all-white feral cat that had been following me got caught in a snare. I heard the struggle and the shrieking of this furry carnivore so I went to release it. In the process, the cat freaked out and was clawing at me as if its life was at stake, which it was. I saved its miserable life. It thanked me with scratched and bloodied hands.

Another time, I spotted a bobcat sitting on the limb of a tree, sphinx-like, completely motionless. He had frozen to death in that position.

When I'd come out of the woods after a two-hour or so trek through the wild, I'd emerge with a string of dead, often bloodied, rabbits slung over my shoulder and with the hair of a madman, with twigs and all manner of forest debris tangled up in it. At those times, I was a very young and skinny Grizzly Adams.

It was during this time of hunting and snaring that a young lady named Elaine McDermott moved in just a short walk from our house. She was about my age and had dark, shoulder-length hair. I fell in love for the first time. In those days, it was called "puppy love." In this day and age, "puppy love" might mean doing it "doggy style," for all I know. Oh, well. Times are different.

Her father drove a small, black early-model Austin automobile. I remember it well because it was *different*. You had to crank the engine to get it to catch, and it was real finicky. There was a cranking iron, I guess it might have been called, that fit into a place at the front of the engine. You then put your weight into it, as they say, and turned that crank as hard and as fast as possible to get the motor to start. Sometimes that took a while. It was the first and the last one I've ever seen, and good riddance.

Elaine was a tomboy. A few times she would go with me when I went into the bush to collect my snared rabbits. She was the only one my age who lived nearby, so we quickly became good friends. Only a year after moving to Waverley, they packed up and moved to Halifax. I missed her a lot. She promised to visit and finally did a year later.

I was off in the woods as usual, and she waited for me to appear over the wooded knoll leading down to the house, knowing where I was and what I was up to. So, there I was, trudging out of the woods, a string of dead rabbits slung over my slim shoulders, a rifle in one hand and my trusty knife secured in my belt. My hands and face were filthy and my hair a mess with bits of branches and such. It was an awkward moment.

She looked fantastic. Older. Sophisticated. What a difference a year older and a year of living in the big city had made in her. Wow! As she looked me over, I swear she knew at that moment she had made a mistake coming to see me. I was embarrassed. "Aw, shucks, Miss Elaine!" It wasn't long before she was on her way and I never saw her again. That was my first of many romantic heartbreaks.

I was very successful in snaring rabbits. Cleaning the rabbits I did not enjoy. Gutting them and peeling the skin off, leaving a very white and scrawny, bald, cat-like cadaver, was not to my liking. The smell of the guts of these unfortunates really turned my stomach, so much so that I'd get my brothers to do the job for me for twenty-five cents a rabbit.

The rabbits we didn't eat ourselves I sold at the side of the road that passed by the house as a way to make some money.

Lake William had a lot of freshwater clams. Unfortunately, they were inedible, so I used to carry buckets full of those bivalve molluscs up from the shore to the house and use them for shooting practice in the backyard. We got especially good at it. I was pretty nifty with a rifle to begin with from my time spent in the woods shooting at inanimate objects in the forest and of course living targets such as pheasant, rabbits, and other small game.

Crows made great targets, whether on a distant branch or even while in flight. You had to be good to judge the distance, the wind, and the flight of the crow, leading a bit so that once the shot was fired, the bullet and the crow would collide. I make no apologies to all the crow huggers out there.

Back then, it was no big deal to shoot pellet rifles at floating cans, wood, and such down at the lake. Today, of course, you'd be arrested for doing this on the lake, and your shooter confiscated. You'd be slapped with a stiff fine for good measure. But it was the '50s. It was great fun to throw a bottle far from shore and take turns—usually sharing the same gun—at hitting the bobbing target. We were young with steady, strong arms and a firm grip and doing something fun, so it was not surprising that our marksmanship was uncommonly good.

Although I spent a lot of time hunting and fishing alone with only my thoughts for company, I really and truly enjoyed those early years in Waverley. I felt that I really was halfway to heaven.

We were poor, a fact that was reflected in the way we lived in those days. We had no plumbing and therefore no running water. Heat was supplied by a single wood stove situated in the kitchen. So not everyone would consider it their Utopia.

The bathroom was a strong five-iron shot away from the house. It was a crude two-seater with an old Sears or Eaton's catalogue left there for those using the facility. Of course, there was no heat year round, no nicely padded seat to make the experience even a little bit comfortable, or to help reduce the cold, hard reality of shitting in a hole in the ground in the dead of a Nova Scotia winter night.

In the summer, we washed ourselves in the lake. It wasn't convenient, and the water might have been a tad cool a lot of the time, but it was clear and we could drink from the lake. In the winter, Dad would fetch barrels of water from a hole in the ice and drive the barrels home in the back of his car/truck. This vehicle was a second-hand early '50s Chevy that he chopped down the back of and added a flatbed for hauling water and lots of other stuff. I often went with Dad to fetch that water, which was heated on the wood stove for *warshing*, as my grandmother would say.

During those early years in Waverley, my intense love of the woods remained strong. There are many creatures, large and small, in the woods of Nova Scotia, and I got to know many of them, none more so than snakes. It's kind of ironic that today they give me a severe case of the heebie-jeebies or, as they say in Britain, "the screaming habdabs." (I dislike frogs and toads even more . . . did I mention that? No? Well, I do!)

But back then, I'd find snakes lying about casually catching some sun on a rock, or in the shade of an old stump or tree, or in the green grass. Of course, I'd proceed to put a crimp in their otherwise mundane lives by snatching them up and whipping them into a tote bag. And, yes, they'd get more than a bit irate with yours truly. It must have been humiliating and a hard adjustment to make, all things considered, and they let me know that a line had been crossed.

One of the games we used to enjoy as youngsters during the summer months was identifying cars. This is how the game worked. I would sit with a friend or two down by the road at a point where we could see cars from a fair ways off. The first to identify the vehicle would win. We not only had to guess the car maker—as in "It's a Ford!"—but name the model and the year. For example, the first of us to shout out, "It's a 1954 Ford Fairlane!" would win all the marbles, figuratively and some-times literally.

This was a game you could play anywhere and anytime you wanted to. All you needed was a road and some traffic. Aha, traffic! Therein lies the rub at times. If you were waiting for the tiebreaker on Waverley Road on a Tuesday summer afternoon back then, the wait could go on for a long, long time. Waiting for the next vehicle to come by could become tedious, so we'd go for a walk, often to Shupes, an insignificant walk back then—perhaps a mile or two away—all the while keeping an eye and ear out for the next car, the tiebreaker that would reward the winner with a nickel to spend at Shupes.

Shupes was a small canteen on the side of the road that sold junk food, pop, and cigarettes mostly. That was basically it. We went there often during the years I lived on Waverley Road. On the way home from school, we'd go in and buy a soft drink or a treat of some kind if we had some change. It was also a bit of a hangout for us. The canteen was attached to a one-storey bungalow in back, and next to it was another house. They shared the same driveway. The guy who lived in this other house next to Shupes was an Armed Forces man, and one day he killed his wife and two children, set the house on fire, and then committed suicide. Very tragic.

As a young teenager, my mode of transportation wouldn't be a Studebaker Golden Hawk or a Chevy Bel Air, obviously. It was in fact a bicycle, and my first was a real stinker. It was an old second-hand CCM, about two sizes too big.

This bike that Dad gave me was so big, I couldn't sit on the seat and pedal at the same time, or apply the brakes, which was awkward and often more than a tad embarrassing when trying to stop quickly. It would have been easier to ride if it had been a girl's bike without the top bar that ran from the front part of the frame where the steering is located to the section attached to the seat. I could only sit on the seat when coasting because my legs weren't long enough for my feet to reach the pedals. All efforts to control this big, dumb, clumsy vehicle, which included, but was not limited to, speeding up and slowing down or the all-important stop, and often the sooner the better, required that I stand at a spirited, brave, spastic form of attention. It was also necessary to "stand tall" on the bike in order to pedal up a steep hill. Usually one needed to be standing vertically only to relieve the pressure on "the package."

Because of the inconvenience required to move both pedals in tandem, an additional passenger would sit on the knobby metal handlebars, which if I think about it, were likely more comfortable than the rock-hard seat.

Did I mention that the dim bastard didn't have frigging fenders? That was a treat on a wet or dirty surface, leaving me, by the end of the trip, looking like some kind of mutant skunk with a nasty stripe of brown running from my "package" up and over my entire body. The uncontained mud from the surface of the roads flew at me with a force that even parted my hair for me. Ha ha. Real attractive, not to mention hard on the eyes. I am now rolling my peepers in mock sarcasm, folks. Oh, well . . .

I claimed ownership of this two-wheeled roadster from hell for about a year or so before it was replaced with a newer green-coloured, three-speed Raleigh bicycle.

There was a noisy, attention-seeking, fun trick we used to play that, in fact and fiction, produced loud, rapid fart-like sounds. This was something that played heck with the spokes, so please don't try it at home, kids. Clothespins attaching hard, folded cardboard from the front and rear wheel forks to the wheel spokes produced this irritating noise pollution. It was supposed to simulate the sound of a motorcycle.

Life was usually simple and easy-going when I was a young fella, but not without some occasional drama. One day, I fell from a ladder and landed on a cinder block. That summer's day, my father was doing some work on the roof of our house. He asked me to bring him something: a drink, some nails, some tiles, or some such thing. After passing him what he needed, I turned to climb back down but I slipped and fell. My left foot struck a cinder block on the inside near the ankle bone and punctured an artery, causing the blood to spurt out as if it were being expelled by an old-fashioned drinking-well hand pump.

If that happened to me or one of my kids today, I'd wrap the leg just above the ankle itself and apply pressure to the puncture while I got to the hospital *promptement*. But Dad, probably having watched too many *Dr. Kildare* shows on TV, decided to deal with it himself.

Somehow, he managed to stop the bleeding and got it wrapped up. I had even stopped crying and making a fuss. After a time, I needed to go pee, so I limped inside—we had indoor plumbing at this point—and into the bathroom where I closed the blanket we used for a makeshift door. Then, because my eyes were turning yellow and I needed to piss like a race horse, I recklessly yanked down my zipper—and screamed.

Whoever was nearby came running to the rescue thinking the worst had somehow happened to my injured foot and therefore it was an emergency. Well, it *was* an emergency, but not what they were thinking. My cocktail wiener was meshed into the zipper.

I realized there was only one thing to do; well, two actually. First, I had to keep the enquiring do-gooders out of the crime scene area. I managed to say something like, "I'm good. No worries. I got it."

Then my only choices were either to cut my penis off, which I thought hard about for a second—I can't help but wonder what my ex-wives are thinking reading this bit—or to further lacerate my unfortunate friend by undoing my zipper. I went for option two, which was to put my meat and two veggies back through the blender.

That was *not* a great day, and all these years later, that vulnerable soft area on the side of my foot is numb and uncomfortable to the touch.

Living on the lake, we'd find things washed ashore; not as much as if you lived on the ocean, but some interesting stuff nonetheless. There was a seaplane club at the end of the lake, and the planes used to crash the odd time. One of them washed up on the shore and it was there for a couple of days in about ten feet of water. As kids, we'd swim like fish and we'd go down there, inside the cockpit, and look around the plane. It was a lot of fun until they dragged it away.

Another time, a very long, narrow wooden boat came ashore. We pulled it up and it wasn't seaworthy at all, so Dad and I repaired it. We dried it out completely in the sun, and then my dad made a steel rudder at the shop where he worked. We put in all the caulking and everything so it wouldn't leak. We got the boat to the point that it would float, and then we made a sail out of canvas that he brought home from work. I suspect he really "borrowed" all of this stuff from work. He also acquired some metal pieces and then welded them together, loaded them in the trunk of his car, and brought it all it home.

So, we built this long, skinny, impossible sailboat equipped with a homemade rudder and a steering mechanism made with big knuckle-like joints of solder. What could go wrong?

We happened to pick the windiest day of the year to launch it.

Lake William is a long lake and we were almost at one end, so we had a lot of lake in front of us. I managed to row this sailboat out into the middle despite the stiff wind and the erratic, pounding chop. I'd never sailed before, and even a seasoned sailor wouldn't have attempted to go out in such a ridiculous excuse for a sailing craft. Eventually, up came the single triangular sail of thick canvas with a loud whoosh, and because there was no resistance from my flat-bottomed sliver of a boat, I was soon doing about forty-five miles an hour in heavy winds with no clue how to stop the boat or even how to steer it. I yelled out, "Dad, I'm sailing!"

At that point the boat was like a torpedo, slicing through the waves, the sail pinned and taut from the force of the wind. I had to stop or turn it around soon or do something or I was going to keep going right through whatever structure or building I might hit at the end of the lake. As soon as I turned the rudder to try to turn, the whole boat went out of control, doing a fierce 180-degree roll, snapping the mast instantly. I dove off the boat just before it came apart. I surfaced only to see it, bottom up, continuing on down the lake without me.

Though it could have had a disastrous turn, afterwards I looked back on the incident and laughed.

But our lake adventures in those days didn't always have happy endings. One day, when my buddies and I were in our early teens, we were going camping. It was early evening and there were five or six of us walking along Waverley Road. As we came around a bend, we saw police cars and an ambulance with their lights flashing.

A couple of people had been sailing up the lake from Waverley, and the sun was directly behind them. A seaplane coming in didn't see the sailboat. We knew both of the boys in the boat. The fellow who was killed was Dennis Manley, who was about our age and a guy we had gone to school with. The other person saw the plane coming and jumped off the boat in time. Dennis froze and he was decapitated. The propeller just went right through him. When we got to that spot, the water was all red and like chum, with pieces of flesh floating here and there. There were pieces of the boat and the plane along the shoreline. It was so nasty the police didn't want us to see it. Although we could see what had happened, we didn't get the full details until later. We didn't go camping. We just went home. We were freaked out.

3

—

After my mother died, I can say without a doubt that music was my salvation. It saved me from being a lost soul with no purpose or direction at a vulnerable time in my life. Of course, at such a young age, I had no idea what that direction would be exactly. Odd to me now is the fact that it would be many years before I realized that music truly was my calling and to attempt any other profession, as an adult, would have been a big mistake. But at eleven years old, all I knew was that music spoke to me through the silence of devastating sorrow, and it's clear to me that music helped me deal with the loneliness and the feelings of abandonment I was going through. It gave me hope. It comforted me.

Behind our house in Waverley was a massive white granite rock. It was embedded at the top of a forested hill overlooking Lake William, and that's where I would go when I needed a place to think. I never thought of it back then as meditating, but I guess it was, at least in part. That's also where I would hide out and escape from the world when I was overwhelmed. That huge white rock that sparkled in the sun from the components of quartz and mica in its makeup would be my place of solitude. It would become more and more important to me as I got older and life became more complicated. I would go up there by myself, sit on that rock, and just look down over the lake.

That's where I went with my guitar. That was my place. No one else went there, just me.

I enjoyed music from my childhood days. My dad always had a radio playing when I was growing up. Even when we were working outside—and Dad was forever working on, or building, something—music was on in the background. We mostly listened to country music, artists like Webb Pierce, Eddy Arnold, Tennessee Ernie Ford, and Patsy Cline, among the many other country greats of the mid-1950s. Later on, there was Johnny Cash, Marty Robbins, and a slew of other guys and gals, mostly American artists. But one of the most successful country artists of all time was Hank Snow, also from Nova Scotia.

I learned to play Hank Snow's hit songs along with other country hits when I was kid. He was *the* guy from the Maritimes. We could relate to that, but Hank Snow was huge everywhere. He joined the Grand Ole Opry in Nashville in 1950 and was later inducted into the Country Music Hall of Fame in Nashville as well as the Canadian Country Music Hall of Fame and the Canadian Music Hall of Fame, making all Canadians and especially us fellow Bluenosers very proud.

I knew how to play and sing that country stuff, more or less. That's what I heard at home, so that's what I learned to play growing up. When we went out to see live country music performed locally in Dartmouth, which was not that often unfortunately, it was a great experience. I loved live music. I never guessed then that performing live would eventually become a way of life for me.

But I have be honest, folks, I do not remember when I picked up a guitar for the first time. Apparently, I could play a bit from the time I was about five years old or so, and that ability came from my mother's side of the family.

I've been told that almost everybody on my mother's side played an instrument and sang, and I understand that Dad was able to diddle about with a guitar a bit. They say my mother had a very nice voice and was always singing. Her personal musical ability extended to singing harmonies behind her brother Bob's vocals. The ability to sing vocal harmonies is not easy and usually requires natural talent and a good ear.

This natural ability apparently rubbed off on me, I'm grateful to say, and it is my mother I thank for this wonderful gift of music that not only defines who I am spiritually and has made my personal journey so blessed but also has given my life purpose. Thanks, Mom. I have missed you so, and I will love you for always.

My uncle Bob was perhaps the most accomplished musician in our family. He actually toured the Maritimes with a country music group called Tex Shaw and the Rocky Mountain Rangers, attired in full country and western outfits. They played Nova Scotia, Prince Edward Island, New Brunswick, and even parts of northern Maine.

Uncle Bob taught himself to play guitar from books at about the age of six when no one else was around to show him how it was done. His older brother Evertt had a Gibson acoustic guitar that Bob taught himself on, and I like to think Uncle Evertt showed his younger brother a thing or two from time to time. When Uncle Bob got a little older, he bought his own guitar and started playing at social functions. Later, he moved to Brantford, Ontario, where he met some guys from Springhill, Nova Scotia, made famous as the hometown of Canadian singing star Anne Murray, and they started to play music together.

They gigged in the area and even performed on radio. Bob was asked to go to the Grand Ole Opry at one time by country music legend Roy Acuff but felt he was too young. How about that, folks?

Like so many Canadian country and western singers of the time, Uncle Bob aspired to the type of success achieved by Hank Snow. Snow was a very successful country artist at the time, of course, and almost everyone I remember hearing sing his tunes all those years ago tried to sound like him. He had that nasal sound of his that I guess was quite distinctive, and for my money, it only worked when he did it. He sounded awesome. To me, as a kid, others sounded like they had a head cold or sinus allergies.

Clearly, another great thing about Hank Snow was his ability to write a hit song, and he wrote many of them including "I'm Movin' On," which was covered by a number of rock artists, including Elvis Presley, the Rolling Stones, and Steppenwolf, with Snow's version spending a record twenty-one weeks at the top of the Billboard country chart, as did other compositions such as "The Golden Rocket" and "Rhumba Boogie."

I visited the Hank Snow Country Music Centre in Liverpool, Nova Scotia, back in 2005, and although it was closed that day, Lauren Tutty, the centre's manager, did me a favour and not only let me in but gave me a personal tour as well. She then let me go through the place alone and at my own pace. It was fascinating to me. I know of no one else at that time, or few since, who achieved more fame in the United States musically by relying solely on his own personal talents, personal drive, and originality than that man.

I eventually learned all the hit country songs of the day. I knew how to play the music on guitar, and I would sing the words to myself, in my head. I was far too shy to sing in front of anyone. These songs that I got to know and enjoy had a tremendous effect on me musically. Some of my favourite artists back then were Marty Robbins, Buck Owens, Don Gibson, Hank Williams, and Jimmie Rodgers.

Hank Williams was special. I knew that when my age was still a single digit and my voice more suited for the Vienna Boys' Choir—in pitch, I mean, not in my ability to sing. He was the other singer who had a long-lasting influence on my relatives who were passionate about their music. Hank Williams was, and still is, an enigma to the music world. He transcended all styles and had an uncanny ability to write important, sometimes happy, often sad, songs that were reflections of himself and the time in which he lived. His songs have been covered by countless artists over the decades. His most notable compositions include "Jambalaya," "Hey Good Lookin'," "Your Cheatin' Heart," and a personal favourite, "I'm So Lonesome I Could Cry." And there are so many more.

A few of the songs at the top of the charts in the mid-'50s included Bill Haley's "Rock Around the Clock," Tennessee Ernie Ford's "Sixteen Tons," Bill Hayes' "The Ballad of Davy Crockett," and Pee Wee King and His Golden West Cowboys' "Slow Poke." Okay, this last one I don't remember; catchy song title, though.

Elvis Presley seemed to come out of nowhere and take the world by storm. I watched his first appearance on *The Ed Sullivan Show* with my father and my brothers on September 9, 1956, on a second-hand black-and-white television. (In remembering that night, I can't help but realize I have no recollection of my mother watching that famous *Ed Sullivan Show* broadcast with us, but she must have been there with Dad and us kids. It would be only three more years before she succumbed to cancer.) It was the season premiere, and that night British actor Charles Laughton was filling in for Sullivan, who was recuperating from injuries he sustained in a head-on car crash that August. Elvis was not in the studio in New York either. His four songs that night — "Love Me Tender," "Don't Be Cruel," "Hound Dog," all chart-topping songs in 1956, and "Ready Teddy"—were performed from the CBS studios in Hollywood where he was filming his first movie, *Love Me Tender*. I was eight years old and, boy, what a year for rock 'n' roll it was. Elvis had six songs in the top ten that year, five of them number ones, including the three he performed on *The Ed Sullivan Show* as well as "I Want You, I Need You, I Love You" and "Heartbreak Hotel."

I was in grade 4 at Waverley Memorial and loving the music I was hearing. I was experiencing it for the first time like everyone else. I remember the excitement of that *Ed Sullivan* telecast. I don't know if anyone else in our home that night was as pumped as I was, but my dad must have been interested in seeing what all the hoopla was about. Besides, he liked Elvis's country-flavoured hit tune "Love Me Tender."

When I finally saw *Love Me Tender*, I was mesmerized watching Elvis's every move; I hung on to every word. I knew he was the real deal musically and that the girls were crazy for him, and I was fascinated by it all. I can remember people saying, "Well, he can sing all right, but let's see if he can act." Fair enough.

I was honestly nervous for him. To me, he seemed like a good guy and I wanted him to do well. I enjoyed the movie, but he dies in it. I watched with sadness as "Elvis the Pelvis" bit the bullet. To me, it was tender and it was cool. Of course, Elvis would go on to make many more movies, and frankly, a great deal of them weren't very good artistically. He wanted better roles and to make quality movies but that never really happened, and he would come to hate Hollywood and movie making. But his music rocked!

There was no question Elvis was King, and he ruled the popular airwaves in 1956 and 1957. Then it all came to an end. He was drafted into the army.

But there were lots of great performers and marvellous songs on the radio at this time. A song called "Blueberry Hill" by Fats Domino really stood out to me. I just loved the feel; the sixteenth notes he played with his right hand, the low bass notes in half time, and his rich New Orleans vocal styling were wonderfully rhythmic. It was rock 'n' roll magic that immediately cast its lasting spell on me. Fats had hit after hit and I was a big fan.

In 2007, fifty-one years later, I asked blues singer and piano player Kenny "Blues Boss" Wayne, who was about to play on a mid-tempo blues song of mine titled "Tell Me Where I've Been, So I Don't Go There Anymore," if he could give me that Fats Domino, "Blueberry Hill" feel. He smiled and said, "Oh, yeah!" He nailed it. Kenny is also a big fan of "The Fat Man" from Louisiana. Fats would have a string of hits in the '50s and '60s with the instrumental and vocal stylings that were uniquely his own.

My first radio was a small cream-coloured Philco transistor with three burgundy dials, and I was able to seek out some of the stations available to us in that part of rural Nova Scotia. There is something extraordinary about lying in bed at night and hearing faraway voices coming to you from distant places. It was kind of surreal. Every kind of audio entertainment you can imagine was at your fingertips during these final days of the golden age of radio. The weekly radio programs were great fun: *The Green Hornet, Amos 'n' Andy, The Roy Rogers Show*—all different styles to enjoy with just the turn of the Bakelite dial.

As I write these memories down, I get to relive those times with a more intellectual curiosity. As well as being cathartic, it instills in me a need to understand why things were the way they were and why I was the way I was back then. That, in turn, helps me appreciate, in a more informed and benevolent fashion, the person I am today.

With that in mind, I can recall the mood and the sounds of life back then. Listening to the radio broadcasts, it was almost as if I was eavesdropping on others in far-off places as they went about their daily business. At times I felt I needed to hold my breath in order to avoid being discovered, fearing that that profound intimacy we shared, though miles apart, would suddenly be shattered.

Besides music stations, there were other programs I listened to. One of my favourites for a time in the mid-'60s was the hugely successful hour-long radio talk program called *The World Tomorrow*, a show of reflections, philosophy, and commentary on the times by American evangelist Garner Ted Armstrong. In the '70s, *Penthouse* magazine noted that Garner Ted provided "late night companionship to thousands of truckers, the voice of the morning to millions of farmers, the living room preacher to a subculture of lonely frightened disoriented Americans."

The show was mixed with political, economic, and social news with Bible-based commentary. Armstrong's voice, style, and presentation, with his low-keyed iconic delivery, were more in the style of a comedian's monologue than the didactic fashion of the standard evangelist.

I listened to this very entertaining program for some years. There was a period later on when Jim Henman, a founding member of April Wine, and I would sit in his dad's Buick at night and smoke "pinched" cigarette butts from the ashtray, listening, captivated by his voice, his words, and mesmerizing delivery.

But mostly it was the music on the radio that I tuned in to. I enjoyed the different styles of music, the sounds of different instruments, and the variety of vocal sounds and performances. The sound that intrigued me the most was the electric guitar.

My musical skills on the guitar were slowly developing and switching more and more from country songs played on an acoustic, steel-string guitar to electric guitar riffs and rhythms that I had learned on the acoustic. I was constantly adding songs to my "repertoire" through 1957 and 1958, the nascent years of rock 'n' roll and pop music.

The popular songs of the day were a strange mix of the great songs ("Smoke Gets in Your Eyes"), bad ones (Tab Hunter's version of "Young Love"), instrumentals like Boots Randolph's "Yakety Sax," and downright silly tunes like "The Chipmunk Song."

But the music that I heard and enjoyed the most back then was rhythm and blues. Of course, that meant Motown. There are too many artists and songs to list here, but the music of Motown ruled the airwaves for years starting in the 1950s through the '60s and even into the '70s.

***

I learned to play the guitar on an inexpensive acoustic that belonged to my father. I'm not sure what make it was. It was harder to play than it had to be. The strings were a bit too far from the neck, and you had to press firmly on the strings for it to sound okay. When you know what you're doing, and you're doing it on a quality instrument, just a little pressure is required in order for the instrument to sound as it should. With this guitar you needed to be firm. Playing it made my fingers ache. The guitar was a plain brown model, a six string with a black pickguard. It helped fill the hours when I wasn't floundering about at school or fishing for flounder or tending to my rabbit snares.

I played that guitar until I was mentally tired and my fingers were sore. The strings were also tired. I played them until they sounded dead and a tad rusty from my sweaty hands. I had to boil the strings from time to time to keep them clean and sounding as good as could be expected. It also helped to keep them from breaking. Strings cost money and money was scarce. I used bread ties and other pieces of plastic for a plectrum (or guitar pick).

I liked to play the drums as well, and I used pots and pans for drums, and pencils and long-handled combs and other similarly shaped things for drumsticks.

I would spend many hours sitting there all alone on that large granite rock behind our house or down on the shore of the lake or in my room, with the guitar in my hands, working on songs. I was trying to be a better player, a better singer, as I learned the hits of the day.

I find it funny to think that years later, kids would learn how to play and sing songs that I wrote and sang, songs that were hits for April Wine over the years, many of them now referred to as classics.

4
—

carried on like this over the next few years, working on play-ing guitar, listening to what was popular on the radio, and going to school. And then for me, in the summer of 1963, life on Waverley Road changed. We had neighbours move in next door, the Henmans, when I was fifteen years old.

On June 23, these new folks settled in our community, a short walk down the road or through the woods that separated our house from theirs by about a quarter mile. At that time, that kind of distance between your house and your neighbours' houses was common enough. I was just coming out of my Davy Crockett period and taking notice of other things going on around me. Up until then, I wasn't looking for friends, really. Elaine McDermott was an exception.

There were ten kids in the Henman family. Brothers Jim and Bob Henman were to become my best friends. They still are two of my dearest friends today. Jim Henman, in particular, was into music and playing guitar, and he was good at it. This com-mon interest is what brought us together with a special purpose that only music can sometimes inspire.

Jim is a year older than I am and Bob a year younger. Bob's

nickname was Dinks. When I spoke to Jim about how we first met on the day we became neighbours, he told me a story that I've heard since then, from others who were there at the time.

Apparently, I burst out of the woods that separated our house from the Henmans' house, wild-eyed and breathing hard and asking, quite emphatically, of everyone standing there, "Does someone here play the guitar?"

I sounded like a desperate person indeed, and in a way I was. I had no real friends who played guitar, or any other instrument for that matter, and I was at a point musically where I needed someone to play music with. The possibility of having a buddy next door who shared the same passion to play was a thrilling prospect. Jim remembers that at the time he felt like a freak, as he was isolated and a loner. I felt the same way.

I knew the Henmans were coming to live next door. Jim and Bob's grandparents had lived in that house for years. They were living there long before the Goodwins showed up, so we knew there was a family, with kids, moving into the house and they, the grandparents, were moving out and into a small cottage across the road on the lakefront. I was told by them that one or two of their grandchildren played the guitar.

When we met, Jim had an acoustic guitar and so did I. Mine was called a Norma, a Japanese copy of a Gibson Hummingbird. My dad bought it for me about a year before from a department store in Dartmouth called Nieforth's. The store sold everything from TVs to beds, washers and dryers, and even musical instruments. When I left our home in Waverley, I gave that guitar to Dad. I never asked him later on what he did with it. I guess I never did because I never needed it again, and so I didn't think about what happened to it.

In 2013, I was doing an April Wine gig in Vancouver, and when I arrived at the hotel from the airport I was told there was something being held at the front desk for me. Someone brought out an old, dusty guitar case. Not knowing what was in the case or who it was from, I opened it. It was Norma, my old acoustic guitar. For many years, a woman named Mary Hannaberry had been a dear friend of my father's, and when he died, she took this guitar and held on to it. And then she decided to give it to her son, who lived on the west coast, intending that he give it to me when I was in town. So here it was, some forty-five-plus years later, back in my arms. How remarkable is that, folks? What a wonderful thing for Mary to do. It was in great condition, needing only a good cleaning and a fresh set of strings. I'll never part with that guitar again.

I called Mary when I got home and thanked her from the bottom of my heart. She said that my dad kept the guitar in a closet for years, making sure it was not broken or perhaps stolen. Thanks, Dad.

Jim and I spent so much time together during those years, jamming at his house. We never jammed at my place because it was smaller, and besides, my grandmother was there. And although the Henmans were a family of twelve in total, we found more privacy and felt less noticed at Jim's. In the winter months we used his bedroom as a place to learn and create, and during the summer we hung out in a small shed situated at one side of the main house. The shed was called *Club Duschene*. There was no reason for the name other than we liked the sound of it. It had a small stage and streamers on the door, and we planned to sell tickets for twenty-five cents to watch Jim and me play. That never really materialized, though. We got together after school on weekdays and on weekends to practise and play music.

Jim and I sang songs that were popular at that time, including folk, country, and pop songs. Our favourite artists were the Everly Brothers. Their songs were catchy and relatively easy to learn, and the vocal harmonies were perfect for two guys learning to sing together. One of the first songs I wrote was inspired by the Everly Brothers and was called "You Won't Dance with Me." It later became a hit for April Wine.

But in 1964, when the Beatles arrived in North America, all the rules changed. Like the rest of the modern world, we were blown away by the whole British Invasion and the changes in the direction of popular music.

It was thrilling to see the Beatles on *The Ed Sullivan Show*. I knew their music, I had seen their pictures, and I was pumped to see them perform live on television. It was life changing, I can honestly say. This was what I wanted to do more than anything else, and watching the show that night steeled my resolve to work hard at being a singer, writer, and musician. I wanted to be in a band that would be the next Beatles.

Instead of learning songs by artists from the '40s, '50s, and early '60s, we were now learning Beatles songs and trying to figure out how they wrote them. Jim's brother Bob would beat out an offbeat rhythm on his mother's pots and pans, much to her dismay.

The Beatles songs were much harder to learn on guitar and the harmonies more difficult to reproduce than most of the stuff we had worked on up until that time. And we loved the challenge. We were trying to play like the Fab Four, sing like them, write great songs like they did, and we even tried to look like them by eventually growing our hair longer, and we wore Beatles boots. Of course, we were learning other British bands' songs that were starting to dominate the charts as well.

In 1965, I put together a three-piece group called Myles and the M.G.s. It didn't last long. I was in other outfits briefly back then but I hardly remember them, so I won't guess at those details here and now. I played at the old Waverley Hall for a while, but it was ill-fated, probably because, whatever band it was, we sucked.

The big song in our repertoire was a slow ballad called "Donna." The original was done by Ritchie Valens. "Donna" was the last song of the night, and it was the only song that had the dance floor full. Young, desperate people clinging to each other, the gals looking for romance perhaps and the guys hoping to get laid or at least the opportunity to cop a feel.

The most memorable thing about the gigs was that there was drinking and, of course, eventually fighting, which I tried to ignore. The fight would start inside the hall and it would be finished outside, so the hall would be empty while we continued playing. When the fight was over, everyone would come back inside. The violence I saw outside that particular venue at times, when I wasn't on stage but there to see other bands, was sickening. Guys with brass knuckles duking it out. The sound of a fist hitting flesh is terrible, and I heard it many times over the years. The Maritimes was behind the times in many ways, especially in smaller rural towns such as Waverley, Windsor Junction, Fall River, and the like. Marlon Brando's character, Terry Malloy, in the 1954 movie *On the Waterfront* was alive and living in Nova Scotia in 1965. The guys had ducktail haircuts, wellington boots, and a pack of smokes tucked under rolled-up sleeves, with a Zippo lighter in a pocket somewhere. The mentality of the men and the women was based on the rebel, bad boy types from that genre of films. Not everyone, of course, but many. When the British Invasion came to that part of the world it was like two worlds colliding, kind of like the Mods and Rockers in England. It got unnecessarily complicated at times.

My life, other than the music side of it, was difficult. There wasn't much joy and happiness at home, but there were some nice moments and some good memories. It was great when relatives would visit us from Ontario. These were aunts and uncles, nieces, and cousins from my dad's side of the family. Relatives from my mother's side of the family never came by, that I remember, not after she died.

My uncle Ray, Dad's brother, was a *very* funny man. He made everybody feel lucky to be in his company; he was a lovely character, full of life with a terrific sense of humour. It was a sad day when he died of cancer in his thirties.

The first time I ever played a Fender Stratocaster was when my cousin Vern brought one by the house in 1964. He was in the Air Force at the time, and he was travelling down east visiting friends and family. He also had a white Fender amplifier with him, a Tremolux I think it was. That handsome Strat had a sunburst finish, a white pickguard, and a rosewood neck. It was pretty new, and the guitar case had a brown tweed covering. To this day, the sunburst Stratocaster is my favourite Fender guitar model.

A fellow named Roger Feener lived in Waverley, near Waverley Memorial, where I first attended school in 1956. Roger was a great guy, and he gave me free lessons in his house from time to time. He was in his early twenties and living with his mother. One day, I dropped by his house knowing he'd be at work. I told his mother when she answered my knock at the door that Roger said I could borrow his Stratocaster for the day. She handed me the guitar and I rushed home and played that thing for hours. I was sure to get it back before Roger got back home. But his mom told him what happened. I heard that he was really pissed and looking for me. I avoided him for a few weeks. When I finally saw him again, he was over it and gave me a few more lessons.

It's important to remember the good times and not just the difficult ones as we go through life.

Some memories of those days are quite humorous, and now, years later, they still make me shake my head and chuckle.

For about a month one summer, I worked at a place that refurbished school desks. Our job was to scrape and sand the old desks to remove initials and chewing gum and anything else that was there so they could be restained and made to look good again for the next school year. We were paid a dollar for each chair we completed. We each averaged two or three chairs a day.

The large building that housed all the desks and other types of used furniture was built next to a large pond that was said to be bottomless. Legend has it that two horses and a wagon went into the pond and were never seen again, even after many attempts to retrieve them from the bottomless depths of the dark, sinister-looking water.

One day the son of the man who owned the business got angry at a derogatory remark I aimed at him, and he told me he was going to kick the shit out of me and toss me in the pond when he got back at the end of the day at five o'clock. I told him to bring it on, that I'd be right there at five waiting for him. His name was Moose. I was a dead man.

I waited all afternoon for Moose to return, mindful of the bottomless pool of mystery that was all too visible as I worked that long, hot afternoon sanding a desk. My friends told me to leave ASAP in case he came back early, but I held my ground. I refused to let this ape get the best of me. But I had a plan and I prayed it would all work out in my favour.

Finally, five o'clock arrived, and at exactly 5:00 p.m., I hurried off the lot, saying, "Tell Moose I was here till five! Tell him he was a no-show and that I win!"

My plan was simple. I knew that Moose would end up at a tavern as he always did on Fridays and that he'd show up late. I'd be gone by then and able to save face. My last look back that day was at the bottomless pond with its wild bulrushes and the countless skitters franticly skimming the fearful surface of the water; I shuddered at the thought of what might have happened. I didn't go back to work on Monday.

I heard a story years later that at one point Moose had been missing for two days before he was found hanging from a fence in a wooded area that he tried to cross at night when he was drunk. His shirt got caught up and he was unable to free himself.

School was hard for me, and I didn't like it much. I was mostly daydreaming in class and not listening to what I was being taught. I failed a few grades starting in grade 7 when I was twelve years old. My mother had died the year before.

A tough memory for me, folks, is remembering my dad's disappointment that I was losing a year of my life repeating the same grade. I finally passed grade 7 the third time and went on to grade 8. Then I spent two years in grade 8. I heard my father crying in his bedroom after he'd seen my latest report card where, at the bottom, it said that I failed. Again. I was breaking his heart.

I was very self-conscious for a few reasons.

One, I was considered poor and therefore different because of it. My mother was dead, and that was an uncomfortable truth that made my brothers and me different.

We were lower income, a charity case. Folks were kind, but it didn't really help fitting in. I was a skinny kid with frizzy hair and pimples. The pimples were the main reason for my lack of confidence in my teens. I had them bad.

I remember that the school principal at L.C. Skerry had me meet with a dermatologist to see if that person could help me with my skin condition. The principal was a tall, shapely raven-haired woman with a big space between her two front teeth. She drove a noisy, grey four-door diesel Mercedes-Benz. This intimidating creature told me that it was a shame, but because of the severity of my acne, I would be scarred for life. Gee, thank you for making my day, Teach!

The dermatologist I was sent to was a woman who looked like she'd been up all night. What a mess she was with her mouse-coloured hair, her splotched makeup, her puffy, blanched face, and her rumpled clothing. She was clearly hungover. I just stared at her thinking, what the fuck? After barely looking at me, she told me to shave in one direction—I didn't shave when I was fourteen—and to put some Clearasil on my zits. What a waste of time she was.

Boils. I had boils everywhere. On my arms, my back, and my neck. But the worst were the ones under my arms, big nasty things filled with pus, so uncomfortable I couldn't lower my arms for the pain. Many a time I would find myself sitting at the kitchen table in Waverley, my arms held up, looking like the upper part of a scarecrow hanging from an invisible cross. My grandmother had homemade poultices of bread and milk positioned on the boils. Their purpose was to suck out the poison and that long, wormlike cord that went deep into the infection. It was an awful business.

By the way, that insensitive principal was correct. I still carry the scars.

When I left L.C. Skerry, I went to Sidney Stephen High School in Bedford, Nova Scotia. I was finally in a school where there were students my own age, regardless of the fact that they were all several classes ahead of me. Jim and Bob Henman were there already. Finally, there were music programs and a glee club and a variety club and theatrical events. And girls my age! That all was pretty sweet after the crap at L.C., where there had been no music programs offered at all and the girls were more like children than young adults.

An odd thing happened when I arrived at Sidney Stephen High. The powers that be decided I should be in grade 9A. Now, back then the grades were identified by a letter and a number, depending on the abilities of the students. For example, the smart students were in grade 9A, while the less accomplished students were in 9B, all the way down to 9E. So what the hell was I doing in 9A, you ask?

Well, they gave me an IQ test and based on the result decided I was failing school because I wasn't challenged enough. What a crock! The reality should have been obvious: I was failing because I didn't care about school after my mother died. Our family was a mess. There was no academic discipline at home, and there was no direction. I cared more about music than I did about school studies, anyway. My brothers were also doing poorly in school.

Here I was in 9A surrounded by fellow classmates—some of these kids had even skipped grades—four and five years younger than I was. Regardless of their collective professional opinion that I would likely flourish academically now that I was faced with real challenges, I floundered.

Although I didn't repeat a grade again while attending high school at Sidney Stephen in Bedford, I sucked nonetheless. I was no longer welcomed in "A" classes. The second year I was in 10B for a while and then 10E, where I belonged, I guess.

Music was now all I really thought about. I was constantly daydreaming and hearing music playing in my head, current music, all kinds of music. I wanted to learn more about it. At the risk of sounding overly theatrical, I'd say that music was my magnificent obsession.

It was when I went to Sidney Stephen High, where Jim was a senior student by this time having started going there in 1964, that I had the opportunity to join a real band. It happened quickly. Jim was in a school band called Creatures, and he recruited me as a guitar player. We changed the name of the band, and that's how we started Woody's Termites, which also included Doug Grace, Dave Dodsworth, and Greg Stephen.

Woody's Termites was a decent cover band and we did well.

There were lots of gigs, the main one being a regular Saturday night show at the Bedford Fire Hall. We had that gig wrapped up for two years. My memories of the band are mostly good, but nothing really jumps out at me aside from the fact that I got to play some great tunes on the guitar, sing background harmonies, and make money. The songs we played were the latest songs to go Top 40. Our singer was great at picking out the songs for the band to learn.

Woody's Termites was a vehicle for Jim and me to try out original material. I had two songs back then, a song called "Why" and one named "You Won't Dance with Me," the latter a slow Everly Brothers–styled ballad. Later they became one. "You Won't Dance with Me" was written because of my experience of having a girlfriend and being a musician in a band. Because I was in the band playing at the dance, I could not be with my friend dancing and hanging out. Eventually that friend would go off with someone who could give her the attention she needed.

By this time, Jim and I were playing electric guitars. Jim owned an Eko six-string electric that his father had bought him. One day he went to his father and explained that I didn't have an electric guitar and that he would like a bass guitar because that's what he wanted to play. He intended to give me his six string. His father agreed to buy him an Eko bass guitar. Thanks to Jim's dad, we both had electric instruments. Jim was very appreciative of his father's understanding, and I appreciated Jim's kindness to me.

We made good money in the Termites by playing on the weekends. The longer we were together, the more we were in demand, and therefore we earned more money. After a time, we were doing three or four gigs a week and travelling outside of our immediate area. There were two trips to Prince Edward Island, for example.

The money was decent and we bought better band gear, like Fender amplifiers, a Thomas organ for Greg, and Ludwig drums for Dave, as well as good-quality microphones. We bought stage outfits to wear, including reversible vests with white shag on one side and brown suede on the other. And, of course, Beatles boots.

Greg was, and probably still is, a good musician. He was a quiet fellow, as was I most of the time, but we were different otherwise. I never knew what Greg thought of me back then. I was surprised when he put pen to paper at the request of a friend of mine. Surprised that he'd take the time to reminisce with us, but more surprised by his comments.

Greg Stephen said he was introduced to me through siblings of the John Henman family, who were parishioners in our local church, and that it was rumoured that I was a homegrown version of James Dean, a rebel, my cause being music. According to Greg, to his astonishment, he discovered I did fulfill that billing somewhat. I had the aura of a loner, but at the time, he was more impressed by the fact I had somehow paroled myself from Sunday services, in fact all pious admonishment, a truly miraculous achievement of which Greg was highly envious.

In an interview, Greg indicated that the James Dean mystique had only deepened over the years as our relationship developed. "In common with many others, I felt an instinctive affection for Myles," Greg revealed. "As a teenager, there was more poignancy in his melancholy than pessimism, and although a solitary figure, he didn't evoke pity but rather admiration similar to the emotions people feel seeing young soldiers off to war. There was a touch of heroic in Myles, and I observed that resiliency put to effective use many times. It's a cliché, but Myles Goodwyn was an original. He often ruffled feathers, but that's *de rigeur* with people who remain true to themselves."

I lost track of Greg after the Termites, but I know he continued to play keyboards and travelled a lot. Apparently, he has jammed with some fine musicians in Canada and the U.S.

From what I understand, Greg departed Nova Scotia permanently as early as was practical and wasn't overly concerned with the route or, for that matter, its terminus. He played on and off in an ad hoc band performing Motown music, so he landed in Detroit. He says it's hard to picture now, but Motown in the late 1960s was quite polished and aristocratic, reminiscent, or at least so he imagined it, of the bygone era of the big bands. In fact, the first musician he met in Detroit was Duke Ellington. Through a friend, a respected musician in the Smokey Robinson band, Greg was accepted into the local club scene and played with some of the Motown greats. Later, after everyone moved to Los Angeles, the Detroit scene, like the city itself, deteriorated dramatically until fond memories are about all that's left. If you mention Motown today, it's like speaking of the Holy Roman Empire.

It's very interesting sometimes to hear what others think of you. When I started this book, I had no idea of the image I projected to others at different times throughout my life. Some folks have nice things to say about me and others, well, not so much. I take it all as it is intended and carry on. It is what it is, as they say. When I read what ex-Termite Greg Stephen said about me, I couldn't help but wonder how he came to see me as a James Dean kind of character. That remark stayed with me and I thought about it for a while, shaking my head and chuckling as I did. Then it came to me.

Greg mentioned that he heard of me through folks at the church. That makes sense. I sang in the choir and taught Sunday school for a while. That's a goody-goody image for sure, but there was another side of me that was quite different, so perhaps it's the other guy he was referring to.

You see, back then, I was known in the area as a bit of a car thief. Not *Grand Theft Auto* kind of shit, just small-time "borrowing." During the time that I was borrowing cars I was in my teens and living at home in Waverley with my dad and brothers. I don't think they knew about my need to borrow.

Most weekends I went to Halifax to see bands, often alone. The distance from where I lived on Waverley Road to where the dances were held in Halifax was about twenty-five kilometres in total. One way. That's a long way to walk, folks.

After attending the dance or a club to see a live band, it was time to get home. I'd walk, all by myself in the dark, through the streets of Halifax and across the old Macdonald Bridge to Dartmouth. When I got to the Dartmouth side of the bridge, I'd visit a large used GM car dealership, which was just a short distance farther on. Then I'd find a Chevy or some such General Motors vehicle, start it up, drive it to Bedford, park it in the parking lot of the bowling alley my friends and I frequented, and then walk the rest of the way home. I'd get in around two or three in the morning.

The reason I usually had no problems starting a car was that, back then, if the ignition switch wasn't turned all the way to *lock*, the car could be started without a key. Easy as pie. Back then a lot of cars—not a luxury car like a Cadillac mind you, but the less expensive models—were often left open and the ignition switch in the unlocked position. All I needed to do was find one. Oh, yeah, and not get caught. And I never was caught, but one time, it was *unbelievably* close.

One night at about midnight, I found a four-door Chevy in the dealership that was unlocked and I started it up. I was always careful that there were no police around or a witness who might grab me and hold me until the police could be summoned. I'd watch from a dark area of the lot, and when I was certain the coast was clear, I'd move stealth-like, from car to car trying door after door. When I found the right one, I'd start it and drive slowly, with the headlights off, out of the lot and onto the street. I preferred the automatic transmission because they were less likely to stall.

Anyway, this particular night, I had that four-door Chevy, with an auto transmission, going down the street next to the dealership where I'd just borrowed it, in the direction of the old bridge to Halifax, when the son of a gun stalled. There was a curb, so I couldn't pull the car over out of the lane. Luckily there was no traffic. I sat there in the car and decided to wait a few minutes before trying to start it again.

I was just about to try firing up the engine when a police car came out of nowhere. It pulled up behind me and an officer got out. He walked up to the driver's door and motioned for me to lower the window.

"What's the problem, son?"

"Not sure, sir, it just stopped running."

He took a step back, looked at me, then looked at the car from one end to the other. Then he said, "Okay, pop the hood!" I felt around, found the hood lever, and pulled on it, hoping to hell it would release the hood. It did.

I was shitting a brick. Here I was at midnight, sitting in a stolen car, with no keys in the ignition—if he had looked carefully, he would have noticed—and not even a driver's licence. Did I mention that I'd been drinking?

The officer was now bent over the engine, sniffing and poking around, touching shit and whatever. He then stood up and motioned for me to turn the key.

"Try starting it," he said and stood back.

I took hold of the part on the steering column where the ignition key goes in and gave it a turn. The fucking thing started!

I was stunned. The officer looked pleased. He closed the hood and proceeded to walk completely around the stolen Chevy. He then asked me to get out of the car.

"Come 'round here, please." He was now on the sidewalk facing the rear passenger door.

"Open the door and take out that beer bottle." It was an order, and at this point, I figured I was going to jail. I opened the back door, reached in, and picked up the beer bottle, an unopened bottle of Schooner. I stood up with the beer in my hand.

"Here, open it." He handed me a bottle opener. Was he going to make me drink it? I felt like I could have used a pull or two, that's for sure.

I took the opener and opened the bottle. I held out my two hands before me, the bottle in one hand and the opener in the other. He took the opener.

"Pour out the beer, son." And you know I did. When the bottle was empty he took it from me.

"Now get in the car and go home. Do not stop along the way."

He walked back to his car and stopped with one hand on the door handle of his cruiser, looked back at me, and said, "Drive carefully, son."

Then he got in and drove away. He didn't even watch me pull out, and he never followed me.

Like I said, it was *unbelievably* close.

I'm not sure if this kind of behaviour is what Greg meant when he said I was a homegrown version of James Dean. I sure as hell didn't look like him.

When I was about sixteen and going to L.C. Skerry in Waverley, I used to buy a pack of cigarettes for sixty cents or so and run a cigarette lottery. I would buy the pack over the weekend and then sell tickets at school starting on Mondays, with a draw at noon on Fridays. It was very lucrative. Not many kids my age could buy smokes because they were either too young or they didn't want their parents to find out from the local vendors that they were smoking, but I had my ways. James Dean had *his* ways, right?

Back then, and probably today still, kids under legal age would get beer and liquor by standing outside a liquor commission with money asking a friendly or cool-looking guy to buy them a mickey-sized bottle of rum or rye or some cheap wine and, of course, some beer. Single bottles were easier to carry than, say, a case of beer. Mickey-sized bottles were quite easy to hide in a pocket or tuck into the waist of a pair of jeans. Lemon gin was a popular purchase because the girls liked it. We called it panty remover.

For the smokes lottery, I simply used narrow strips of plain paper about five inches long that I would fashion myself with scissors. They had a number written on them twice so that when a student bought a "ticket," I would keep the corresponding number with the name next to it for proof. The tickets cost twenty-five cents, and I would sell ten or so tickets during the week. After costs, I was making about $2.00 profit off my sixty-cent investment. Not bad. A six-pack of beer at that time cost a buck.

But eventually I was called into the school office and told to stop selling cigarettes. It might come as no surprise to you, but I was expelled from school a few times for one reason or another. A rebel without a clue.

Breaking and entering was another pastime.

Breaking into cottages was a thing I did for fun. I tried not to do damage to the property, but that wasn't always possible to avoid. Usually, though, people would save me, or us, the trouble of a forced entry by leaving a door or window closed but unlocked. Windows especially. Access to the house through the basement was also often doable. We usually chose weekend cottages that were empty during the weekdays, and we went at night.

One day, a guy named Colin and I heard about an old farmstead that was in the woods near Waverley, and we went looking for it. We found it easily enough but had to force open the front door to get in the main house. There were some outbuildings and a large, faded red barn. We found a shotgun inside the house and some shells. We blew a couple holes into the barn. From the look of the old building, I doubt we were the first to do so.

We finished up our fun and were about to leave the main building when the door flew open. It was the owner of the farm, and was he ever pissed off.

He looked at us and then to where he knew his shotgun should be. I'd put it back in its place on the wall when we were done shooting at his barn. He went straight to it. He pointed the shotgun at us and proceeded to tell us he was sick of us breaking into his farm. I don't know if he thought the gun was loaded; I don't think so. It wasn't when we found it, but we were scared nonetheless.

He threatened to call the police, but that was not likely, given the fact that we were this far back in the woods. It would have been a long wait. He wasn't going to physically take us to the cops, so he gave us a warning.

"You assholes set foot on my property again and I swear I'll shoot ya both. Get out of here! Now!"

So, I escaped going to jail. Again. But my luck would run out one day and I'd find myself locked up behind bars. James Dean would be proud.

With money coming in from gigs with the Termites, I was finally able to indulge in my passion for wheels that had nothing to do with borrowing a ride. I had a Honda 65 motorcycle for a while, and I used it to earn extra money by getting a job weekdays clearing land with a small company about a half-hour or so out of Halifax. Work would start very early in the morning and the locations were deep in the woods, accessed by truck usually, but in my case, I drove my bike in. My job, along with a half-dozen other guys, was to drag the cut trees and bush and pile it all up to be burned. There was lots of bush and fallen trees of different types and lengths, and some stuff was heavy. It was a hot, sweaty job.

On the second day of the job, one of the pumps wouldn't work. The pumps brought water to extinguish the remains of the fires being set so they wouldn't flare up and start a forest fire after we were gone. When the guy in charge couldn't get the pump going after a while, he asked if anyone had experience with this kind of machine and was able to fix it. No one raised his hand or came forward to say he could fix it or even give it a go. So I shouted to the boss man that I'd give it a try. What the hell, right?

I took a wrench and a screwdriver and messed about with the thing for a while, not knowing what the hell I was doing. I tightened anything loose and tapped parts of it, and when I turned the ignition key, that damn thing started up. Who knew?

I was put in charge of the pump. No more hard labour for me. After two weeks at this job, I quit because these guys were ripping us all off. So I said, "Screw you!" and moved on.

I bought myself a red 1962 Corvair Spyder convertible. It was the only rear-engine, air-cooled American car produced back then. This car, new, cost under $3,000. Mine was second-hand and in less than stellar condition, so it was relatively inexpensive for me to buy, probably a couple of hundred bucks, tops. That car never started easily. It almost always needed to be push-started. My dad used to watch and laugh at me and my friends trying to get that damn car running. It was real pretty, but it was not a good car.

I was involved with the local church, teaching Sunday school and singing in the choir at the time I was in Woody's Termites. We would play Saturday night, and the next morning I'd hitch-hike or walk to church if I couldn't get a ride, both ways, for a total distance of about six kilometres, summer and winter.

When I tried out for the church choir, they had me singing structured parts, like the tenor part or the main melody or a third part that didn't deviate from start to finish and on its own was boring. I didn't enjoy that kind of discipline and I couldn't read music, so I got confused and frustrated. I wanted to enjoy myself, so I would stand more or less in the middle of the choir and sing whatever part I felt like. That worked for me, and I enjoyed the practices and the performances on Sunday with the robes and all.

We belonged to St. John's United Church in Waverley. It was not a big church. It was built of wood and painted white, with a single black steeple. Sunday school classes for six- and seven-year-olds were held in the basement, right before the full service on the main level. The kids were cool and I enjoyed being with them, and occasionally they made me laugh with their naive curiosity.

One morning, I was tired from the gig the night before, and the kids were giving me a hard time. They were restless and talking all at once, and one or two were trying get their little hands in the pockets of my sport coat. What they expected to find I don't know. They were just having fun.

Finally, I told them that was enough and to sit still, close their eyes, and repeat after me the words of a prayer I was about to read out loud. I started.

"Lord bless us with your kindness." They repeated after me, "Lord bless us with your kindness."

"Thank you, Lord . . . *aahhggg*, excuse me." (I was clearing my throat.)

And they repeated, "Thank you, Lord . . . *aahhggg*, excuse me." That made my day!

I went by to see that old church some years ago, and sadly, it's gone.

All in all, the Woody's Termites experience was a good one, and it's real nice that I'm still friends with some of the guys all these years later.

Cheers, mates!

When I left Woody's Termites, it was because I was moving to Brantford, Ontario, in 1967. As I said, my grades weren't great at Sidney Stephen High School, and I was getting more caught up in what was happening out on the streets and was not home much. My brothers and I were not getting along well either, and so my dad was speaking to his sister, my aunt Vivian, about his concerns about me. My aunt Viv and uncle Arnie, parent and step-parent of my cousin Vern, the Air Force fella with the beautiful Stratocaster, thought it might be a good idea to have me move in with them in Brantford and go to school there in the fall. They figured it would be a geographical cure for what ailed Myles. It was very considerate of my aunt and uncle.

I had visited Brantford once, years before, and I liked it there. I liked the way the properties were kept nice and neat, with lovely hedges and manicured lawns.

The city of Brantford is sometimes known as "the Telephone City" because former resident Alexander Graham Bell invented the phone there, and the first long-distance phone call was from Brantford to a Tim Hortons location in Paris, Ontario, in 1876. (Okay, I'm not sure about the Tim Hortons part.)

The city was named after Joseph Brant, an important Mohawk chief during the American Revolutionary War. Other notables from the city include the late actor and comedian Phil Hartman, Group of Seven member Lawren Harris, hockey great Wayne Gretzky, and Canadian writer and poet Pauline Johnson.

So I packed up my things after finishing Sidney Stephen in June of '67. I said goodbye to Jim and the rest of the Henman gang, quit the Termites, and moved west that summer to start a new life. I had no problem leaving friends and family. I needed a change; I've never been afraid of change.

I hadn't been thinking about what I wanted to do for the rest of my life. I was nineteen that June, and although I loved music, I had no thoughts of being a professional musician. I wanted to be as good as I could be in terms of being a guitar player, singer, and songwriter; maybe even very good. But that was it as far as I was concerned. Unbelievable as it may seem now, I do not remember having a guitar during the time I lived in Brantford. All the gear I bought while in the Termites remained in Waverley waiting on my return.

It wasn't until I moved to Ontario that I finally made a decision regarding a real vocation for myself. I decided I wanted to be a mechanical draftsman in the Air Force. Up, up, and away!

I'm sure my cousin Vern was part of the reason for that choice. He looked cool in his uniform. He was travelling around the country with his guitar and amp. He represented adventure. My uncle Gerald, husband of my mother's sister, Aunt Lola, was also in the Air Force.

Yes, I figured I'd learn how to design airplanes and airplane engines and more. It all sounded exciting to me and I went for it. I enrolled at Pauline Johnson Collegiate in Brantford that September, a vocational school, and I signed up for mechanical drafting and design. It was an intense two-year course. When I graduated at the end of that time, I would enlist in the Air Force and begin life as a mechanical draftsman. That was the plan.

My aunt and uncle lived in a plain white house at 292 Grey Street in Brantford, with a garage on the right side of the house at the end of the driveway. The backyard had a good-sized lawn, with hedges on either side, and a set of train tracks at the back of the property that ran behind all the houses on that side of the street. I recall that there were many trains passing by each day, and they used their brake horns a lot.

There were two bedrooms in this unpretentious post–Second World War bungalow. My bedroom, which was cousin Vern's old room, was small. There was only one bathroom, shared by all, and a living room. The downstairs basement area, which had green wall-to-wall carpeting, was furnished with a sofa and a table, some chairs, and a TV. This is where I hung out. I loved *TV Guide*. I'd never seen that back home. These days, there are too many channels and choices for a book format like this to be practical.

My uncle always had bottled beer on hand, and I raided his stash every evening and would drink several each time. They never said a word.

I had a part-time job in a beauty salon, washing hair and cleaning up, thanks to my cousin Alice, who worked there. Alice tells me it took a while for me to get some things right. One time I washed a client's hair with cream rinse. Another time, I lost control of the rinse hose and it was like a scene out of a Peter Sellers movie. The renegade hose danced around like a serpent, spewing water everywhere and getting everyone quite wet before I finally got the faucet turned off. No tip for me, I guess.

Alice says I was a good worker but not really enthusiastic about working in a ladies salon. But one day, a strikingly beautiful woman entered the shop, and I almost knocked Alice down to get to the lady first. All I needed was motivation.

I also lived and worked at a farm on the weekends for a while. I was given a room to stay on Friday and Saturday nights and was expected to put in twelve-hour workdays on Saturdays and Sundays. This job was a challenge in that we needed to be up at five in the morning, have a big breakfast, and then get busy. We'd stop for lunch and then get back at it till suppertime. I actually enjoyed the job, except for the pigs. The stench from a pigsty is not to be believed. It took my breath away and made my eyes water, not to mention the wave of nausea that washed over me the instant I entered their area. The stink of the pigs was the reason I eventually turned in my slop bucket and went back to town. I'm amazed I can still enjoy bacon after that.

The course I took at Pauline Johnson was difficult. First of all, I had no idea there was so much math involved in mechanical drafting and that one had to be precise and incredibly neat when drawing. I had to figure out complicated math problems based on size, materials, mass, stress factors, function, purpose, and so forth.

There was a drafting machine attached to my table that consisted of a pair of scales mounted to form a right angle on an articulated protractor that allowed for rotation. I drew with pencils mostly, and there are different types of pencils with a variety of lead types and sizes. Same for drawing in ink. As you can imagine, making a mistake on a large, complicated drawing can be a pain to erase and correct. Back then there were no computers and computer programs to make the job easier.

Although I didn't bring my guitar with me, I was still into music and going to see bands. I befriended a couple of guys, and we talked music and went to see live bands in the area. I don't remember their names, but one guy was a smaller fellow and the other was tall and skinny with dark frizzy hair, and he wore heavy makeup to help hide his acne. His eyes were dark and sharp. He knew a lot about music and bands.

It was the second guy who suggested we see an Ontario band called the Lords of London. I'd never heard of them, but they had radio play with a tune called "Cornflakes and Ice Cream." That night, I heard for the first time a band that was miked and going through a P.A. It wasn't a particularly large venue, but they were miked nonetheless and I was floored. The thing is, I knew something was different but I didn't realize what it was right away. The band wasn't just loud; the group had power and punch. After a while, I understood what I was hearing, and it was an epiphany. I was used to hearing what was coming off the stage, and often the acoustic sound of the drums was buried behind the sound coming from a wall of Fender amps. The vocals were sometimes going through a simple one- or two-speaker public address system, if we were lucky, otherwise the vocal mikes also were plugged into an amp just like a guitar. Sometimes in the same amp as an instrument. What a difference! I couldn't wait to tell the guys back home.

So I went to school, drank beer in the evenings, and went out to see live music every chance I could on the weekends. Once or twice my cousin Alice would take me with her to a licensed club at the Graham Bell Hotel where the drinking age was twenty-one, although I was nineteen. I would bug her until she relented. It was swell of her to take me along with her because she knew I only wanted to hear the music that was going down. I would sit quietly in the corner sipping my Coke and appreciate the live music that was filling the room. I was listening, watching, and making mental notes almost unconsciously as I absorbed what I was experiencing first-hand. And what I was seeing was some great players, different instruments and arrangements, showmanship, and presentation. I loved it all.

In the spring of 1968, just before I returned to Nova Scotia in July, Pierre Elliott Trudeau was on the campaign trail to becoming the fifteenth Prime Minister of Canada. I was fortunate to see him speak at the Bell Memorial Park in the centre of downtown Brantford. He was wearing a suit and tie with a red rose in the lapel of his jacket. He was charismatic and a brilliant speaker, of course, and I was very impressed. So were the majority of voting Canadians as he was elected in June of that year. In 1977, April Wine would perform two shows with the Rolling Stones in Toronto, with Margaret Trudeau in attendance both nights. That caused a bit of a stir as the media speculated on the state of her marriage to the prime minister. They would divorce in 1984. Their son Justin would become the twenty-third prime minister of Canada in 2015. And the beat goes on.

After finishing a successful year at Pauline Johnson Collegiate in Brantford, I returned to Nova Scotia and to my family and friends whom I had left the year before. But I wasn't staying long.

When I got back to Waverley, I collected the things I'd left behind at home, which wasn't much when it came to my personal stuff, really, but there was my gear, and I wanted that right away. I moved out on my own after I landed a job in Halifax a few days later and eventually ended up renting a room in the south end with Jim Henman. Jim had finished Sidney Stephen High, and there was no more Woody's Termites. After I left the band to go to Ontario, I was replaced and they carried on for a while, but it didn't last. That fall Jim was going to start at Saint Mary's University.

My job was at Henry Birks and Sons on Barrington Street in Halifax, and it was the greatest "straight job" I ever had. I was in charge of maintenance for the entire building. I wore a white shirt with *Birks* embroidered on it and a few pencils sticking out of my pocket and a utility belt with some tools hanging off it. I don't know how I got the job because I'm not the useful handyman type. Far from it. I don't think I've ever been able to properly install a doorknob let alone be in charge of the maintenance of such a prestigious landmark as the Henry Birks and Sons building. I guess they liked the look of me or they were desperate. If you chose "desperate," you're probably correct.

My first task of the day was to hand-polish the large brass door handles on the front and back entrances. The handles were thick letter Bs, one facing the normal direction (the one on the right) and the other facing the opposite way.

The rest of the day I was at the beck and call of anyone needing me to change a light bulb or tighten something coming loose. There was some dusting and polishing to do, but not much. After all, I was there during business hours, and I'd just be in the way of folks shopping.

As you can imagine, there wasn't really a lot to do and I was my own boss. I liked going up on the roof on warm, sunny days to check the drains to be sure they weren't blocked up with leaves and such. The views of the harbour from the rooftop were very nice, and it was a good place to pass the time. I carried a hand radio of some kind with me so I could be reached if someone needed my services. It was a cool gig, but after a while I got restless and moved on.

Next, I tried my hand as a salesman at a men's clothing store called Jack's Clothing just down the street from Birks. Jack was cool and it was a decent job, and I was okay at selling. Some of the other kids stole stuff from Jack, but I never did. I liked Jack. He was a hard worker and a fair boss. He was much older than he looked, something I realized when his actual age was mentioned to me. He had straight, black hair, combed back, a tanned Mediterranean complexion, and perfect teeth. There was a stern, old-country, gangster look about him, but he was an easy guy to work for if you did your job diligently. I worked there a couple of months but "retired" when it was time to go back to school.

Back to school meant enrolling at the Halifax County Vocational High School for the second and final year of mechanical drafting and design. I was still wanting to join the Air Force, so getting a diploma was important to me.

I was working at an IGA stuffing bags when Gordie Mahar and Paul Aucoin walked in one day. They came up to me and asked if I wanted to join their band. They told me Jim Henman had suggested me for the group. I said, "Yes!" and followed them out of the store, never to return. The band was called Squirrel, with Jim, drummer Gordie, guitarist Paul, and a

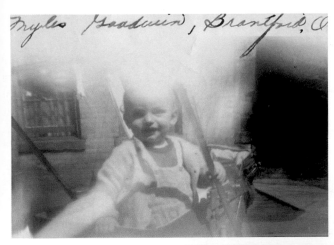

Me, as a baby. I was born Miles Goodwin in 1948. I would later change the spelling of my name to Myles Goodwyn.

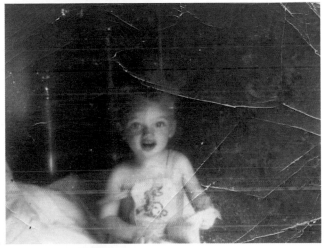

Adorable me, at age two.

Sledding with brother Barry in Tufts Cove, Nova Scotia, 1954.

In Tufts Cove, a poor, rough neighbourhood in Dartmouth, Nova Scotia, in 1954. The following year Dad moved the family to beautiful Waverley, Nova Scotia, into a house overlooking Lake William.

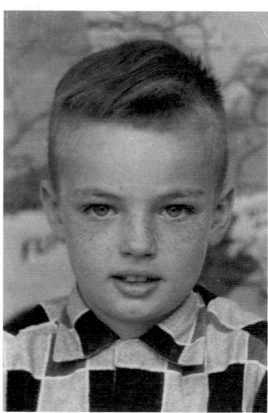

A school picture taken when I was six years old.

My mother, Roberta Anne, passed away from brain cancer much too young, at the age of twenty-eight. I was not yet a teenager.

Dad (left) with his brother, my Uncle Ray.

My brothers and me on the day of my
mother's funeral, in 1959. We had no
idea Mom was being buried that day.

With my brothers Barry (left) and
Allan (middle) in Brantford, Ontario,
in 1961.

My Aunt Lola (centre) with my grandparents on my mother's side, Gertrude and John Turple.

My grandparents, Nan and Bomps, on my father's side. Nan looked after us kids after Mom died.

Relaxing in the backyard of our home in Waverley, Nova Scotia, in 1967.

Jim Henman (left), Dave Dodsworth (on drums), and me when we were with Woody's Termites, circa 1966. The guitars, Italian-made Ekos, were a gift from Jim's dad.

Woody's Termites, circa 1966. From left: drummer Dave Dodsworth; bass guitarist Jim Henman; lead singer Doug Grace; yours truly; and keyboardist Greg Stephen.

Goofing around with Woody's Termites. From left: Doug Grace; John Baron, temporary bass player for Jim Henman; Dave Dodsworth (seated below); me; and Greg Stephen.

Backstage at a high-school gig in the early days of April Wine, in 1972. From left: Jim Clench, Ritchie Henman, David Henman, and me.

Playing the very same piano that had been used by Duke Ellington, Cab Calloway, and other artists of that period, at Kee to Bala, Ontario, in 1972.

An early April Wine poster, circa 1972.

singer named Neville Roberts. Actually, the group was called the Flintstones when I was asked to join them on Jim's recommendation, but it was changed to Squirrel shortly after. The band didn't last very long, but one experience I had was life changing for me.

I was staying in a small, narrow room in Halifax at the time. The ceiling was quite high. A single light dangled above my lumpy bed, suspended by a long, spear-like arm. It was unnerving having that thing pointing at me while I slept. There was a small, distressed bedside table and not much else in the room. A hot water radiator, painted the colour of old cabbage, was anchored against one wall. The toilet was down the hall.

In those days, the whole drug-culture hippie thing with the peace, love, and long hair was going down and had been for some time. I was not a hippie and I didn't wear beads and smoke marijuana or hash or anything like that. I preferred cold beer in a tavern, but I decided, what the hell, I'll try drugs. So I dropped acid.

I did the tab of acid in the afternoon, in the Public Gardens in Halifax. I remember that the streets suddenly had deep ruts and the vehicles looked like they were cruising along with their wheels caught in these ruts, and it was all in a slower time than it was in the real world. The colours were brighter and everything had a bit of a cartoon feel to it. I started to freak out, and I went to my room and locked the door and then got into bed.

I'd forgotten I had a gig that night. When someone started pounding on the door to my room, the freak factor went through the roof.

After coming back to my room that afternoon, high and paranoid, I made myself relax through slow, deep breathing and sheer willpower. Mercifully, I drifted off to sleep. I was sleeping when Paul started hammering his fist on the door, shouting, "Goodwyn, get the fuck out here!"

I was terrified for a few seconds as I stared at the door incredulously.

"Goodwyn, are you in there?" The man was persistent and disagreeable.

Then I recognized the voice.

"Yes, I'm here, Paul. What do you want?" I managed.

"Get your narrow ass out here, we were looking for you! Let's go, we gotta gig!"

Damn.

When we headed out a few minutes later, I noticed it was dark outside. What I didn't notice was that I had left my only guitar in the room.

We went to the gig.

Up until this point, I had played only two electric guitars in my life. One was Jim's original Eko that his dad had bought him, the one he let me use when he got his Eko bass. I had bought a Hagstrom guitar while I was in Woody's Termites. So, when I arrived at the gig without my guitar—and after the guys stopped telling me what a fuck-up I was—we needed to borrow one, pronto.

The guitar they handed me, which I think belonged to the guy who owned the club, was a Gibson. That night I was blown away by the feel and the sound of this great instrument. It had a thick, rich sound with growl and yet it was musical. The weight and balance of this single cutaway guitar was perfect, and the dark rosewood neck was a dream to feel in my hand—and it played like a dream, too. I was smitten.

I was enjoying this instrument so much that after one of our songs finished, I kept playing without the other guys. When I realized I was the only one playing, I stopped and looked around me. Everyone was staring. I knew then and there that I had to make some real money and buy myself a Gibson guitar. Oh, yeah, and no more acid for me.

Squirrel didn't last long, and I was busy with school and just surviving. I found the drafting thing hard for all the reasons I did when I took that first year of training at Pauline Johnson in Brantford. But I kept at it.

I was now living with Jim in one large, unremarkable room. Unremarkable, that is, if you didn't have mixed feelings about two adult men sharing one double bed. It sucked to be honest, but we made the best of it. Jim was studying at Saint Mary's University while I attended the vocational school. We didn't have much money, but we managed.

In the fall of 1968 I became a professional musician. You see, I was having doubts about being a draftsman, but I was still interested in being in the Air Force. I went to a recruiting office in Halifax in December and started asking questions that I'd never gotten around to asking before. I told them I wanted to sign up to be a mechanical draftsman when I graduated in the spring. Well, I learned something that day. I learned that almost all the drafting, mechanical or otherwise, was not done by Air Force personnel at all. The drafting and designing work for the Canadian military was done by civilians. I suddenly had a vision of me wearing corduroy pants, a cheap sport coat, brown, sensible shoes over grey socks, and thick glasses like the ones worn by Buddy Holly, sporting a breast pocket full of pens and pencils. Oh, my. No Air Force, no uniform, and no adventure.

I left that office that day with a big decision to make. Did I want to be a civil draftsman? What else could I do? This is what I'd been training for. All that friggin' math, which I hated, and learning to be painstakingly neat and precise, learning to think a certain way with regard to form and purpose. And now it felt like my life had no real purpose anymore, or at least not one I cared to follow. I was depressed and I was confused. I slept on it.

When I awoke the next morning, I knew I could not go back to school. The dream was dead. The romance and adventure had been sucked out of it. You're probably thinking, how much romance and adventure would a draftsman possibly see anyway, even one in uniform? But you know what I mean. It was once again time for change. Did I mention I wasn't afraid of change?

I was in Squirrel in October 1968 when I met Pam Marsh, a singer and piano player from the Halifax area. I gave her my number and suggested she give me a call sometime. It wasn't long after I decided to leave vocational school that Pam did in fact call me.

Squirrel was no longer together and I wasn't doing much of anything, so her call was a timely one for me. She was in a band in Sydney in Cape Breton called the East Gate Sanctuary (EGS), and they needed a guitar player. She asked if I would be interested in joining the band. I said, "Yes, of course! Thank you!"

Meanwhile, I'd told Jim I had dropped out of school and the reason why. So after the call from Pam, I informed him that I was taking my stuff and boarding a Greyhound bus for Sydney. Off I went with an old suitcase, my guitar, and my amp—all my worldly possessions.

When I arrived in Sydney, I had a place to stay. Pam had arranged for me to rent a room in the same boarding house where she was staying. It was within walking distance of the main park in the centre of town, and I spent time there reflecting on the recent decisions I'd made. Quitting school was a big choice and I hadn't yet experienced the consequences. Time would tell, of course, and I was a tad apprehensive. But when I met the new band the day after my first night in Cape Breton, I was in for a shocker.

"His hair's too short. I don't want him in the band." This from the bass player, whose dad owned a major drugstore in town.

"It'll grow," Pam replied, in my defense. "Besides, Myles can really play." She was relating to me the conversation that took place after my audition. It never occurred to me that I might not get the job and be stranded on the Cape.

"He's an asshole! What if I was to drag the little prick around the block a few times by the hair?" I had said, half-serious. "Maybe he'll see things differently." I was upset.

The bass player's hair was very long, and his girlfriend or wife, whomever, ironed it every day, I was told.

After some heated discussion between the group members, with Pam and the drummer, Pat MacDonald, and the other members vouching for me, it was decided that I would be their new guitarist. Bass-dude wasn't in the band long after I joined.

We rehearsed at a place called Chesterton Alley in Sydney, a square, one-storey, flat-topped building on the main drag in town. It was a hippie club that was painted black on the inside, with DayGlo posters and black lights everywhere. It was very psychedelic. We also gigged there.

Pam has said she could tell I was serious about music and that she could feel my intensity right away. "He was entirely devoted to his craft even then and was eager to do anything to bring himself closer to his goal of mastering his instrument and furthering his career. He had a sardonic sense of humour, and when he made a crack out of the side of his mouth, it would be a good one. He was shy to a certain degree but wouldn't hesitate to speak up when he had an opinion. Myles always treated me as an equal and with the greatest of respect, and I felt we were both on the same wavelength both personally and musically."

Our repertoire included songs by Janis Joplin and Big Brother and the Holding Company, the Electric Flag, featuring Buddy Miles on drums, Procol Harum's "A Whiter Shade of Pale," and the Young Rascals' "Groovin'" and "I Ain't Gonna Eat Out My Heart Anymore." Good tunes.

We also did a few gems from Led Zeppelin's debut album. Covering Zep tunes was great fun for a guitarist.

EGS rehearsed until we sounded ready, and then we started doing shows in the area. We hadn't been together that long when we met an engaging young man named John Duart MacDonald from the west coast of Cape Breton. He lived in a small town called Strathlorne in Inverness County, and he wanted to be our manager.

John's parents had been killed in a horrible car accident on Christmas Eve 1967, leaving John and his nine siblings parentless. The story was heartbreaking, and it was reported by the media right across the country. John Duart was the eldest and he was a strong, positive young man, and I liked him immediately. Most of us did. He lived in an old farmhouse with his brothers and sisters.

So, John Duart became our band manager. He wanted us to move to Strathlorne, but not everyone was convinced. Regardless, it was eventually decided that Pam, Pat, and I would follow John Duart to Strathlorne, where he said he knew a bass player who would be a good fit for the band.

Now *this* was a change I looked forward to.

5

—

As I try to remember events that happened in the past, in this case moving to Strathlorne more than forty-five long years ago, I tend to remember only events that were extraordinary or unusual for one reason or another. For me, meeting the MacDonald family from Strathlorne that year was both those things.

When Pam, Pat, and I followed our new manager, John Duart, to Strathlorne, on Cape Breton Island, we ended up living in the family's farmhouse for a couple of months. John was the eldest at twenty years old, a year younger than me. The next oldest was his sister Lena, a year or two younger. The youngest sibling was only four years old or so.

Lena was the "mother" in that family in terms of taking charge and taking care of most everything that needed to be done to maintain some kind of domestic order and discipline. Lena was remarkable and would continue to take care of "her" children for years to come. They were a group of beautiful young children, and it was a wonderful experience living with them, even for the short time that I did.

I realized they were learning to fend for themselves pretty

much. My understanding was that there was some financial help in the form of a trust fund. Regardless, it was obvious to me that it was a challenge for the family to manage on the small amount of money they were given weekly.

And so it was into this delicate domestic situation that John arrived one day with us three vagabond musicians in tow. It must have been quite incredible to everyone, except John Duart, I guess.

At first, I was the only band member who lived with the family, but eventually the entire band moved into the farm. Because only three of us from EGS came from Sydney, we needed a few new members, and as John Duart promised, he had a few guys in mind. Stevie Basker played bass. Jody Cleary played very good rhythm guitar and keyboards. Pam Marsh was on vocals and piano, and Pat MacDonald played drums, with me on guitar. We all contributed to the vocal work, although I fought having to sing at all. I was stubborn and wanted only to play guitar. Reluctantly, with John Duart's persistence, I sang some background vocal parts.

The band's few days' stay turned into the summer, or what was left of it. Once Lena realized the new band was staying for longer than a few days or even a few weeks, she decided to move the kids out of the farm and away from the long-hairs and the loud music. I didn't realize this at the time, or I believe I would have insisted that the band move out of the farm, not them.

After Lena left with the youngest of the kids, that left John Duart, five of the older kids, and the five band members living together. It was fun for all of us. It was different, and it was at a time when music was exciting and original. Free-spirited people in the late 1960s experimented with lifestyles and choices in new and provocative ways. Of course the kids enjoyed the new freedom of living without house rules. I believe they got a kick out of the local notoriety of living with a rock band. It all worked for the short time we were there.

John Duart made sure we rehearsed every day, and we became a decent live band. Meanwhile, John was on the road hustling gigs for us. He had us performing in Battle of the Bands competitions, and we did well enough to earn some gigs. Mostly we played dates in the area and even travelled to St. John's, Newfoundland, and shared the stage with Smokey Robinson and the Miracles. That was the highlight for the EGS band, in my mind.

Although we were working and making a bit of money along the way, we were far from becoming the international act John Duart and the band were hoping for. There was nothing original about us. We were a bar band doing cover tunes.

John Duart was an amateur boxer and, I believe, a darn good one. I saw him in a street fight once in rural Cape Breton. One night after a gig, some drunk guy started a fight outside the dance hall. John and the guy squared off as a bunch of people, including the band, watched.

I figured the bout would be over in a few seconds, but that fight dragged on and resembled more of a dance than a fist fight. Eventually, the fighting started for real and punches were thrown. After a few minutes, John knocked his opponent out. The guy was an ass and deserved it.

After the fight, I asked John why it took so long to flatten the guy. His explanation was that he had no idea who he was or if he could fight. So John took his time, watching the guy for a while, determining what kind of opponent he was dealing with, and then, once he felt comfortable, he moved in and knocked him out. Made sense to me.

I don't like fighting and I hate the sound of a fist hitting flesh. I've heard it a few times too many in my life, and I can live without ever hearing that sound again. But sometimes a guy does what he has to do, regardless.

During the time that the band and Lena, along with her youngest siblings, were still living together at the farm, we had an unwelcome visitor.

As Lena MacDonald tells the story, it was one of those lazy, sunny summer days on the farm, probably a Sunday. She was hanging clothes on the line, with several of the kids playing around the apple tree and swing area. I was sitting with my guitar near the front door.

"A big car drove up into the yard and a large, angry man in a suit—no lie, I remember—got out," remembers Lena. "He was looking for his son. I am pretty sure his son's name was Johnny: little guy, baby face, wanted to be a hippie in a band. He yelled out, 'Where the hell is my son?!' and 'He had better get his ass home!' 'His son better get in the car now or never come home,' that kind of talk. 'Goddamn hippies!' he said several times. This big, angry man I think had a beer bottle in his hand, which he drained and then flung over onto the grass beside the children's swing set. 'Goddamn hippies!' he said again . . . but, just in a flash, Myles, who had been sitting quietly to one side, was out of his chair, right up in front of this big, angry fellow, with his finger up to the guy's face, saying, 'Who the hell do you think you are to come here and insult this family; you pick up that bottle and get the hell out of here!'

"The man was shocked. He didn't expect that. Everything

seemed to stop. I stopped hanging clothes. The kids stopped playing. Myles didn't move from in front of this man, and he told him again, 'I said, pick your damn bottle up and leave.' The man sort of straightened up, looked at Myles, then went and picked up his bottle and left in a hurry. We never saw him again.

"Myles went quietly, as usual, back to his guitar. I continued to hang the laundry on the line. The kids went back to playing. But I knew at that moment, Myles had, on the inside, real character, something that big, angry man would never have. This early recollection is one of those moments I will never forget. I think if you want to know who and what Myles is, this moment, all those years ago, on a farm in Cape Breton, tells you a lot. And that is why I will always consider Myles a stand-up guy and a friend."

I have a vague memory of that incident. All I can say for sure is that I'm glad things did not get any uglier that day.

The story also reminds me of the prejudice and the hate there was for young men with long hair and for all guy and gal hippie types back then. There were many times I feared for myself and my bandmates, including later on with April Wine, when we'd stop at a restaurant or a truck stop. More than a few times we just turned around and walked right back out when heads turned our way and these dim, homophobic, redneck characters glared at us with hate and the possibility of real violence. One time we were chased by a car after we left a truck stop. We got away unscathed.

The days of East Gate Sanctuary and living at the farmhouse in Strathlorne were numbered. The children needed their home back, and so we needed to move on. When September rolled around and school season started up again, we had to leave the farm. A long-haired rock band was too much of a distraction to have around once that summer was over. Lena and the kids needed to get serious about the upcoming school year and dealing with life as normal as possible under the circumstances.

As much as we worked at getting better as a band and with John Duart as our manager, all current arrangements were about to change quickly. The band would soon move out and John Duart would move on.

The members of the band had their sights set on an old farmhouse near Antigonish—not sure who chose this farmhouse or why—back on the mainland of Nova Scotia, about a ninety-minute drive southwest of the Inverness area where we were living with John Duart and his family.

When it came time to move out of the MacDonald homestead, John Duart decided he wasn't going to manage us anymore. He wasn't fond of one of the band members, who he felt was childish and self-serving. To be perfectly honest, I didn't care for the guy that much myself. One story John Duart told me, which I had forgotten about, was of the guy inviting two or three girls to a show and then, when they all turned up at the gig, the guy would feign being really sick. John Duart would have to carry him out, claiming he had to get him to a hospital. Unfortunately, that silliness wears thin.

I also believe John Duart began to realize that EGS was not going to be the next Beatles or even a successful recording group. As I said, if you're a cover band, you're going nowhere important, in terms of a real career. John Duart also had a spirit of adventure, and there was a world to see outside of the

Maritimes. He was eager to move on and live life on his terms. No flies on Mr. MacDonald. I liked him then, and I still do.

At any rate, when the band left Strathlorne and moved to the Antigonish area, we were without a manager.

Unfortunately, when Lena MacDonald returned to the farm, the telephone was disconnected and there was about a $300 bill outstanding. She apparently found out where the band was living and mailed us a copy of the bill, asking us to please pay. It wasn't paid. She now knows that we were not getting a lot of work at the time. Around the end of September, EGS played at the Inverness Dance Hall. Lena went in and waited at the door. When the event was over, she reached into the cash drawer and told us she was taking the money that was owed to her. She says one of the band members came over and told her she couldn't, that the band needed the money, that she had no right, and so on.

Lena recalled during a chat as I was writing this book that I came and told that band member, "We owe her the money!" I then told him to go load up the van.

We split the admission fee, which came out to be about $50 or $60 each.

Lena added, "There was a reason I trusted Myles, a reason I would give him the respect I sure didn't feel towards other band members."

I was gratified to hear that the reason Lena held me in such high regard was because I had always behaved in a quiet, respectful way around her and the family while I lived at their farm in rural Cape Breton.

***

When we arrived in Antigonish from Strathlorne, we moved into a derelict farmhouse that should have been condemned.

Besides falling apart, it had no running water and we had to use an outhouse. (Just like the old days living at home back in Waverley.) But the most pressing issue by far was the dead flies, thousands of them covering the floors.

We had little money and lived in that ramshackle farmhouse with little furniture and little food. You might be thinking that our life kind of sucked at this point. I'll agree with that.

We did perform some gigs, though, and actually did a wee tour (two dates) on Prince Edward Island. But there's nothing really worth writing home about as far as a musical career goes. We were just paying our dues. Despite the dead-end road we were on, there were some laughs—and a few at my expense, I must confess.

One day I decided to go hunting in the woods around the farm, by myself. I left that morning with an old twelve-gauge shotgun I had found on the farm and the few bullets that were with it. The rifle worked. I tested it by tying it to a tree, loaded and cocked, with a string tied to the trigger. When I pulled on the string attached to the trigger, the shotgun went BOOM, and when the smoke cleared, it was still in one piece. I tried it again, this time with the brown, wooden stock tucked under my chin and my face pressed against the slightly rusted metal loading chamber. I had one hand firmly on the stubby barrel, the other nearer my narrow chin, hoping to hell it wasn't ready to blow up on the second try.

It didn't, and without a second thought, I was off on a hunting adventure. I was hunting for meat to feed myself and the band. I was on a mission.

I thought of the one and only deer I had shot some years back, in Waverley, as I went casually into the unfamiliar woods. I walked for hours, seeing nothing much along the way, just small game, but that was not what I was looking for. There were deer signs, though, and I had hope. There were also bear tracks, and that gave me some feelings of apprehension, but I carried on. For hours.

Then it started to get cold, and I was getting tired and hungry and I'd been thirsty for a while. It was time to head out of the woods. With a few hours of daylight left, I needed to get a move on.

I started to work my way back but realized I wasn't sure exactly how best to do that. After backtracking for an hour, I admitted to myself that I was lost and that my best bet would be to climb the tallest tree I could to see if I could determine a way out of the woods. I rested my trusty twelve-gauge against a tall tree and started climbing. I got well up into that tree and started looking in all directions. There was nothing but 360 degrees of thick forest. No sign of civilization, at least not from that height. I was lost.

I'd been in the Boy Scouts as a kid and had badges for survival. Better still, I had experience in the woods and knew how to hunt. I knew I could survive if the bear didn't get me.

Seriously, I thought about hunkering down for the night as there was little daylight left. I spotted a big spruce tree that was upended, its network of roots still desperately clinging to the ground with the false hope that maybe the tree would be okay again and able to right itself. The fallen tree's wide base of roots, moss, and dirt made a lean-to shelter that, with a little work, would serve my purposes for the night. I started gathering the wood of long-dead tree branches and breaking off some low-hanging wide boughs of evergreens nearby. I was going to crawl in under this fallen tree and use the branches to cover myself to keep warm but also as camouflage in case a deer came by. I could get a good shot away with the deer up close and unsuspecting. I'd then gut the deer and pull it inside the shelter, and then fit my body inside the deer's cavity for warmth. It would be messy, and I was still wary of the bear. I knew for certain that it was going to be a long, dark, cold night.

But, as luck would have it, as I was gathering small, dry, lighter wood for a fire—I had no matches so I'd make a fire the old-fashioned way if need be—I came upon a dirt road. I reckoned it to be an old logging road. If there was a possibility of getting out of those woods that night, this road was the answer. Of course, roads go in two directions. One way was out of the woods and the second would take me deeper into the unknown. I stood there, in the middle of that rutted dirt road, with the sun disappearing quickly, trying to make a decision. I had one shot at this, at least for this night.

All was still and quiet. Then I heard it.

I followed the distant sound as it grew louder, until I could see it. The bear!

No, I'm kidding. It was a wide, fast-running brook. I was on my knees on the bank of that stream, careful not to get my gun wet and drinking deeply the cool, refreshing water.

As I knelt at the stream, I watched the flowing water with new hope. Water runs downhill towards the ocean or a lake, to civilization. If I wanted out tonight, I was going to follow the road in the direction the brook was running. That was my only chance.

I started walking, and after trekking about an hour, it became entirely dark. When I finally stepped out of the woods, I was on a small hill overlooking a valley. A few hundred yards in front of me and down the hill was a small house with the lights on.

The couple who greeted me were nice, and after a quick sandwich and some tea, they drove me to the farm. I was tired and grateful. And safe.

Life in East Gate Sanctuary had become predictable. There wasn't a lot of work and I was restless. I needed inspiration, and I needed to move on. My friend and bandmate, Pam Marsh, was ready for a change as well.

One day, in December 1969, a car pulled up to our farmhouse in Antigonish. It was my dear friend and neighbour from Waverley, Jim Henman.

Jim came to visit us because he and his two cousins, David and Ritchie Henman, were planning to put together a group, write their own material, and head for Toronto or Montreal. They were in a group called Prism—not to be confused with the Vancouver-based group that gained notoriety in the late '70s and early '80s—and were itching to do their own thing, to write their own music and shoot for the moon. They wanted me with them.

I asked for some time to think it over, but it took no time at all, really. I was in a cover band and I wanted much more. From the beginning, I wanted to be in a group that wrote and recorded their own material. By this time, EGS was fading away. Jim's timing was perfect. There was only one gig in our immediate future, and we had eaten pretty much all of the food that was left in the cupboards. There was no way I could continue living in the unheated farmhouse in December, and besides, we had very little money left between us.

Also, an important factor in my decision to leave immediately was Jim Henman's involvement. Jim and I were the best of friends back then, and we had lived next door to each other for years growing up, sharing the dream of making it in the music business as composers and performers. I looked forward to this budding music project because of his involvement.

A few days after Jim's visit, Pam and I boarded a train for Halifax.

Did I mention that I wasn't afraid of change?

PART TWO

April Wine

6

___

I arrived at the old Halifax Railway Station on Hollis Street with a blue, road-weary, hard-shelled suitcase with a black strap around the middle helping to hold it closed. It was filled with all my personal possessions: letters, pictures, poetry, and other assorted bits and pieces of my life up until then. To this day, I still have that small, old suitcase, which was given to me by my grandmother, Nan, when I left our home on Waverley Road for the last time, and it *still* contains most of the same personal contents as it did back then, almost fifty years ago. I also had my beloved Gibson Melody Maker and a Fender combo amplifier with me and a garbage bag containing all my clothing. I had about sixty dollars to live on and that was it.

David and Ritchie Henman, along with their friend George Mack and, for a while, Jim Henman, had been in Prism, but the Henmans were at an impasse with their band and were frustrated. David had just gotten sick of the situation: If you wanted to play gigs, you had to play covers. There was little room for originality. So David and Jim were writing songs and getting serious about music. They wanted to be more than a cover band, and they were trying to commit to writing their own music full time. They needed a new vehicle.

According to Ritchie Henman, that was the seed that was planted, so at that point David and Jimmy just went into full-time writing. Jimmy dropped out of university—Ritchie and Jimmy were both at Saint Mary's—and they asked Ritchie if he was in.

"Ritchie told us he was going to stay in school," recalls Jim Henman, "but if we were going to be working at home, he'd see us every night, hear what we were doing, and make his decision. Once we started playing him our songs, he told us that compared to what he was doing in university, he'd rather take a chance on this. But we all knew we needed a fourth guy with a strong voice, and we also wanted to get into doing lead guitar."

David Henman's recollection of how the band was formed was that he and Jimmy Henman got together at the Old Mill Tavern in Dartmouth on a weekday afternoon and ordered a jug of beer. They started talking about their frustrations with music and bands and what they were trying to do, and they decided to put a new band together. David said he would break up his band, Prism, which included his brother Ritchie and Jimmy Henman. Jimmy said he would call me in Cape Breton, where I was playing with a band in North Sydney called East Gate Sanctuary. The idea was to get me to leave East Gate Sanctuary and come immediately to Halifax by train.

In late 1969, when it came to music and lifestyle influences, the province of Nova Scotia and its capital city, Halifax, was pretty much the same as anywhere else in North America during that post-Woodstock winter.

The Vietnam War still dominated the news, while albums such as *Led Zeppelin*, the Beatles' *Abbey Road*, Simon & Garfunkel's *Bridge Over Troubled Water*, and *Let It Bleed* from the Rolling Stones, now minus Brian Jones, provided the sound-track of the day. Vocalist Nanette Workman, who has lived in Montreal for many years and is a friend, sang backup on tracks from the *Let It Bleed* album including "You Can't Always Get What You Want" and "Country Honk." She was also on the group's 1969 chart-topping single "Honky Tonk Women." Grand Funk Railroad, Chicago, Plastic Ono Band, and the Who's rock opera *Tommy* debuted, while America got its first taste of King Crimson. Jimi Hendrix made the headlines as he went on trial in Toronto for hash and heroin possession, and John Lennon and Yoko Ono were very much in the post-Beatles' public eye, as among other things, they met with Prime Minister Pierre Trudeau for an Instant Karma summit. There was actually a lot going on musically in the Maritimes, in Halifax in particular, through the '60s as well.

It wasn't exactly the centre of the musical universe in Canada, although back in the mid '60s, Canada had been given a taste of some of the local talent through the CBC-TV musical variety show *Frank's Bandstand,* the Halifax segment of the network's national *Music Hop* series, hosted by Frank Cameron.

His regular guests were local artists such as Patricia McKinnon, Karen Oxley, D.J. Jeffries, Davie Wells, and Anne Murray, who during that period was teaching gym classes in her hometown of Springhill, Nova Scotia, and driving to Halifax to tape the shows. The show also provided national exposure for local bands like the Five Sounds, Spring Garden Road, the Axemen, the Brunswick Playboys, and the Great Scots, who, in the mid-'60s, decked out in traditional Scottish dress including kilts and sporrans, appeared on the popular TV music show *Shindig!* as well as *American Bandstand,* hosted by Dick Clark.

Brian Ahern, who would later become Anne Murray's producer, was music director and guitarist with a house band that
consisted of some pretty talented musicians destined to make
their mark further afield in the years to come, including saxo-
phonist Keith Jollimore and trumpet player Bruce Cassidy of
Lighthouse and Dr. Music, Juno Award–winning jazz pianist
Joe Sealy, and drummer Jack S. Lilly of the Great Speckled Bird.

In the late '60s, the very popular CBC-TV show *Singalong
Jubilee*, which had been the summer replacement for *Don
Messer's Jubilee*, was still being produced out of Halifax (the
show ran on the CBC from 1961 to 1974), featuring among its
many singers Anne Murray—who had just recorded her 1968
debut album, *What About Me*, produced by *Frank's Bandstand*
and *Singalong*'s music director, Brian Ahern—Gene MacLellan
(the composer of Anne's international hit "Snowbird"), Ken
Tobias, Catherine McKinnon, Edith Butler, Tom Kelly, and
show hosts Jim Bennet and the late Bill Langstroth, who would
later become Anne Murray's husband.

As the Swingin' Sixties were coming to a close, I was living
with Jim Henman in his grandparents' cottage on Waverley
Road, just down the hill by the lake from Jimmy's parents'
house. It was really just a summer place on the shore of Lake
William, the lake I grew up on. You'd walk down the hill and
there was this tiny little cottage—not much more than a
changing room to use before you went swimming. I don't know
how his grandparents had managed to heat the place.

The best part of living in the cottage, which was owned by
Jim's parents, was that the rent was free. It was small, but it
worked for us. Jim slept in the one bedroom, and I slept in the
living room on a sofa. We had no money for oil and it was bitter

cold. We had a couple of space heaters and some blankets, and that was it. There was a tiny toilet but no bath or shower. We ate a lot of peasant food and our fair share of junk food, but from time to time we also got to eat at his mom's. We would have gone to the house I grew up in next door to Jim's parents, but my dad and my brothers had moved out a year or so after I did.

That year at the cottage would be the last time I'd ever live in the Waverley area, although, years later, I would buy a house on that lake, a house that belonged to Dad at the time, which I immediately gave away to one of my brothers and his family.

I didn't know David and Ritchie Henman that well before we got together in Halifax in late 1969. We had met once or twice at Jim's parents' home in earlier years. They seemed to be more middle class than Jim and me. It's funny, but living in a subdivision with neighbours all about, with a nice lawn, a backyard, and a car garage, seemed pretty snazzy to me at the time. My aunt Viv's place in Brantford was like that. It had that *Leave It to Beaver* vibe.

I was used to living in the woods, not only when I lived in Waverley but also at the band house in Cape Breton that EGS lived in. I've heard it said that you can take the boy out of the country but you can't take the country out of the boy. I'm down with that. I still have a place in the country surrounded by trees, along with a meadow and an orchard where I sometimes witness deer eating apples in the early morning. I call the place Roberta's Way, in memory of my mother. My love of nature also extends to the ocean, and I'm fortunate enough to have a place on the water as well. My view is the basin where my grandfather, Bomps, used to take me fishing for tinker mackerel. I'm blessed.

David and Ritchie were city slickers to me. They had a paved driveway.

We were trying to forge a style and a new sound, having never played together before. Jim, David, Ritchie, and I began practising as often as we could—often all day—in David and Ritchie's parents' basement in Lower Sackville. I thought that David and Ritchie's folks were disappointed they had both dropped out of university to chase this pipe dream, although they managed somehow to remain supportive of the band. I was wrong—according to Ritchie, at least.

Ritchie Henman recalls that their parents were 100 percent behind their doing this thing full time, and they always were. He didn't know if they would have recognized one way or the other whether the band had great potential. They were going by the fact that we worked so hard at it. Right from the beginning, Ritchie and David's dad and mom always said, "If they're working that hard at it, they are serious about it and it's not a passing fancy. This is something they want to do and they want to be successful at it."

There's no doubt my dad was very proud of me, though, and I'm sure he felt a parent's relief, knowing his eldest boy took the right path and followed his destiny and things turned out well.

I wonder if he realized the guitar he bought me in the early '60s, Norma, was, in part, my ticket to fame and fortune.

By the way, and while I'm thinking about it—it just popped into my head—the answer to a question that's been put to me many times over the years goes like this: David came up with the name

April Wine. It means absolutely nothing. You're welcome and thank you. Let's move on, shall we?

With April Wine, the idea that we would play only original material and not other bands' tunes right from the get-go is true, kind of . . . at least, I think so. Jim remembers that we wanted to do only originals. He said he didn't think I would want to join the new band otherwise. I believe Ritchie feels the same way in that we decided to do only original tunes and no cover tunes. But David remembers things a bit differently.

David recalls that we had our first rehearsal in his mom and dad's basement in Lower Sackville and that our plan was to be original but to play it safe and still do cover songs. The decision to go entirely original happened—or at least was put forth— when they heard me play a riff of a song I was working on. He says they were floored by how heavy it rocked, and that was the inspiration for the declaration by all of us that we would, henceforth, be a 100 percent original group.

"We sat down and Myles started playing a riff he was writing, and right away, the four of us looked at each other and said, 'Okay, that's it . . . no cover songs! This is what we want to do.' We were so excited by this riff; it opened up all the doors."

This is the way I remember it—David's version. As a new band, April Wine needed to build a repertoire from nothing, so doing a mixture of original and non-original songs made sense. That was the initial plan, but that changed after I played an idea I had for a new song at that early band rehearsal.

The bottom line is that April Wine decided to perform only original material, and therefore, in the beginning, we didn't have ninety minutes of original music for a concert or even enough for several sets working in clubs. We needed lots of songs in order to make a living as a live band. We didn't have lots of songs in the beginning, but we did have some.

Ritchie Henman says the band was pretty clearly defined from the start. "David and I were the avant-garde side of things, Jimmy was going to contribute the folky aspect, and Myles was going to keep us grounded in rock 'n' roll."

I thought of April Wine as a rock band. I wanted to play music that was rock, and it didn't matter to me at the time whether it was a fast tune or slow tune, heavy or otherwise, as long as it was in the rock vein. But I think I was the only one who felt the direction should be that simple.

I thought this new band was worth a try, as I wanted no part of a cover band. In my entire career, to date, I only spent approximately one year playing in a cover group professionally, which I consider an accomplishment of no small claim. I wasn't great at learning other people's material, I don't think. I didn't mind giving a song I liked a new arrangement, but recreating a musical piece, note for note, was not my cup of java.

April Wine played original material all right, and the new material was the result of the diverse influences and writing styles of David, Jim, and me. Ritchie would later recall in an interview with *Music Express* magazine that "the sound of the band then was very heavy, very complex, a hybrid of a dozen different styles filtering through three very different songwriters. Definitely a band with no direction."

I disagree that early April Wine was really heavy, although I concur with Ritchie that we were without a unified direction. We never really did find common ground during our short time together. The only time we came together in a singular style was when we recorded songs brought to us by producer Ralph Murphy, for our second album in 1972.

A great early example of how different we were in terms of style and direction was the score we wrote and recorded for a stage play performed at the internationally renowned Neptune Theatre in Halifax.

Ritchie Henman says that in the time between when we formed in December of 1969 and April 1, 1970, when we left for Montreal, we mainly practised and worked on the original songs. "Myles and Jimmy were getting more and more prolific every day as songwriters, so we worked on the original material. David and I still had an involvement with the Neptune Theatre, and Myles and Jimmy couldn't figure out this thing David and I were doing, with this business of writing music based on fifteenth-century themes and Gregorian chants and stuff like that to accompany a stage play [*The Lion in Winter*] set in the year 1300 or something. They went along with it and contributed what they could, but they were pretty mystified right up until the night the play premiered. We all went to the opening night with our families. We had recorded the music at the CBC studio, and they got to see how it works. It was segues. When a scene ended, some of this music we had written would fade in. It was a whole series of short pieces we had written and recorded that were all key to certain scene changes and elements of the play. Myles and Jimmy were rock 'n' roll and R & B guys. They were used to the three-and-a-half-minute song. They were kind of mystified by some of this weird shit that David and I were into."

The optimal word there, folks, is *shit*.

I sat there in the audience at the Neptune that night without saying a word. And then I tried not to laugh. Was it just me or was the whole music score ridiculous? Years later someone sent me a CD of the music that April Wine contributed to the score for *Lion in Winter*, and I was right. To be kind (and truthful), we were young, over-ambitious, pretentious, and not accomplished enough as players and as composers to really pull it off. It was silliness.

Oh, well, things could only get better.

We continued to write and rehearse with the intention of being good enough to head west and get a recording contract.

David Henman recalls that we got crazy with the writing, and the material piled up. Eventually we played in public; if we played for an artistic audience, we were embraced, but if we played for a drinking audience in a bar or whatever, they would be yelling out for stuff. Right away we knew we didn't belong there. We knew we had to get out of Nova Scotia. We knew we'd have to go west.

We had been recording demos in the basement on David's reel-to-reel tape recorder and sending out feelers to clubs, agents, and managers, having gotten names from our local booking agent, Entertainment Contacts, looking for even the smallest spark of interest. Mostly, we rehearsed in the evening after Ritchie got home from Saint Mary's University. Jim had already left Saint Mary's, so David, Jim, and I wrote during the day. Once Ritchie dropped out of SMU, we practised longer hours, always preparing to hit the road if fortune and fame beckoned.

We had sent one of our demo tapes to an agent in Montreal named Donald Tarlton, a.k.a. Donald K Donald (DKD). Although we'd sent our demo tapes to different people and companies in Toronto and Montreal, DKD was the only one we heard back from.

"What the people at DKD essentially said was—sort of a polite rejection—send more demos," Ritchie Henman later explained. "They didn't send back our original demo, and they didn't say screw off. They really didn't say, don't call us, we'll call you. They did say, 'We're interested; send more demos!' We just interpreted that as, well we had better get up there and see if they want us!

"We were restless. I was pretty anxious to get moving. Halifax had become a sour place for me. Still too many rednecks and not enough tolerance for long-haired artists such as me. I was damned glad to get out of there, personally. When the guys said we were going to move to Montreal, I said, 'Fine! When do we leave?'"

It wasn't long after the ambiguous encouragement from DKD that April Wine piled in a van one night and said farewell to Halifax. The city's lights twinkled in the darkness and then faded into the distance behind us.

7
—

We arrived in Montreal on April 1, 1970. We had no definite plans and therefore no place to stay. The first few nights Jim and I stayed at a YMCA while David and Ritchie stayed with a friend from Nova Scotia now living in Montreal.

Somehow, we found a small hotel in downtown Montreal that was owned by a guy named Peter Geary. The four band members and George Mack, a friend of David Henman's and a roadie for the band, stayed there in one room for a while. Geary and his boyfriend had a German shepherd and may have been partners in the hotel.

Peter was an amateur photographer. One day, he brought us to a location in old Montreal and took a bunch of pictures of the band. We viewed the pictures, and I'll never forget him saying that I wasn't photogenic. That remark hurt and it stayed with me. It affected me so much that it would be years before I could smile in front of a camera without fear of looking bad. I hated having my picture taken, and I'm still not comfortable with it. Man, was I in the wrong business! It's amazing how an off-the-cuff remark can psychologically scar a person for life. Even a careless, backhanded compliment can hurt someone's confidence so that self-image suffers needlessly. I was foolish to take Geary's comment so seriously, but then again I was a serious young man, somewhat shy and insecure.

Now that we were in Montreal we needed to work, and that meant a trip to see the folks at DKD's office.

Ritchie Henman's memories of that period are very clear. "The very next day we got into the van and drove over to the DKD offices and said, 'We're here!' They sent us over to Laugh In, a club in downtown Montreal where Donald Tarlton of DKD was doing a press conference. We went over there and all of these people were coming in. We could tell there was something big going on; this was on a Wednesday afternoon. The place was empty when we got there except for Tom Hansen, who was the bartender. Hansen went on to work with Donald. He was the 'Doctor Tom' in the title of the song from the Montreal band Freedom.

"We introduced ourselves and he told us there was a big press conference going on there that afternoon and that Donald should be there any time now. 'Why don't you get a table and I'll get you some drinks and when Donald gets here I'll point him out to you.' He was very nice. We were sitting at this table and people were coming in and we kind of got this fantasy notion in our heads: What if this is for us? Which of course was completely ridiculous. They weren't even expecting us, but you know, we were pretty young and naive. The thing got going and it turns out the press conference was to announce this big pop concert and the artist lineup. In the end, I don't think it ever came off, but that's what the press conference was about.

"When it was over, we said, 'Okay, that's Donald!' So David went up and said, 'Hi, I'm David Henman and we're April Wine.

We sent you a demo.' He was taken aback and said, 'Oh, I didn't think you were going to come up here.' David replied, 'Well, we want to move up here and see if we can get a record deal and get some gigs.' He told David that we should come down to the office tomorrow. The next day we went back to the DKD office and met a fellow by the name of Bob Ramaglia, a.k.a. Rags, and he said, 'Gee, we didn't think you'd drive up here, but as long as you are here, we'll help you find a place to stay and get you some gigs.' I have to say, everyone was so nice to us."

It went from there. Eventually they got us a gig so they could send somebody out to hear us play, and I guess we impressed them enough to get another gig and on and on and on. And we found permanent shelter.

We ended up living in a shabby ski chalet in a small town called Saint-Sauveur, north of Montreal, for about $60 a month that had four bedrooms, one bathroom, and a kitchen area/living room. My bedroom always had about an inch of water on the floor when it rained. What was cool about the place was that there was a nice brook that ran down from the ski hill behind the chalet. I would fish successfully for trout in that brook, which ran between our place and the chalet next door. It was next door that I first met Jim Clench. A band called the Coven were our neighbours, and Jim was the bass player. The drummer in that band was Richard Cezar, and he had great feel and a good singing voice. Richard remains a friend to this day. Jim Clench would become the bass player in April Wine in late 1971.

"Up in Saint-Sauveur, we got into a routine right away," Ritchie Henman recalls. "The guys would write during the day. We mostly slept in the mornings, although at first Jimmy and Myles and I used to go up into the hills fishing. By the end, I was the only one who was still getting up early enough to go fishing.

"They would write in the early part of the day and part of the afternoon, each one in his own room. Occasionally Myles and Jimmy would work on something together or Jimmy and David would write together. Starting at three or four in the afternoon, we'd plug in the amps and I'd get behind the drums and we'd ask around, 'Okay, what have you got?'

"Each guy would present a song in turn, and we'd work on that. If it didn't gel, the writer would just put it aside. These guys were writing a couple of songs a day, so by the end of any given week, we had another batch of songs to choose from. We did this seven days a week. We just practised all the time."

Write, practise, and, oh, yeah, get stoned. Smoking grass and hash was part of our normal routine back then. The parties and jam sessions with our musical neighbours, the Coven, were frequent, and because we had no other neighbours, the music usually went on all night. It was a lot of fun, and I learned a lot from jamming with other folks.

Someone introduced mescaline to the chalet while we were living there. Now that was kicking things up a notch. Mescaline for breakfast was an eye-opener to say the least, and I'd have mine with slices of bananas and a glass of juice. The first time I tried mescaline, I went for a "walk" that started by me getting on my knees and crawling as soon as I got out of the door. The colours were spectacular and 3D-like. I'd be crawling around observing the gravel in the driveway, the grass and flowers in the yard, and the bugs and insects. What an adventure the day had in store when one was stoned out of his gourd.

But that drug, or any other of the popular hallucinogens,

didn't become a problem for me, and I didn't partake in hard drugs for all that long. I was still young, though, and I did experiment from time to time.

Listening to music stoned was a gas. There was so much great music at the time, and listening to records by artists such as King Crimson while high on hashish or marijuana seemed to make the listening experience more acute and more meaningful. Even crappy music sounded pretty good.

Speaking of gas, there was a band named Natural Gas staying and performing at a lodge called Nymark's situated a short walk from our band house. It was a great band that included the amazing lead singer George Oliver and a fine drummer by the name of Graham Lear who went on to play with Santana, Gino Vannelli, REO Speedwagon, and Paul Anka, among many others. Every member of Natural Gas was a player.

I still have their self-titled debut recording in my record collection. There's an interesting instrumental on it that consists of multiple layers of overdubbed bass tracks, written and performed by the bassist, Leon Feigenbaum, called "Tribute to Rubber Boots."

Ritchie recalls that it was a while before we got a gig. "The first place we played was Nymark's Lodge. That was an experience. We saw Natural Gas play some gigs there. I guess there's a lull when the ski season ends, but when the good weather starts coming in, they start having bands in the bar. We got the chance to see what the room was like. The very next weekend it was our turn to play. We had a favourable response that night, and that led to a gig at a club in Montreal called Laugh In. People from DKD's office came down to see us play, and they decided to book us more and more.

"When we arrived in Montreal, the first priority was to get some gigs, although even in April when we first arrived, we were going around to the record companies. I think the first one we went to was PolyGram. We were a little fixated on PolyGram because we liked their roster. Unfortunately, we went first to their record pressing facility. David was going through the phone book and writing down names and addresses. We went into the reception and the lady there said, 'This is the pressing facility.' She gave us the address of the main offices. One thing led to another and eventually a music publisher."

It was soon after this that we were introduced to music publisher Brian Chater at Summerlea Music. We liked his attitude right away because he wanted to talk about the music. For him, it was always about the music.

Brian became a revered member of the Canadian music industry over the years as a vocal and persistent advocate for Canadian songwriters, composers, and musicians. He had arrived in Canada from England about four years prior to us meeting him in 1970. He saw the potential in April Wine and some other local artists, like Montreal-based rocker and songwriter Michel Pagliaro, and was also the first to recognize the talents of Bryan Adams and his writing partner Jim Vallance in the early days of their careers. Sadly, Brian died after a courageous fight with cancer in September 2013 at the age of 73.

Looking back, Brian was the first one to explain to us the actual figures—here's what a publisher gets, here's how royalties work—and he knew all about the people at Donald K Donald. He mentioned that they had a new record label, Aquarius Records.

Once we went back to DKD and were able to tell them that Brian Chater was interested in signing us for publishing, things changed quickly. In the end, everything was pretty much in-house at DKD, other than our music publishing, which was with Brian at Summerlea Music. A fellow named Bob Lemm had a graphic company, Promotivation Art Studio, and he would do our graphics, Terry Flood would manage us, and Donald would book us.

In retrospect, our naivety led us to signing away far too much of the publishing, and we found ourselves locked into a spider's web of interests under the DKD umbrella. We would pay the price as the years went by.

8

I n 1970, we signed a publishing contract with Brian Chater and Summerlea Music, an arm of Much Productions, as well as a recording contract with Aquarius Records and a management contract with the president of the Aquarius Records label, Terry Flood. How's that for interconnectedness, folks? I don't even know if that kind of practice is legal anymore. There's far too much potential for conflict of interest. But what did we know?

We no longer lived in the ski chalet in Saint-Sauveur. We now had a band house in the suburbs, in a place called Saint-Hubert, Quebec.

We arrived in Montreal in April, and by August of that year, DKD was booking us full time. They sent us off on a small tour that summer opening for a local Montreal band named Mashmakhan. Mashmakhan is a type of marijuana. The drummer for that band was Jerry Mercer, and he would join April Wine in 1973, replacing Ritchie Henman. It was when we got back from that particular tour that we signed our contracts with Terry Flood Management and Aquarius Records and DKD.

David Henman recalls our first big show. "We opened for Stevie Wonder at the Montreal Forum. There was a sax player on first, then April Wine, and then Stevie Wonder. During sound check, we were running through one of our songs and we heard this clavinet playing a riff, and we looked over and there was Stevie Wonder. We all walked over in single file and shook his hand and thanked him."

The Stevie Wonder show was in February of 1973, and it really was an uncomfortable situation for me. I was beyond nervous. I felt that we were not worthy. I was a big fan of Wonder's and in total awe. I was embarrassed because I knew we were far from being a great band and on the wrong billing as well. The folks in the audience that night were into R & B and soul music, and we were a light rock/pop band. A poor attitude on my part I know, but that's how I felt at the time, though it was nice meeting Stevie Wonder during the sound check that afternoon.

A show that really stands out for me in those early days of April Wine was playing with the Guess Who on June 5, 1970, at Place des Nations in Montreal. It was a beautiful summer's evening, cloudless, with a full moon shining brilliantly behind the stage during our opening set. That was a magical night.

Most of our gigs were not as glamorous. There were lots of shitty bars and clubs and odd-ball gigs like a strip club or two, a golf course—I would later become a longtime member of that private golf club—and a yacht club, of which I also became a member later on. But these gigs paid the bills and gave us an appreciation for success. We needed a song on the radio to achieve that next level of success. It was time to record.

"We were okayed to start recording at RCA Studios in Montreal in the fall of 1970 so that we could release the album the next year, just in time for the CRTC 30 percent Canadian content regulations," Ritchie later remembered. "They chose as our record producer Bill Hill. He was new at record production and had been the guitarist in an excellent local Montreal group called J.B. and the Playboys."

The Canadian Radio-Television Commission's Canadian content regulations, which Ritchie referred to, were implemented by the Liberal Canadian government in response to the reticence by Canadian broadcasters to program homegrown music, preferring to go with the tried-and-true hits coming from the U.S. and the U.K. at the time. It was controversial legislation, but for the most part it was embraced by Canadian artists. In the summer of 1971, Kelly Jay of the Canadian band Crowbar presented Prime Minister Trudeau with a small plaque inscribed, "Thank you for making it possible through CRTC for Canadians to be heard in their own country."

But this was the fall of 1970, and we were about to enter a new phase of our career as recording artists.

"It was kind of awe inspiring because this was a real serious studio," David Henman explains. "The only other studio we had ever been in was the CBC studio in Halifax to do the *Lion in Winter* stuff. That thing was antique. The equipment there looked like it came from an old Buck Rogers movie, gigantic knobs and dials.

"We went into the RCA Studios in old Montreal. Bill Hill was a funny guy. He kept us laughing. He had a great sense of humour. For that first album, they didn't tell us what to do. We were kind of on our own; they just let us go. They just said, 'Play your stuff and we'll record it!' So there are some really unusual songs.

"The one song that stood out, of course, was 'Fast Train,' penned by Myles. It was a brilliant piece of music. It went Top 40 in Canada. It really got us noticed. A signature song, and to this day, it really holds up well. Myles' vocal was great. He has a very intense vocal style that gets noticed."

Adds Ritchie Henman: "Everybody was so excited to be in the studio and finally making a record. When you're growing up out in the suburbs of Halifax and listening to your idols on the radio, you start to wonder if that's something you can do one day. And here we were, doing it for real."

I was as excited as the next guy at an opportunity to record, and although I don't remember many details of the project, I do remember Gaetan, the recording engineer, doing a lot of old-fashioned tape splicing on two-inch, twenty-four-track tape during the session. It was necessary, but disconcerting, to see butchered recording tape lying about on the floor. (Today, digital editing replaces physically cutting tape.) He did a great job of trimming fat and other such unwanted bits, however.

The fact that we got no much-needed direction during the session should have had us questioning the record company's choice of producer, but we were too naive and inexperienced to know better at the time. Bill's a nice fella and a fine guitar player, but I think if we'd had a more experienced producer on that record, it wouldn't have been, musically, so all over the place.

Ritchie Henman later talked about the group's first taste of success. "We knew you had to have a single to get on the radio, and you had to get it on CKGM or CFOX. The first single was 'Fast Train.' That was one of those songs that I call the Thunderbolt. You know, in the *Godfather* movie when Michael Corleone first sees Apollonia up in the hills of Sicily and his Sicilian friend says, 'Oh, you got hit by the Thunderbolt!'

"One night we were practising in the band house in Saint-Hubert and Myles came down and played that song for us. He said, 'I wrote this one this afternoon,' and he played those open-ing chords for 'Fast Train' and me and Jimmy and David went, 'Okay, that's it, we have a single! We are complete. We are now ready to go.' We just knew that was the one—the one that was going to open all the doors. It was so obvious right in those first three chords."

That first record took several weeks to record and was released in 1971. When it came out and our single release, "Fast Train," was being played on radio stations in Canada, we started what would become a relentless routine of going in the studio, recording an album, then touring, recording, touring, recording, touring. For April Wine, that pace would go on for over a decade. It was hard work, but mostly it was fun.

While working on our first album I discovered Elton John's first record, which stirred my imagination and renewed my appreciation for piano, very much like when I had first heard Floyd Cramer and Fats Domino years before. But I was even more impressed with Elton's hip, modern approach to pop rock music and songwriting. I decided I wanted to play and write on the piano, so I rented an old, brown Canadian-made upright Dominion piano and had it moved into our band house.

Ritchie Henman continues the story. "We were writing for the second album in the house in Saint-Hubert. We each had our own bedroom, but it was only a three-bedroom house. Myles had the living room for his bedroom, and he had a big curtain for a door. That was his room, and he rented a piano. Back in those days, you could rent a piano from Andy's Pianos and they would deliver it for about $20 a month. That's when Myles started branching out to other instruments.

"I play a little piano, so I played a little keyboard on the first album. Jimmy and I would always work out the stuff I was going to play on his material, but it was Myles' piano we were using to practise on. He was practising on the piano every day when he wasn't writing, and by the end of the month, he was doing these Leon Russell licks on the piano. He picks stuff up so fast.

"The big difference between David and me and Jimmy and Myles is that Jimmy and Myles have that innate talent for music, especially Myles. It just comes to him. He's a little bit like Mozart in that way. He just figures it out so fast. David and I had to really work at it and practise and practise and practise. It didn't come easy to us. We had to dig deep and work hard at it. Myles worked equally as hard at it, but it came easier to him. By the end of that month with the piano, he was just wailing on the thing. From the second album on, Myles did all the piano and I never did any more of it. I think there was one point in 1971, besides playing guitar, he had a keyboard on stage with him, a set of congas, and a flute. He went out and bought a flute and I swear he was playing it within barely two weeks. The sax gave him some trouble. He gave up on that after a while.

"He was good on drums, too. When he wrote a song, he'd ask me if I had a plan for the drum part. He'd say, 'Let me just play something!' On *Electric Jewels*, for instance, on the title track, there's a persistent drum roll that goes all the way through it. I played it on the recording, but he played it for me when we started working on the song. Same thing with 'Lady Run, Lady Hide.' Kind of an odd pattern on the snare drum, dragging the stick between the beats. I said, 'Yeah, that's cool, I'll do that!' He's got a better ear than David or I ever had. When Myles and Jimmy went to sing, they hit that note right on. We'd get close enough to tickle it, but they could hit those notes."

Of course, every good adventure should have romance woven into the fabric of the tale, and our story was no different. Not long after we arrived in Montreal, Jim was dating a girl and I was introduced to his girlfriend's friend, Phyllis Pascas. Jim's relationship with his girlfriend didn't last, but my relationship did. Phyllis and I would be together eighteen years and have two children.

Our second record was called *On Record*. I have no idea who came up with that title, the label probably. There were some significant changes this time around, the most impactful of which was Jim Henman's decision to leave the band.

Jim decided that the lifestyle was definitely not for him. The hours, the stress, and the inevitable drinking and carousing and the other seductive temptations that were part and parcel of being in a professional rock band were too much for him. I knew Jim was becoming increasingly restless and not focused on the band that much after that first album. He then announced one day that he had decided to return to Halifax and Saint Mary's University.

"When I left April Wine in 1971, the only thing I remember now is the depression and loneliness I was feeling and the inability to talk to anyone about it," remembers Jim Henman. "In hindsight, I see that I was a kid who had some emotional issues and used drugs and alcohol to self-medicate myself to be able to cope. I was also the acoustic guitar player who played bass in a rock band. You can hear that on the first album. Jimmie Rodgers, Taj Mahal, James Taylor, and Crosby, Stills & Nash, with a touch of Led Zeppelin, were my favourites in those days.

"I had lost much of the motivation and discipline to write the tunes that April Wine's move into becoming a successful commercial band would require of me. My songwriting was becoming self-indulgent and therapeutic, fueled by alcohol and drug use, which became unpredictable and somewhat danger-ous. Life on the road was physically and emotionally hard on me because of my excesses in those areas.

"Somewhere in early to mid-1971, I went into a depression caused by my own self-doubts, Catholic guilt, and excessive alcohol and drug use. The way out of this state of unhappiness, I thought, was to leave the band. That would fix it. That was a coping mechanism of my youth, to leave a situation—a geographical cure.

"I told the boys on the way to a rehearsal that I was thinking of leaving, and Myles, who knew something was up, said, 'Well, do it then!' I didn't say why. Ritchie and David said nothing, to my recollection. I don't think any of us talked about it. We didn't know how to, perhaps. Now I can see I was running away 'from me,' but at twenty-four years old I wasn't ready to see that.

"I spent a year bouncing around between Montreal and Halifax. I even had an offer to join a vocal-focused group in Quebec before I decided to study medical lab science in Halifax, and my life's journey continued."

"Jim Henman and I lived together at one point after April Wine became more financially successful and we could afford our own places," remembers Dave Henman. "Jim and I wrote together and we spent a lot of time together. Jim always con-fided to me that his Catholic upbringing was at odds with the rock 'n' roll lifestyle of booze, drugs, and partying. It was getting to him, so finally he came to us and said, 'Look, I can't do this. I've got to go back to Nova Scotia and find myself.' We certainly understood. We were all from the same place. We all grew up together, so we understood his feelings. This is what we want but if you don't, we understand. We were really enjoying ourselves.

"I don't recall there being any animosity. Jim did a lot of singing, but none of us was the lead singer at that point. If we didn't say it, we all recognized that Myles was the strongest voice. We tried to be democratic. That I think drove Myles crazy. With everything Myles wanted to do, we had to have a meeting, and that must have been difficult for him at times. He was the guy with the drive. We all had the creative spirit, but Myles had intense drive. Anyway, I don't recall any animosity towards Jim. We felt bad for him because he was going to miss out. We were practical about it. We just said, 'Okay, we've got to find a bass player!'"

9
—

Sure enough, having a song on the radio changed a lot of things for the band. There was more work available and therefore more money at stake, a point not lost on management.

When Jim Henman left the band, we needed to move quickly and find a replacement in order to maintain the momentum we had worked hard to achieve. An obvious choice, as far as I was concerned, was Jim Clench, who was our neighbour in Saint-Sauveur and bass player in the band the Coven. The other guys in the band agreed that he was a good choice as our new bass player. The Coven was no longer together, and so Jim accepted our offer to join April Wine.

The first gig with Jim Clench was September 1971 at John Abbott College, in the Montreal area. Jimmy was intense on stage, with a gritty bass style that was aggressive and powerful. For all his years as a player, Jimmy played a Fender Precision bass through an Ampeg SVT amplifier. He used a pick most of the time instead of his fingers, and he pounded on his instrument, wielding it like it was a guitar. His voice was also distinctive and he had great stage presence. Jimmy was a great new addition to the band.

When Jimmy joined us, we continued to gig but the main focus was on the next record. We needed a record producer, and we were introduced to a fellow Canadian who was living in New York at the time. His name was Ralph Murphy. In 1971, Murphy had a number two country hit with Jeannie C. Riley titled "Good Enough to Be Your Wife," which gave him his first introduction to Nashville. Ralph was a song man, and that's what we needed. He actually became quite successful as a song-writer over the years.

In 1978, Ralph moved to Nashville and began a joint venture publishing/production company with Roger Cook, an English singer, songwriter, and record producer who had co-written a number of international hits including "You've Got Your Troubles" (the Fortunes), "Long Cool Woman in a Black Dress" (the Hollies), and "I'd Like to Teach the World to Sing" (the Hillside Singers), which began its life as a Coca-Cola jingle in 1971. The Cook/Murphy co-venture achieved its first number one hit within a year of opening with a song by Crystal Gayle called "Talking in Your Sleep," written by Bobby Wood and Roger Cook. In 1978, Ralph co-wrote "Half the Way" with Bobby Wood, which was recorded by Crystal Gayle and held down the number two position on the Billboard country chart for three weeks. In 1980, he co-wrote "He Got You" with Bobby Wood, a chart-topper for Ronnie Milsap. Randy Travis, Ray Price, Don Williams, and Shania Twain, among others, have also recorded Ralph's songs.

Ralph Murphy was, and is, a very likable fellow and obviously an excellent writer, and as such, his emphasis in the studio is on the songs, and he brought us some great ones. "You Could Have Been a Lady" and "Bad Side of the Moon" were the two "outside" songs that Ralph brought to the band for the recording of *On Record*. Both became hits. Thank you, Ralph! "Lady" hit number 32 on the Billboard chart in the United States, remaining on the chart for eleven weeks. It reached number 5 on the charts in Canada.

Ralph liked to find songs in England that were successful there but not released here. "You Could Have Been a Lady," produced by Mickie Most, known for his hit-making ways with British artists such as the Animals, Herman's Hermits, Donovan, Lulu, and the Jeff Beck Group, among others, had been a hit for the British soul band Hot Chocolate across the Atlantic. They were best known in North America for their disco-era hits of the late '70s: "You Sexy Thing" and the number one song "Every 1's a Winner."

"Bad Side of the Moon" was a song written by British superstar Elton John and his songwriting partner, lyricist Bernie Taupin. The song had originally been recorded to appear on Elton John's 1970 self-titled debut album in North America, but it didn't make the cut and subsequently showed up as the B-side to Elton's single "Border Song." A concert version was included on his live album *11-17-70*.

The studio experience with *On Record*, our sophomore album, was more like what I expected a recording session to be. The studio had great equipment, we had a great engineer, and we had a capable producer in Ralph Murphy. *On Record* was recorded in Toronto at Toronto Sound. The engineer was Terry Brown, who in his native England had engineered, produced, and mixed for Jimi Hendrix, Traffic, Joe Cocker, the Who, Procol Harum, the Moody Blues, and many others before moving to Canada, where he is best known for his production work with the Canadian Rock and Roll Hall of Famers Rush, with whom he worked on nine albums.

Besides the two cover songs, in my opinion, the only other noteworthy tunes on the album were David Henman's "Drop Your Guns," which became a regional hit in Canada, and Jim Clench's haunting ballad "Didn't You."

"For our second album," David Henman recalls, "the record label teamed us up with a producer from New York, a Canadian guy by the name of Ralph Murphy. What a hoot that was! To this day, he's one of my favourite people; a real character. He was a tall, slick, fast-talking dude. We had a freezing rehearsal room in Verdun or Ville LaSalle, wherever it was, and Ralph would meet us there at nine o'clock on a weekday morning with a bottle of Johnny Walker Red. That's how he started his day, drinking it straight from the bottle, not that it affected his ability to work at all.

"We recorded 'Could Have Been a Lady,' and I remember Ralph came up with this idea for that 'na, na, na, na, na, na' section. I don't think Hot Chocolate did that part on the original version; that was a Ralph Murphy creation. We all thought it was the most bubble gum part . . . and we refused to do it. We stood our ground and we said, 'No. We're not doing no 'na, na, na, na' chorus!' so Ralph was like, 'Screw you! I'll do it!' Myles then said okay, so Myles went in with Ralph, as did Jimmy Clench.

"Ralph was a fairly adventurous producer too, so when we got the finished album we were shocked to hear this between-songs string quartet. We said, 'What the hell is that?! We didn't sign off on that!'"

That in-between "orchestral" thingy was weird. But otherwise, Ralphy boy did a great job and we owe him a lot.

Pam Marsh, my dear friend from the East Gate Sanctuary days in Cape Breton who was living in Toronto at the time, sang background vocals on "Bad Side of the Moon." Keith Jollimore played flute on "Moon." Keith was from Nova Scotia but was then living and working in Toronto and was very successful as a studio session player performing on recordings by Ray Charles, Anne Murray, Bob Seger, Gordon Lightfoot, and many more. He was also a member of Doug Riley's Toronto-based band Dr. Music.

By the way, if anyone out there knows what the hell "Bad Side of the Moon" is about, please let me know.

All in all, it was a positive experience, and Ralph was fun and serious at the same time, and that's how it should be. Making music should be a joyful adventure.

We went back to touring and certainly did a lot of that in Canada. We were playing clubs, bars, high schools, and even a few small arenas back then. With songs on the radio in Canada and a song charted in the United States on Billboard, things were looking good. Or so you'd think.

Ritchie Henman looked back at that period of our career: "We started to get some U.S. action after that album and single were released and that was because of Ralph. Rosalie Trombley is a Canadian, and she was the music director at CKLW, the powerhouse Top 40 AM radio station in Windsor, Ontario. Her ability to select the songs that would become big hits contributed to the success of the station and earned her much respect in the music industry both in Canada and the U.S. Ralph got Rosalie excited about the *On Record* 'project,' and once Rosalie got on it, the door to the States was opened for April Wine. This was with the tune 'You Could Have Been a Lady.'"

The problem was, we were busting our balls here in Canada with a single on the charts in the U.S., and we were doing nothing to support the record and album down there. Our management didn't have a clue what to do about breaking into the U.S. market, and the opportunity eventually passed us by.

"We didn't do any touring down there," Ritchie recalls. "It was frustrating. Every once in a while, in '72 and '73, we'd go through a crisis point where we would kind of threaten to self-destruct, and towards the end of '72, it was because of the fact that we were on the charts in the U.S. on Billboard and Record World and so on. They're playing our record down there and we've got a Top 30 song, but we're playing in a club for a week in Oshawa for factory workers from the GM plant with no clue as to who we were and no interest in us at all. Why weren't we down there?"

At this time, there was a lot of frustration. We were wasting an excellent opportunity to chase after success south of the border at a time when it was so hard for a Canadian band to break into that market. Why were we in bars doing absolutely nothing about our American airplay? The other bandmates were feeling the same way.

"This is when we would get into it with our management and the people at DKD," Ritchie notes. "We'd keep saying, 'Why are we here when we should be down there promoting this record?' They kept telling us, 'Oh, we'll get you there. We just can't get you there right now.' We were doing well, but we weren't happy with the way we were being handled. We were seeing where there were chinks in the armour and potential flaws. Things should have been done better. We should have been in Detroit or Philadelphia, maybe in a club, but someplace in the States where they were playing our record and where people were going to listen to the band."

By the way, it was during these days of touring eastern Canada that I was busted in Ontario and went to jail.

We were driving to a gig at the time, with Ritchie behind the wheel. David sat next to him, and Jimmy and I were in the back seat. We had finished smoking a joint, and David wanted to pull over to the side of the road and squirt.

Right after David finished relieving himself and got back in the car, a police cruiser pulled in behind us. He was checking to see if we were in need of assistance. We lowered the windows in the car, and it was obvious by the sweet smell of marijuana and the cloud of smoke that wafted out that we had been recently smoking dope. The officer asked us to get out of the car and then asked if we were carrying any illegal drugs. It was useless to deny that I was. The two hand-rolled joints on board were mine, and I had tossed them under the back seat when I saw the cruiser pull up behind us. I courageously confessed to possession, and I was off to jail.

Once in the police car, the officer asked me if I minded going with him for a quick cruise around town before we went to the station. I said, "Sure!" I was in no hurry to be booked. When we got off the highway and drove into this small Ontario town, the cop, who was nice and friendly, started driving slowly up and down some of the local streets on the lookout for any possible crime in progress or any other incident that might need his attention. I was in the back seat.

"I got your back, officer, if there's any trouble," I said, half-joking. He liked that and laughed.

"Good to know," he replied.

When he was finished with his drive around town and certain there was no mischief afoot, he took me to the jailhouse, where I was fingerprinted and then taken to a cell for the night. Jokingly, in my best James Dean, I enquired if he had a cell with a view, cause that'd be cool.

He said, "Sure!" and led me to a concrete room with a glass, opaque window that let in a bit of light.

"There you go, son. Enjoy!" I was left alone.

The next morning my manager in Montreal was called, and I was released after paying a fine. The money was hand-delivered by our tour manager at the time, Lloyd Brault, and I was set free. Besides the fine, I was put on probation for a year after which time I was given a full pardon.

Meanwhile the gigs kept rolling in. One of the more interesting concerts happened in the summer of 1972 at a historic Canadian music industry event called the Maple Music Junket (MMJ). This ambitious undertaking took place at a time when the Canadian music industry was coming of age and an infrastructure was slowly being put into place to support it. The CRTC Canadian content regulations for radio had come into play in January 1971. The regs basically required AM radio stations across the country to play a minimum of 30 percent Canadian music between 6:00 a.m. and midnight. Before the rulings, stations (especially the powerful urban pop stations that controlled the bulk of listenership) played relentless streams of American and British music, and many Canadian musicians and songwriters went unheard. They were also driven south of the border to get their songs recorded.

To give an idea of how tough things were for Canadian

artists prior to this, you have to look no further than our fellow Canadian Music Hall of Famers the Guess Who, who were given their name by Quality Records, their record label in the mid-'60s, to disguise the fact that they were Canadian and to create a bit of a mystique around the release of their upcoming single "Shakin' All Over." They were a Winnipeg-based group called Chad Allan and the Expressions, but when the record became a number one hit in Canada, the Guess Who name stuck. Of course, the song may well have become a hit without conjuring up the mystery group concept, but this was the mentality at work in those days when it came to approaching Canadian radio stations with homegrown tunes.

By early 1972, April Wine had earned a limited national profile in the wake of the regional success of my song "Fast Train" from our self-titled debut album. In the spring of 1972, we were on the radar in North America, having achieved Canadian and U.S. chart success with "You Could Have Been a Lady" from the *On Record* album, which, along with our debut set, got picked up for release in the U.S. by Big Tree Records, a label formed in 1970 by current Sony Music Entertainment chairman Doug Morris.

The concept of the Maple Music Junket arose out of the frustration felt by many in the Canadian music industry that media from outside our borders were oblivious to the fact that there was an exciting and rapidly growing music scene in this country. This was a topic of discussion over tea at a little restaurant on the Strand in London, England, between Toronto-based Aussie music journalist Ritchie Yorke, who at the time was read by more people in more countries than any pop writer in the world, and Andy Gray, editor of *New Musical Express*, one of Europe's largest music papers. Andy, listening to Ritchie rave on about the vast amount of talent to be found across the big pond, threw up his hands and made the suggestion that rather than have Ritchie meet with him each year and rant on about the talent cache to be found in Canada, the government should be convinced that it would be a canny business proposition to have a number of journalists flown over from Europe to see exactly what was going on in the colonies.

By the time Ritchie got back to Canada, the idea had become an obsession. The government said yes. The Canadian Record Manufacturer's Association, known as Music Canada today, were in, too. CP Air also came on board. Slowly the support grew until Maple Music Junket was no longer a slogan but a reality.

The media guests from the U.K. and Europe flew in and were treated to a series of concerts in places like La Butte à Mathieu in the village of Val-David, Quebec, sixty miles north of Montreal in the Laurentians, one of the most important showcase venues for the province's singer/songwriters through the '60s and early '70s, and the Place des Arts in Montreal, where over two nights some of the top talent in Quebec and English Canada was showcased, including Anne Murray, Julie Arel, the Poppy Family, Marc Hamilton, Luc and Lise Cousineau, and the Stampeders. The following day, the media guests left Montreal for Toronto by train in preparation for the last two shows at Massey Hall. The first night featured folk and country artists such as Bruce Cockburn, Murray McLauchlan, and the Mercey Brothers. The second night, June 7, 1972, was the much-anticipated rock showcase on which April Wine shared the bill with Crowbar, Edward Bear, Fludd, Lighthouse, Mashmakhan, and Noah, who replaced Chilliwack on the show after their last-minute cancellation.

Even though the hall was hot and humid, the crowd never sat

still, dancing and clapping themselves into exhaustion. Crowbar stole the show and provided the madcap ending to the evening with a girl popping out of a cake and kilted bagpipers marching around the venue and onto the stage.

One very unfortunate incident during that week professionally hurt April Wine unnecessarily. Let's call it the Walt Grealis Affair. The late Walt Grealis is considered one of the pioneers of the Canadian music industry as publisher of the now defunct Canadian music trade magazine *RPM Weekly* and as co-founder, with partner Stan Klees, of what came to be known as the Juno Awards, Canada's answer to the Grammy Awards. The Special Achievement Award presented annually at the Junos bears Walt Grealis' name.

"There was a big reception during the Maple Music Junket week," explains Ritchie Henman. "We were expected to wander around and mingle and introduce ourselves to people and promote ourselves, something we weren't particularly good at. We weren't salesmen; we were pretty low-key musicians. Somebody introduced us to Walt Grealis and we sat and talked for a bit. Myles had idly written something on a napkin. What he wrote was 'Don't drink the water because fish fuck in it!' We had just heard that, I think, from Ralph Murphy. We thought it was the funniest joke we had heard that week, so Myles wrote it on a napkin. Somebody else came along—nobody knows who— and started adding things and kind of went over the top with it. It originally said, 'Don't drink the water because fish fuck in it,' and somebody else wrote '. . . and shit in it, and piss in it,' intentionally trying to be crude and lewd. Somehow, Walt Grealis associated that with us and thought, 'These guys are a bunch of low-lifes; a bunch of assholes from the Maritimes' or something like that. That's how it was told to me. This napkin had ended up in Walt's possession. It was a really stupid, juvenile sequence of events that really had little or nothing to do with us.

"Apparently a meeting was called, and Ralph Murphy sat us down and said, 'Walt Grealis is pretty upset with you guys.' Grealis was a powerful man in the Canadian music industry, not a man to piss off. This was a bad situation, and we certainly paid the price for his spite over misunderstanding the situation, and apparently he was the kind of guy who held on to those things. I understand he had something similar with Anne Murray because of something she had said about his sexuality. In her case, there wasn't much he could do about it because her success just overwhelmed even his ability. We didn't understand what that was all about. What did any of that have to do with anything, and especially what did that have to do with a music career just because somebody wrote some crap on a napkin in a fancy hotel that happened to end up in the wrong hands? It all seemed kind of petty and silly."

Other than pissing off one of the most powerful men in the Canadian music industry, it was a great night!

Although the band was working a lot after the release of two records, we were still upset that we were not working outside of Canada. Along with the others, I was feeling pissed and disappointed. It was in preparation for a new, third recording that I wrote a song about how helpless I was feeling at the time.

Ritchie Henman has said that by the time we did the third album, *Electric Jewels*, if you read my lyrics to the title track, you kind of get an idea where our head space was at that point. I referred to the band as "electric jewels" and management as "fools."

Our management's lack of follow-up in the States while we

had a single on the charts was a very serious concern for the band, and the frustration almost led to a breakup, several times.

"Those were always the crisis points in the band where the thing would threaten to self-destruct," Ritchie added. "Then somebody like Ralph Murphy would sit us down and smooth it out and calm us down and say, 'You're on the right track and everyone's working hard and we're going to get it done for you!'"

Despite the words of encouragement and the promises from Terry Flood and DKD, they didn't find work for us in the States at this time in our career, and so nothing happened.

But there was friction in the band beyond not being able to support *On Record* in the United States because of poor management. Jim Clench and I were musically frustrated.

I've always tried to be a better guitar player, a better songwriter, and a better singer. I always worked hard at it. I gave 150 percent all the time. I still work at it. I was totally dedicated to my career, and it was hard to be with others in a band who did not give it their all.

Jimmy did. He worked hard at being as good musically as he could be. Nothing else but music really mattered to us. We were both determined to make it.

David and Ritchie did not seem to have the drive or desire that we did.

When I'm asked by young, struggling musicians, what do you have to do to be successful in this business, I always tell them to work hard. It's not quite that simple, of course, but without the hard work and dedication, one's chances of making it in this business are slim to none.

And, oh yeah, if you're in a group, surround yourself with others willing to work just as hard as you. If there is a person, or persons, holding the group back and jeopardizing the success of the band, then change is necessary.

Therein was the rub for April Wine going into 1973.

Apparently, the band April Wine was only a temporary stepping stone to kick-start the solo careers for its individual members. I did not know this. Until recently. Memo to Myles . . .

David Henman said that one of the interesting things about the band's formation was that we were really naive. "We were going to use April Wine as a jump-off. We thought, okay, we'll form this band and within six months we'll be as famous as the Beatles, then we'll split up and become solo artists. That was our game plan."

Ritchie Henman agreed. "We didn't really start the band to be all for one and one for all. Our agenda right from the beginning was to create a vehicle for the three individual and later the two individual songwriters. Jimmy [Clench] did start writing, so I should say there were still three songwriters. The whole idea was to create a platform from which those three songwriters and all of us as musicians could move on to whatever other things we wanted to do and have the doors open for us because we had been April Wine."

Well, folks, I do not remember ever having this discussion, but that doesn't mean it didn't occur. The Brothers Henman believe it did. No matter, that's not what happened from where I stood.

As the band started working on the next record, the friendships between everyone were deteriorating.

I was unhappy with Ritchie's drumming, and despite encouraging him to work harder at his craft, the talks meant nothing. Ritchie was driving Jimmy crazy because of his poor playing and lackadaisical work ethic, and it might have come to blows some nights. Jimmy had a temper.

"Jimmy and I would fight tooth and nail after a gig," Ritchie would later explain. "I would jump on him for his performance. I would say, 'Man, you sucked out there tonight. You looked bored and you looked indifferent and you played too loud!'"

The truth is, Jimmy always worked hard on stage. It didn't matter if he was happy or sad or sick, he did his best. Bored? Indifferent? Nope, that does not describe Clench. Those who have seen Jimmy perform can attest to that. The man was simply fed up with being one half of a rhythm section that didn't have a good drummer. And I understood exactly where he was coming from.

Jimmy was a groove guy and feel was everything. Jim Henman, too. Ritchie's feel was less than adequate. Jim Henman told me on many occasions that he found it frustrating and impossible to get a good groove going with Ritchie. And now here we go again—new bass player, same problem.

In all fairness to Ritchie, his calling was not music. He was not destined to be a great drummer.

Meanwhile, a shitstorm was brewing.

"We get from the second album to the third album, and what is happening now is in part because we've been playing and touring so intensely since August of 1970, and now we're getting into the end of 1972," Ritchie remembers. "At the beginning of 1973, we're starting to work on the *Electric Jewels* album. I'm no longer happy with the band's live performances. We kind of lost our spark live."

Ritchie's "no longer happy with the band's live perform-ances." Really?

David Henman sums up the state of mind of the band at that time: "With the success of "You Could Have Been a Lady," suddenly we were booked right across Canada. We did a lot of Maritime tours. It was just constant touring to the point that, in the summer of 1973, we were finally at the end of our first cross-Canada tour, and we were just baked. It got to the point where we were hating each other. Ritchie and Myles never really got along well. They never really bonded. Myles and I were always respectful of each other. He and I never really had that opportun-ity to get to know one another other than as bandmates."

It's true that Ritchie and I never got along very well. We were as different from each other as two playing in the same band could be. We had different work ethics and different ideas of what it meant to be successful. Although David and I weren't best buddies, I liked David then and I still consider him a good friend today.

I alluded to Jimmy's having a temper earlier. Sometimes it was justified and other times, not so much. And he was physical, throwing things in the dressing room, ranting at times and being hard to deal with. He was almost replaced once during this per-iod because he was so difficult off stage. He was a complicated man, Jimmy was. But then aren't we all.

Electric Jewels was our third album, released in 1973. Again, it was recorded in Toronto with Terry Brown engineering the sessions and Ralph Murphy producing. Dave Halbert was the mixing engineer.

David and Ritchie Henman, along with Jim Clench and I, were in the studio when the project was started, but we would not all be in the band by the time the album was finally finished.

10

The songwriting credits for *Electric Jewels* state that all songs were written by Goodwyn/Clench except "Weeping Widow," which was written by R. Wright. In fact, Jimmy and I collaborated on just three songs on the album. At the time we went into the studio, "The Band Has Just Begun" was the only co-written song by Goodwyn/Clench.

During the recording, David and Ritchie were replaced by Gary Moffet and Jerry Mercer, so two more songs were needed to replace the two written by David Henman for the record. To fill out the album, Jimmy and I wrote "Come On Along" and "I Can Hear You Callin'."

There are only nine songs on the *Electric Jewels* album. Today a CD will have about twice as many songs on a single disc, no problem. But when making records, we were limited to the number of minutes we could put on each side of a record before the sound quality suffered. They called the twelve-inch in diameter 33 1/3 rpm microgroove vinyl record an LP (long play) when it was introduced by Columbia Records in 1948, but despite the much finer groove than its forerunner, the 78 rpm disc, which could only play around five minutes of music each side, the LP still had the limitation of approximately twenty minutes a side.

In 1973, as April Wine worked in the studio in Toronto to complete *Electric Jewels,* the record business was going through a period of unprecedented growth and profits, in part because the labels were reissuing their catalogues in these new formats. There was money for tour support, lots of money, which was spent on limos, lavish parties, and luxurious hotel rooms. Many artists realized too late that this extravagance was being paid for out of their record royalties.

Here's a rundown of the songs on the *Electric Jewels* album:

Side One

The first track is "Weeping Widow," a strong tune written by an American fellow by the name of Robert Wright. I believe it was Ralph who brought this song to us. The song has great dynamics between acoustic guitar and heavy electric guitars. Jimmy did an awesome job singing it. He made it his own. For years R. Wright kept sending the band original tunes to record, but we never heard one that was as right for the band as "Weeping Widow."

"Just Like That" is a song that was written for stage. As a writer, I sometimes write a song with a specific purpose in mind. Other times, a song is inspired by circumstance or, sometimes, by a lyric or a riff or a certain feel. In this case, I wanted to write a stage song that was high energy and full of optimism, a song with a driving beat that rocked beginning to end. It was kind of inspired by "We're an American Band" by Grand Funk Railroad. I opened with only the guitar rhythm to set the feel, then added the lead vocal singing the verse, then a vocal harmony halfway through the verse, and into the chorus with the full band. Jimmy and I wrote the bridge sections together. This song became part of our live shows for years to come, often as the first song in a concert set. It was also the first time Jimmy and I sang lead vocals together in the same song. I guess you could call it a duet. I sang the verses and Jimmy the bridge sections.

"Electric Jewels" is the third song on the record. I started writing new songs for the third album while touring with *On Record*. The first tune I completed was "Electric Jewels," which expressed my frustration with management.

Here's a verse from the song:

Electric jewels, in hands of fools, controlling all of me
Here's my life, here's my dreams, now won't you set me free
I'm beggin' with you, please, it means so much to me

Although our management knew this song was directed at them, they never commented on it. They must have known they were responsible for missing a great opportunity to break into the American market given the success of "You Could Have Been a Lady."

Ritchie Henman notes that after the success of the second album and the single "You Could Have Been a Lady," we still never got to work in the States, which was one of the many things that was chipping away at the band. "We weren't always where we should be in terms of performing. Maybe that was a bit management's fault, maybe a bit the record company's, or whatever. Like it says in Myles' song, 'Electric jewels in the hands of fools, controlling all of me.'"

Anyway...

"You Opened Up My Eyes" is a ballad written by Jimmy

and is one of my favourite songs of his and a favourite on this record. It features the late, great Canadian blues man Richard Newell, a.k.a. King Biscuit Boy, on harmonica. Richard was also an on-again, off-again member of Crowbar. I played acoustic guitars and mandolin on the tune, and Pierre Senecal from Mashmakhan was on organ. Pam Marsh sang background vocals along with Jimmy and me.

Side Two

"Come On Along" is one of only three songs that Jimmy and I ever wrote together. The other two songs are also on this album: "I Can Hear You Callin'" and "The Band Has Just Begun." We share vocal duties on "Come On Along."

"Lady Run, Lady Hide" is a ballad I wrote that deals with my concerns for the environment. *Lady* refers to Mother Nature. The message is a good one.

> *Lovely lady, silent lady*
> *Will tomorrow be the last day in your life*
> *I can't free you, only plea you*
> *On the last days of your life*
>
> *Lady run, lady hide*
> *Lady run, lady hide*
>
> *Lonely lady, lovely lady*
> *Do you know, do you know you've lost the fight*
> *'Cause we'll use you, and abuse you*
> *On the last days of your life*

Our tomorrow is now today
And our last chance to find a way
You'd think we'd learn, you'd think we'd try
When tomorrow we all could die

Lady run, lady hide
Lady run, lady hide

Jimmy and I wrote track three on side two, "I Can Hear You Callin'." Again we shared the lead vocal work. Jimmy and I were big fans of early David Bowie records, especially Bowie's *Hunky Dory/Ziggy Stardust and the Spiders from Mars* period. There is an obvious (to me) Bowie influence on "I Can Hear You Callin'."

"Cat's Claw," the next track on *Electric Jewels*, is a great track written by Jimmy. Paul McCartney was another major influence, and Jimmy played a Rickenbacker bass after seeing Sir Paul using one. The melodic part of Jimmy's playing was also a direct influence of the cute Beatle. Of course, Paul was a bass player, singer, and songwriter and Jimmy wanted to do all those things as well. What young musician didn't want to be the next Beatles or Rolling Stones back then? (All you Beatles Babies, raise your hands, please!)

The song has a strong Bowie influence, but it's unique at the same time.

Strange love, torn between the heart and the soul
Laughing while the body grows cold
Somewhere that I should never be
Woman won't you please let me be
Free me, from the darkness here underground

Screaming but I can't hear a sound
Drowning in the pleasures of pain
I can't see the sky, for the rain
You took me places higher than I ever wanted to go
You took me places higher than any man should ever hope
to go, oh no

Reaching for the sun to come and take me home
Sitting in a chair and sinking like a stone

Sweeter than the sweet that comes to the brain
Just upon the threshold of pain
That's the hold you have over me
Woman won't you please set me free

You took me places higher than I ever wanted to go
You took me places higher than any man should ever hope
to go, oh no

Pretty intense lyrics there, James! A powerful piece of music as well. Classic.

The final track on *Electric Jewels* is a positive statement of hope for a young band dreaming of rocking its way to the top. "The Band Has Just Begun" was full of hope, but ironically, it was our last record together with this formation of the band.

Come talk to the band, and we'll tell you our plan
We've got a lot to say
We've worked for a while, to develop a style
On tunes for you to play

We'll sing you a tune, we'll scream and we'll croon
Some rock 'n' roll for you
And we'll give you a rush, with a look and a touch
We'll rock the whole night through

So we never have to worry, and we'll never have to run
Our chance to have a party's just begun, oh yeah, oh boy
The band has just begun

You can sing, you can dance, we can all take a chance
Come on, let's have some fun
Try if you will, to remember the thrill
Of a band that's just begun

And now you'll never have to worry, you'll never have to run
The chance to have a party's just begun, oh yeah, oh boy
The band has just begun, oh yeah

The guitar work on this tune is aggressive and was recorded LOUD.

I played several guitars that I owned then while in the studio. I was a collector, even back then. These days, I have more than sixty guitars in my collection. At the time, my guitars included a 1963/64 Gibson Melody Maker and a tobacco-burst double cut-away that I traded my red Hagstrom for in Cape Breton in 1969. I bought a brand-new Gibson Les Paul Custom in 1971. I also had a 1961 Gibson Les Paul SG—the guitar I most regret selling, ever. I bought a new Martin acoustic '73 but traded it for a 1947 Gibson Southern Jumbo.

It was on the Southern Jumbo that I wrote the majority of

my songs over the next decade, including the hard rock tunes "Roller" and "I Like to Rock." I still own that amazing old guitar.

But the most recognizable guitar in my collection today might be my '60s-model red sparkle Goya guitar used on the cover (an artist's rendition) and pictured on the back cover of *Electric Jewels*.

My amp selection back then was my old Fender Bassman head and a more powerful two-piece Ampeg V4. I would eventually try Sunn amps but then switched to Marshall. Once I went to Marshall amps, I never looked back. Remarkably, I still have my Ampeg rig and my original Marshall and two cabs.

The back cover on *Electric Jewels* is interesting. It's a picture of a man sitting in an alley, one hand on a wine bottle, bent over looking like he's about to pass out. He is clearly depicted as a drunk sitting on the ground against a wall. Standing at the entrance of this alley, which is littered with garbage and other urban refuse, is a man with a dog at his side looking at the man. Against a stone wall, and across from the drunk, is a young woman drinking booze from a bottle. In the forefront of the picture is my red sparkle Goya guitar, lying on its side with the neck and body facing the camera.

The man in the alley really is a homeless alcoholic, the young man with the dog is the man's son, and the young lady is the younger man's girlfriend. The drunk man in the alley is wearing an old red and black, sparkly stage shirt of mine. It is a thought-provoking photograph. And sad. I was not with the photographer when the picture was taken.

Electric Jewels was a difficult record to make (a major understatement, folks) because the relationships between the members went from bad to worse. Total communication is so necessary in making a great record, and in our case it was not there. We were getting the songs on tape, but for me, it all seemed a compromise in terms of performance. I do not mean just the other guys, but me as well. The thing about making a record is that it must be called finished at some point, knowing that is that. The door is now closed, forever. Next.

Jimmy Page once said that a recording is never finished, it's just that you have to stop working on it at some point and move on. True.

The point is, we could not finish the record, not the four of us. I felt like the band tracks were a compromise and not what I wanted. I imagine when I listen to music sometimes that the people recording are smiling when the music feels right. When we finally finished the record, I didn't feel like smiling; I felt like I'd had enough. I wasn't the only one. Although the album was considered finished, it wasn't. In fact, it was the band that was through.

11

—

I n the end, *Electric Jewels* wasn't the album it started out to be," Ritchie Henman has said. "We held up the release by taking the band off the road with the uncertainty of whether we were going to stay together hanging over us. In September, we had a meeting and we all announced we were leaving the band. It was a great breakup. Everybody felt relieved."

David Henman recalls that same period. "I was invited to join a reformed April Wine, but my brother wasn't. Ritchie and I have always been pretty loyal to each other, so I decided to abstain. I have no regrets. I was young and given to temptation. My sense is that I'd have ended up a casualty [of rock]."

What's remarkable looking back now is how things that happened all those years ago are interpreted in different ways today. I can understand that Ritchie didn't realize the band purposely disbanded, only to reform a few months later. The breakup was staged by Jimmy and me, with the plan to reform the band a few months later. I feel bad remembering the deception.

But Ritchie recalls a different version of the breakup: "For me, the first crack came on the cross-Canada tour in 1973. Too many mediocre gigs. We finished recording *Electric Jewels*, and then we took the band off the road at the end of June 1973 because I had already announced that I was going to leave the band."

It's similar to the time he said we got together to break up. That wasn't on my agenda. I have no recollection of Ritchie announcing that he was leaving the band either. Maybe he said it to David; I'm certain it wasn't said to me or Jimmy. It all happened over forty years ago, so it's ancient history and matters no more anyway. Or does it?

The Truth is another name I considered for this book. All my career, I've held my cards close and made no comments regarding members leaving the group over the years. On the other hand, certain ex-members have had a great deal to say about things.

I always stated to the press, and everyone else, that so-and-so left the band because of musical differences. With Jerry Mercer, it was a case of him retiring. After all, he was well into his sixties when he left the band.

The truth would be hurtful to some, and I never wanted to walk that road. I prefer the higher road. I still do.

But now I want to speak the *truth*, without malice, without being hurtful, if I can help it, and just state what *really* happened.

I wanted to continue April Wine back in 1973, but not with the same members. I wanted a new drummer. Jimmy wanted the same thing. So, not long after finishing *Electric Jewels*, we went to management and told them how we felt, and they said they understood and were prepared to stand by us. I told them David and Ritchie did not know what we were telling them.

I also discussed how unhappy Jimmy and I were with

them—the management and the label—and they said they were sorry and that they had made new contacts in the U.S., and next time they'd be ready. We gave them the benefit of the doubt.

And then Jimmy and I formulated a simple plan. As I look back now, I wish we had just had a band meeting and said the band was going to continue but with some changes. But we were chickenshit or something, and so there was some cloak and dagger nonsense that went down.

We would pretend the band was finished, take a break, say for a few months, and then announce that the band was reforming with new members.

Meanwhile, management wanted to be sure the rights to the name *April Wine* were free from possible legal battles later on. They wanted David and Ritchie to sign a release form giving up all rights to the name. And that's what happened.

David never had any anger towards Jimmy and me, as far as I know. He didn't have to leave the band when Ritchie did—that was his choice. David's a stand-up guy, and I'm happy we are still friends.

After April Wine, Ritchie played in a couple of bands before he chose a vocation that had nothing to do with music. He's done well, and I'm very happy he found something he was strong and successful at.

Jimmy and I were ready for the next step, but there was just one problem. We needed to find a drummer and another guitar play. We got lucky. Very lucky indeed.

Actually, the first order of business was to finish the record *Electric Jewels* now that David and Ritchie were no longer in the band. As I mentioned already, Jimmy and I had to write a couple of songs to replace the two David had written and that we had recorded. We also needed to find a drummer and a guitarist, but we had to be careful and find the right people, so we wisely decided to take our time before we made any decisions.

In the meantime, since we were unable to tour without new members, we decided to write and record some new tunes. Jim and I talked the record company, Aquarius Records, into sending us to England to record some new material. Ralph Murphy would come with us and produce.

Because Jimmy and I were such fans of British acts and the entire British invasion led by the Fab Four in the mid-'60s and by the bands that followed—the Dave Clark Five, the Animals, the Who, 10cc, Led Zeppelin, and so many others—we were thrilled to pack our bags and head for merry old England.

Jim and I prepared for the trip. We packed up a couple guitars and some personal shit and we were on our way to England. When we arrived, we stayed in an undistinguished hotel in London. The studio they had arranged for us to write and record in was in a residential building, with the studio downstairs and a tenant right above us. It wasn't exactly Abbey Road Studios or the Manor. Oh, well. We were in England and we were pumped, so off to work we went.

We started each day around noon. The morning doesn't always jive with playing and singing rock music. On the first day, at about 5:30 p.m., we were told to turn things down. The noise was bothering the lady who lived upstairs. Right. The next day we started mid-morning and managed to work until about suppertime, and again we were told to turn it down; we were too loud. This was not all right.

But we could do nothing about the volume problem, and the woman upstairs was getting her knickers in a knot for no good reason. We weren't that loud, really, it was just that the sound was carrying up through the vents, I guess, and therefore we were screwed after 5:00 p.m. or so every day.

We did manage to finish writing two songs at least. Ralph had a session drummer come in one day and he was cool, but we got nothing that would end up on a record.

At one point, we were working on a new song idea I had, and I wanted Jimmy to play stand-up bass. There's a big difference between playing a Fender electric P bass and a stand-up bass instrument, the same as there is a major difference between playing an electric guitar and an acoustic guitar. Very different techniques. Piano and organ, same thing.

Poor Jimmy tried, though. We got our hands on an acoustic stand-up bass and started rehearsing. I forget the name of the song, I even forget the tempo and feel of the tune, but Jimmy bit off more than he could chew. It wasn't his fault. The feel of the instrument was totally foreign to what he was used to, and there were no frets or markings on the neck to help visually. Placing your fingers on the right notes was all guesswork if you're not skilled on this giant-sized bass instrument. At one point, he drew dots and fret marks on a strip of tape that he stuck along the side of the neck so he could see where his fingers were supposed to be.

After giving it time and a good try, we passed on using the pain-in-the-ass fretless stand-up bass.

By now, we were bitching to Ralph about the time restrictions. We wanted to start mid-afternoon and play and record into the night; that's when rock and roll magic happens. Trying to sing and play right after breakfast is just fucking wrong, mate.

I believe Ralph tried, but there was nothing that could be done for us, or so we were told.

Ah, but there was something we could do. Go home. And that's what we did.

I got tired of the nonsense we had to put up with every day because the label wouldn't spend the money to put us in a real studio where we could work properly, so I told them, "We're coming home, screw this!" They freaked out of course and tried to convince us to stay, but we got on a plane regardless and flew back to Montreal.

So much for jolly old England being an inspiration for us.

Now that we were back in Montreal, our priority became putting a band together. The first new member was Jerry Mercer on drums.

I had first met Jerry a few years earlier when he was in Mashmakhan. We saw them perform at Lough In, the club in Montreal where April Wine first made contact with DKD Productions when we arrived from Nova Scotia.

Terry Flood, our manager, mentioned that Jerry might be available. Flood knew Jerry from Mashmakhan, and the Triangle before that.

I said I was interested in approaching Jerry about joining April Wine, so Terry called him. Jerry had just finished a gig playing in a backup band for guitar great Roy Buchanan. He was in New York when Flood reached him, and Jerry said he was interested.

When Jerry got back to Montreal we met up. He said he was available and that he would like to join the band. That was it. Jerry Mercer became our drummer. We were now three.

Right away the new band felt tighter and heavier than ever before. Jamming was fun, and I was sure all we needed now was a great guitar player in the band and we'd be set to finish off *Electric Jewels* and hit the road.

Enter Gary Moffet. Gary is a very versatile player. He grew up listening to music that most rock players at the time didn't appreciate the way he did. He not only grew up listening to this music, he also learned to play the songs.

He loved the classic songs from the early twentieth century by composers George Gershwin, Cole Porter, Irving Berlin, Jerome Kern, and Johnny Mercer, who wrote pop and jazz standards that are now part of what is commonly referred to as the Great American Songbook. Songs such as "Over the Rainbow," "One More for My Baby," "Cheek to Cheek," "I've Got My Love to Keep Me Warm," "Puttin' On the Ritz," "Georgia on My Mind," "Satin Doll," "Summertime," "Bye Blackbird," and "I'm Sitting on Top of the World," to name but a few. Wow, what an incredible well of influences to drink from.

So, as you can see, with Gary we were getting a lot more than your typical rock guitarist. Before joining April Wine he was in a band called Pops Merrily, and before that another Montreal band called the Vegetable Band.

It was Jimmy who suggested Gary. They were friends and they'd known each other a long time. When I got to meet Gary and jammed with him, I agreed with Jimmy that Gary would be an excellent choice for our next new member. Luckily for us he accepted our offer, and we were four and ready to rock.

12

After Jerry Mercer and Gary Moffet joined the band, the very first gig we played was on the Friday of the Labour Day weekend in 1973 at the Canadian National Exhibition (CNE) in Toronto with Three Dog Night and T. Rex. Three Dog Night headlined, and we were second on the bill. I remember that we didn't play very well. As Jerry Mercer stated in an interview afterwards, we played everything about three times as fast as it should have been, partly because of nerves, but also because we had never played together before. We were playing in front of 18,000 people, and that's a lot of pressure. Toronto is like our New York or L.A. If you have one bad show in Toronto, it can slow down your career by a year or two. It can take a while to overcome a bad gig in that town, especially when everyone who can help your career along is watching. The press and everybody who was anybody in the industry was there, and we had a horrible gig. I know it took a long time for us to overcome that in Toronto.

The very next show, which was the day after the CNE gig, was at a two-day festival called Mac's Party in Holland, Vermont, in the northern part of the state almost at the Canadian border.

I remember sitting with Frank Marino of Mahogany Rush, who also played that gig. It was an outdoor event and we were sitting outside our trailer. He was sitting on a lawn chair, and I was sitting on the steps of the trailer. He had a small amplifier and a Fender guitar, I think it was, and he was just playing with no effects. Frank Marino and Mahogany Rush were pretty famous for his style of playing, which is very much inspired by Jimi Hendrix. He used lots of effects and the sound was very overdriven, and there were a lot of delays and all kinds of pedals and stuff that he played through. In this case, that afternoon, he was sitting all by himself with the amplified guitar, straight in, no effects, just a musician playing, and it was wonderful to listen to him play. He could really go. It was in his hands. He had feel and controlled vibrato, all those things that the great guitar players have. It doesn't matter what guitar you play, or what amplifier you play it through, great artists will sound like themselves. I was very impressed.

That's all I really remember about the festival, and the fact that we had a great gig that went really well for us, but it seems we were in the quiet eye of a storm that was raging all around us that weekend.

According to a report from the August 31, 1973, edition of the *Newport Daily News*, the event was "a nightmare for local residents who spent sleepless nights of anxiety; for the law enforcement personnel exhausted from 12 hour shifts; for those who suffered losses from stealing and shoplifting; for the hospital which had a packed emergency room at times; and even for Mac." According to reporter Pat Hunt, shootings and gate crashers were part of the picture.

"Police place attendance estimates at some 10,000 over the

weekend while announced figures from the bandstand were 20,000. The set-up on the 200-acre Mead Hill site provided for parking areas near the road, and with the entrance gate and ticket booth a few hundred yards into the field. The bandstand and toilet facilities were enclosed with a high barbed wire protected with Mac's armed security men."

According to reports, security, many of whom were recruited from the historic Watkins Glen Festival, kept the crowds out on Friday but not on Saturday. There were more people outside than in, and when the fences came down the shooting started. The crowd rushed in and April Wine started playing.

Rick Donmoyer of the band Warpig noted, "My band Warpig from Canada played Mac's Party . . . [and] we were rushed off-site as soon as we finished our set, being told there was gunfire erupting and that we would be in danger if we stayed. April Wine followed us, but we did not get to see their set."

So, we went from one of the worst gigs, critically, to one of the scariest gigs we have ever played.

In October 1973, a month after we played that gig in Vermont, *Electric Jewels*, our third album, was released. Its arrival kicked off the Electric Adventure Tour, with a light show, pyrotechnics, and, unprecedented for a Canadian band at least, emphasis on a visual presentation. We worked coast to coast and back again playing hockey arenas for the first time—2,500- to 4,000-seaters—setting some attendance records at the time. It was also the first time a Canadian band had set out on an extended tour of one-nighters.

While we were touring with *Electric Jewels*, there was interest from Gene Cornish and Dino Danelli of the Rascals in producing the band.

In an interview for the book, Gene noted that he and Dino had a group called Bulldog right after the Rascals. "That was around 1973," he recalled, "and we were looking for production work. I ran into my friend Bob Ezrin, who's from Toronto. He was at the Record Plant doing an Alice Cooper project. He said, 'There's this band in Canada that I really like. They want to do a live album but I don't have any time to do it. Would you be interested?' We told Bob that we'd like to hear the band so he bought us a couple of airplane tickets and hotel rooms in Toronto. We went to see the band and they were lovely. They were very happy to talk to us.

"Terry Flood flew down to have a meeting with me. At the time, I was a big shot. I had a Rolls-Royce. I picked up Terry and he almost shit his pants. We drove through Central Park and I took him to a place called Rumpelmayer's for lunch, which was in the Hotel St. Moritz on Central Park South. I gave him the VIP treatment.

"So we decided the best thing to do, given that we had seen the band perform, was that they would pick the venue and we would send our recording engineer, Dave Palmer [former drummer of the Amboy Dukes, Ted Nugent's previous band], who was doing Bulldog at the time. He was up in Toronto with Jimmy Ienner working on the Bay City Rollers. Jimmy said Dave could leave for a week, and it was decided to do the concert in Halifax in January or February."

Between 1966 and 1968, the Young Rascals, who became the Rascals, reached the top twenty of the Billboard Hot 100 with nine singles, including three number ones: "Good Lovin'," "Groovin'," and "People Got to Be Free," as well as big radio hits such as "How Can I Be Sure?," "A Beautiful Morning," and

"A Girl Like You." The band was inducted into the Rock and Roll Hall of Fame in 1997.

Being a Canadian band, it was great to find out that, in fact, Gene Cornish is a fellow Canadian. "I was born in Ottawa, Canada, and when I moved to the U.S. from Canada when I was four years old, I only spoke French. By the time I went to grammar school, I was getting my ass kicked. My real name is Jean-Paul . . . J-E-A-N, like a girl. I quit speaking French and I changed it from Jean-Paul to Gene, like Gene Autry. The original name is Jean-Paul Gorley. That's the name on my passport. Cornish is my stepfather's name. I pay my taxes, and my social security and Medicare are under Cornish. I have from eighty to a hundred cousins. My biological father was the eldest of thirteen children. They didn't have cable back then. My mother's side is all from Montreal. They all live in Montreal. I have six cousins up there."

Obviously, we were excited that this was actually going to come together, but like any project there were details and logistics to be dealt with. Cornish and Danelli were responsible for the technical side of the recording. We were responsible for the artistic side, and I realized we needed to write a couple of new songs especially for this project to give the fans some new material. Those news songs were "Mama (It's True)" and "Druthers." Also, included as a bonus track was a studio recording called "I'm on Fire for You, Baby." It also was an opportunity for the new members to collaborate together for the first time.

"We got a remote truck, and remote trucks weren't that highly sophisticated at the time," Gene recalls. "Dave had a truck in Long Island. He took the ferry boat across the Long Island Sound, which at the time took a few hours. It was freezing cold.

We flew up to Halifax and had dinner with Terry Flood [April Wine's manager]. We went to the Queen Elizabeth High School auditorium in Halifax, and of course, Myles is from there. We were anticipating something like Beatlemania. The snow piled up about five feet high. They handle it there quite well because they're used to that. I remember, we had Chinese food and we talked about the show.

"So, the next day, there was the set-up, and the damned truck wasn't used to recording in the wintertime. It had a small heater in it. It was like a step van, and the recording desk was called Stephens . . . as in Stephens remote deck. They parked the truck outside and fired it up, so we went in and listened for a while, but we were freezing our asses off. Dave recorded both shows, and we took the tapes back to Electric Lady Studios in New York. [Studio is located at 52 West Eighth Street in Greenwich Village, New York. Originally built by Jimi Hendrix in 1970.]

"We listened to the tapes, and it seemed the audience was not exactly as enthusiastic as we had hoped, and a couple of mikes that we had for audience reaction really weren't working so well, so we had a dilemma here. The band was sounding great, but we thought we were going to have the 'welcome home!' kind of audience. They were a little bit on the reserved side. We never told the band, and to this day, the band never knew what happened. So we had to bring the band to New York to repair some vocals, and there was a buzz in one of the guitar amps. Gary had to redo some guitar parts. We did two days of overdubs, and they went back to Canada because they had to work.

"We were mixing the record and we realized we needed more audience, so Dave Palmer found a Rod Stewart live performance and we found about twelve seconds of nothing but

18,000 people cheering. We didn't have any sampling at that time, so we made these ten-foot tapes and spliced them all together, and we put a bunch of microphone stands around the room and ran the tape from the machine, around the room on these mike stands to the other end of the tape. We kept it going constantly, and anytime we thought we needed more audience, we just pumped it up. We had sixteen tracks. The original audience wasn't actually dead, and the fact that a couple of the mikes that we had weren't working well didn't help."

The live experience worked out great, and Gene and Dino wanted us to go in and record a studio album. To test the waters, I felt it was a good idea to write a couple of new songs, go into the studio, and see how it worked out. Besides, the opportunity to work in Jimi Hendrix's Electric Lady Studios was too great to miss out on.

As a live album, it captured what was going on that night, so in that regard it was okay. There was a lot of energy on stage.

The first two songs on the live album are "Mama (It's True)" and "Druthers." Jim and I were the writers in the band at that point. We wrote "Mama (It's True)," which is a high-energy rock 'n' roll song with three or four chords; not much to it. Same with "Druthers." These two songs were written for stage and for this album specifically. These are songs we played live for many years. (By the way, the credits on the album are Goodwyn/ Clench, but that wasn't the case at all. Most of the songs were written by either Jimmy or me individually.)

The third song on the album is "Cat's Claw," and it's got to be one of Jimmy's best songs ever. This is an example of the credits saying it is a Goodwyn/Clench song when in fact it's a song Jimmy wrote. I did not write the song with him.

The only studio cut on the live album is "I'm on Fire for You, Baby" written by David Elliott, which was recorded in Toronto by Terry Brown. It was brought in by Doug Morris, the president of Big Tree Records at the time, a label he had formed after working as a songwriter, producer, and executive at Laurie Records. When Big Tree later was acquired by Atlantic Records, Morris moved and jointly ran the label with founder Ahmet Ertegun. He would later head up a number of major labels in the United States including Warner Music, Universal Music Group, and most recently, Sony Music Entertainment. He was one of the founders of Vevo, the multinational streaming service for videos, and in 2013 was co-producer and lead financier of the smash Broadway show *Motown: The Musical.*

We learned the song in the studio. Doug was not really a record producer; he was the president of the company. We played the song for Doug and he said, "No, I don't like the guitar. I want something Hawaiian. Can you do kind of a Hawaiian-style guitar solo?" We're all looking at each other, and Gary was out there in the studio with his guitar playing some stuff. I went in to speak to Gary and told him that Doug wanted something Hawaiian. Gary gave me this quizzical look and said, "How about some slide?" Gary's not really a slide player. We had no slide player in this version of the band. Brian Greenway can play some slide. But Gary's a smart guy and a great guitar player. He found a slide and we gave him a little space and time, and he came up with a Hawaiian-sounding slide guitar solo, and we played it for Doug Morris. He loved it. The only version of "I'm on Fire for You Baby" that was ever released on a record, aside from the greatest hits set, was on this live album.

The first song on the second side is "The Band Has Just Begun," which is a song I wrote even though it says Goodwyn/ Clench. This song is about a band starting up, a bit like "Cum Hear the Band" in its theme. The studio version is on the *Electric Jewels* album. We have used that song to open up April Wine concerts for years. It's a great rock 'n' roll song and fun to play.

"Good Fibes" is the second track on the second side of the album. The story behind the song is that Jerry Mercer is known for his drum solos, and that reputation goes all the way back to the Triangle with Trevor Payne and Rayburn Blake, which eventually morphed to Mashmakhan, which had an international hit, especially in Japan, with the single "As the Years Go By." He was also known for the strobe lights that are used in the press roll section of his drum solo with April Wine. That started with Mashmakhan. There was a section in the chorus of the song "As the Years Go By" where they would do peace signs under strobe lights. From that it went to a strobe light placed under Jerry's snare drum so when he was doing a fast high-handed press roll on the snare, the strobe light would catch it in frame so you would see it in slow motion, and at some point you'd hear a very tight press roll, but it appeared that only one of Jerry's hands was playing all of that. People loved his solo, and it became sort of a signature for him.

So I suggested, "Jerry, rather than just a drum solo at the end of 'The Band Has Just Begun,' why don't we call what you are doing a solo, a song, and you'll get a writer's credit?" One of us suggested the title "Good Fibes" because the drum kit he was playing was Fibes, a very popular brand at the time. The song credit on that cut goes to Jerry Mercer.

The last two tracks on the album are "Just Like That," from the *Electric Jewels* album and "You Could Have Been a Lady" from April Wine's studio album *On Record*.

The live album was a moment in time, recorded for posterity, but the band was about to take a giant leap in a new direction.

13

The record company told me that Gene Cornish and Dino Danelli had a great time producing the live record and wanted to do some recording in New York. I loved the idea of going there to record.

I wrote two songs for the session: "I Wouldn't Want to Lose Your Love" and "Tonite Is a Wonderful Time to Fall in Love." I wrote them both on the piano. I had this little hand-held tape recorder that I used to record songs with, which I set on top of the piano. You can hear the wood creaking and the pounding of the foot pedals on the demo. Regardless of the poor quality, they liked the songs and the band went down to Electric Lady Studios to record them. Working in New York with Gene and Dino was special because they are from New York and the Rascals were a New York band.

Dino was Italian, but they both knew where to find the best Italian food in the city. One time they took us to an Italian restaurant and we sat at a large table with them and the band.

Gene told the story of Keith Moon of the Who walking into the middle of a Rascals session while they were recording a song, dressed in a suit, a vest, and a top hat and holding a cane—the English gentleman.

Keith had the Rolls parked outside. He walks in like that, all cheerful and crazy, and he says, "I'd love to play on this song." And they say, "Of course!"

So Keith goes in and sits behind the drums, takes off the hat, and puts down the cane. "Roll tape!" They go through the song, and it's horrible. They look at each other and say, "That was pretty bad. Let's give him another shot!" They ask him if everything is okay. "The headphones are good? You can hear what's going on? Okay, we'll give it another go."

Keith says, "Okay. I'm ready when you are!" He undoes the vest and goes at it again, and it's just as bad. It's almost like he can't hear the track; it's horrible.

So they say, "Well, we're not there yet. Let's do this again!" So Keith gets up, takes off his jacket, loosens the tie, gets nice and loose and flexible, and does it again. At the end of the take, he throws down the sticks, stands up, and proclaims, "That's it! Fuckin' nailed it, mate!" He puts on his stuff and leaves.

They were just speechless. He wasn't even close. They realized after he left that this was his type of humour. He stopped the session, said he was going to cut this track, and completely, on purpose, played all the wrong things and then said, "I nailed it!" and walked out. Crazy.

After they told us this story, the food came to the table and there was a great big plate of steaming hot spaghetti. Gene was still talking as the rest of us started to eat. I guess he was waiting for his food to cool down a bit. Suddenly he turned to everybody and said, "All right, enjoy!" and he buried his face in the spaghetti right up to his ears.

At this point, I was tired of the record company taking us into the studio to record two- or three-minute songs. Of course, that's what Gene and Dino did in New York, but that was an audition of sorts and that was okay. It was around this time that I decided I wanted to write a real album, not just a collection of two- and three-minute songs, hoping they were hit singles.

I got permission from the record company and a budget to produce the next album. This was what I had been dreaming about for a long time, and I welcomed the challenge with open arms. Instead of working in Toronto, I chose Tempo Studio in Montreal, where Ian Terry was the chief engineer. The studio was downtown on Avenue McGill College, just up from the landmark Montreal deli Ben's Restaurant. Ben's was a deli favoured by celebrities such as Leonard Cohen, Liberace, and even former Canadian prime minister Pierre Trudeau. It was renowned for its cheesecake and its trademark smoked meat sandwich. It was open twenty-four hours a day, and every so often, we'd go to Ben's and buy a whole homemade strawberry cheesecake and bring it back to the studio. What a sugar rush!

We worked day and night and pretty much lived in that studio as the album got recorded. We'd start in the afternoon and go all night long and finish somewhere between five and eight o'clock in the morning. There were many times I'd drive home in morning rush hour traffic, get some rest, and then go back in the afternoon and work all night again.

Recording *Stand Back* was a great experience. One of the great things about this album was that we were on our own and we were young and just full of piss and vinegar, very naive, very romantic, and it shows in the songs. It was very experimental as well. We were champing at the bit to try all sorts of things in the studio that we had heard other bands such as Queen, Bad Company, and Led Zeppelin doing, things we had never had the opportunity to do before. What a thrill it was.

Track one on *Stand Back* is "Oowatanite," a Jim Clench song that has been a classic in our repertoire over the years. It starts with sixteen notes played with a drumstick striking the fire bell. Now *that's* a catchy intro, folks. Normally the notes would be played on a guitar or a keyboard, but playing it on a fire bell was a brilliant idea by Jimmy.

The second song on the first side is a song of mine called "Don't Push Me Around."

> *You can call me a punk*
> *I like to scrap when I'm drunk*
> *And I'm just likely to cause a scene*

The song is definitely a song of rebellion, with lots of energy and a cool intro guitar hook.

One day around this time period, our management company got a call from Paul Anka, who at this time was having great chart success with the single "(You're) Having My Baby." He was aware of April Wine, so he contacted Aquarius Records and told them he would like to write a song with me. My answer to Terry Flood, our manager, was naïve, and I now regret it. I said, "I'm not going to write with a guy who's talking about having fucking babies!" Here I was, twenty-six years old but feeling like I'm eighteen, writing songs like "Don't Push Me Around." I didn't want to write about having babies. Thanks, but no thanks. Looking back now, I wish I had said yes and penned a song with Anka; he's a legend.

Me in my Nova Scotia tartan jacket, looking relaxed, with
April Wine bassist Steve Lang in the '70s.

The things I wore (or didn't) back in the '70s—embarrassing, to say the least.

At Tempo Studio working on the *Stand Back* album with chief engineer
Ian Terry (centre) and Billy "The Kid" Szawlowski (right) in 1975.

With engineer extraordinaire Eddie Kramer at Jimi Hendrix's studio in New York City,
Electric Lady Studios. We were mixing *Live at the El Mocambo* after performing
there with the Rolling Stones in 1977.

From left: Bob Rags of Aquarius Records/Donald K Donald Productions; Paul Bronfman, roadie; John Caron, band crew; Peter Lubin, who worked merchandise for the band; Robbie Whelan, band crew; and Leslie Brault , my dear friend and longtime band crew member. Paul Bronfman is now the chairman/CEO of Comweb Group Inc. and William F. White International Inc., as well as the chairman of Pinewood Toronto Studios Inc. Sadly, Robbie was killed in a car accident on his way to Le Studio in 1983.

With my 1967 Jaguar Mark 2, circa 1977. I love Jags and collecting cars.

A group shot taken at Le Studio during the recording of April Wine's *Harder . . . Faster* in 1979. Front row: Steve Lang; Deane Cameron, one of the most respected executives in Canadian music history and longtime president of EMI Music Canada; Brian Greenway; Rupert Perry; Bobby Colomby; me; and Robbie Whelan, assistant engineer. Back row: Gary Moffet; unidentified employee of EMI; Jerry Mercer; and Nick Blagona, chief recording engineer and co-owner of the studio.

At Manor Studio during the recording of *Nature of the Beast*, circa 1980.

Mike Stone and me at the Manor Studio in England. We'd just caught a large trout that was later served up for breakfast by the cooking staff. Richard Branson stocked the pond at the Manor with trout.

Sightseeing in Rome in 1981, when April Wine lip-synched "Just Between You and Me" for a television show.

From left: Allan, Barry, Dad, and me on the *Bluenose II* in the early 1980s. We rented the ship for the day as a special treat for my dad.

Golfing in the Bahamas with one of my best friends, John Sands (far left) and Canadian golf legend and dear friend George Knudson (centre).

Fishing in the Bahamas, circa 1986. From left: Me, George Knudson, Nick (boat owner), and Linda and John Sands.

With my daughter, Amber, in 1984, just before we moved to the Bahamas.

With my son Aaron, in the Bahamas, circa 1985.

With my youngest son, Cary, Christmas 1999.

Archie, my beloved golden retriever. My recording studio, Archie Studio
(also known as Mound Sound), was named after him.

The next song is "Cum Hear the Band." I got the spelling for "cum" from the British rock group Slade, who became known for their deliberate misspelling of their song titles. I was a big fan of the group and especially the *Slayed* album, which had songs like "Mama Weer All Crazee Now" and "Gudbuy T' Jane." "Cum Hear the Band" is a simple song of innocence that really personifies the entire album in a way. It's a song about being in a young band and teenage romance.

> *Billy's called, he's got the van*
> *And Ian's got a set of drums*
> *And I borrowed this old guitar*
> *We're hoping someday we'll all go far*
> *And maybe we'll write a tune*
> *And drive in a limousine*
> *See our picture in a magazine*
> *So won't you be there*
>
> *Cum hear the band on Friday night, oh yeah*
> *Cum hear the band it'll be alright, oh yeah*
> *And baby it's you that's got me burnin' inside*
> *So cum hear the band it'll be all right, it'll be all right*

Billy Szawlowski was the assistant engineer on the record and the Billy referred to in the song. Ian was Ian Terry, chief engineer on the session and the Ian in the song.

The next track is "Slow Poke." It was a very playful song with a sense of humour and sexual innuendo all over the place.

I got something to keep you satisfied
So won't you excuse me, while I slip inside
I ain't gonna rush things, you know I ain't no speed freak
And I like to take my time whenever I eat

Cause I'm just a slow poke, uh-huh, with long strokes
I said I'm just a slow poke, baby
And I like to take my time, poke on

It doesn't actually sound like me singing because the voice is very deep. People often ask us, is that Myles singing? It is, but we reversed what was done with Alvin and the Chipmunks, where they slowed the tape down and recorded a guy singing the Alvin and the Chipmunks part, then when they brought it back up to normal speed, the voices became very high as if they had been sucking on helium. I sped up the tape for this song so it was rolling really fast, and I sang in a normal voice so that when we slowed it down to the regular speed, my voice came out sounding deep and low.

I was told that Keith Richards liked this song. An acquaintance of April Wine's played it for him at the Harbour Castle Hotel in Toronto at the time we played with them at the El Mocambo.

The next track is "Victim for Your Love." The little click heard at the beginning of the song is me moving the pickup selector toggle switch from "off" in the neck position to full "on" in the bridge position with the volume on ten. I did this because I couldn't control the guitar volume any other way. I didn't want to bring up the volume slowly. I wanted the sound to be instant. I was running through a couple of Marshall amps, cranked. The engineers were going to take it out but I said, "No, leave it in!" I'm glad I did, it's cool. We also used tape phasing, which in those days could only be done by manually putting your hands on the tape and slowing it down and speeding it up depending on how much pressure you applied. On this song, it gets more intense as the song progresses. The reverbs and the delays and the phasing equipment are all high-end vintage tube gear, and they sound awesome.

Track number six is the Jim Clench song "Baby Done Got Some Soul." It's a different kind of song for the band, *wah-wah* driven with an R & B feel to it.

"I Wouldn't Want to Lose Your Love," which I wrote for the Gene Cornish and Dino Danelli session in New York City, is the next track. I composed all the slow songs on the piano. I'm not a great piano player, but apparently, after I've consumed just the right amount of alcohol, I can play damn near anything, within reason.

The next song, "Highway Hard Run," was supposed to be titled "Highway Hard On," but the record company wouldn't let me sing that. It's suggestive rock and roll, with power and lots of raw energy. I played an autoharp (chorded zither) in the dream-like pre-chorus sections. Gary played solo lines throughout, and I played the solo and joined Gary in the outro. The guitar I used almost exclusively back then was my beloved early '60s Gibson Melody Maker. Sadly, it was destroyed in a trucking accident in Montreal years later.

Track nine is "Not for You, Not for Rock & Roll," a pop song with attitude. "Wouldn't Want Your Love (Any Other Way)" pops merrily along, a song of youthful commitment.

The final song on the album is "Tonite Is a Wonderful Time to Fall in Love," a great example of using the same simple chord progression start to finish, changing only the melody of the vocal to separate the verse from the chorus. I also used this simple format on "Say Hello" and "Enough Is Enough." I wrote this for the recording session with Gene Cornish and Dino Danelli in New York. It was a big hit for us and a favourite at live concerts.

The album was released in 1975, and it was a tremendous success. It was the first Canadian album to achieve platinum status for sales of more than 100,000 copies, and the first English-speaking album to be certified double platinum. It was the second-biggest seller of our career. With that success came proof for the record company, and everyone else, that we could make our own records. Amen.

The success of *Stand Back* encouraged the band to develop a more theatrical approach to our live performances. The cannon you see on the cover of the *Stand Back* album morphed from an idea I had to use a picture of a twelve-gauge shotgun with both barrels smoking. Then we decided to go big and use a cannon. Everyone loved the idea.

We were preparing for a summer tour to support *Stand Back* when an interesting idea for the stage show surfaced—to build a cannon to bring on stage and fire into the audience. We liked the idea of having the image from the front cover of *Stand Back* presented on stage, and we figured it would be good for promoting the album in a unique way, so we hired the people who designed and built props for Place des Arts, a performing arts centre in Montreal. The Place des Arts complex is also the home of the Montreal Symphony Orchestra and Opera de Montreal.

The cannon was made of sheet metal shaped like a cannon barrel, encased in thick Styrofoam and finished in silver Mylar that simulated gun metal. It was quite large and built on wheels so it could be rolled on and off stage. It was a real cannon, folks, one that really worked. When we used it on stage as part of the show, the barrel was stuffed full of confetti and real gun powder. I would pretend to ignite the "fuse" with a long torch with the business end soaked with lighter fluid. In reality, it was detonated off stage electronically. When fired, it would go KABOOM and shoot confetti out into the audience.

It was absolutely incredible that we were able to do this with no pyrotechnics licence or experience whatsoever. We would cover people in burning confetti, and they would be patting their heads and their shoulders putting out the flaming confetti and loving every minute of it.

Sometimes the cannon didn't go off. That was embarrassing. I'd go out there and lower the torch to the fuse, and the audience would be sitting there waiting for the KABOOM . . . and there wouldn't be one. I'd shout out, "KABOOM!" and try to milk a laugh out of it. That would be our Spinal Tap moment. But it did fire most of the time, and it was great fun.

We had to be super careful that there was nothing in the cannon barrel that we didn't know about. It would be sitting on stage all day long, and somebody could throw a Coke bottle into the barrel, a nail, a little bit of gravel, or something like that, so we had to be very, very protective of it and make sure it was checked carefully before we used it each night.

This cannon thing was so successful live that we carried the idea of a prop for the album cover and stage forward to the next album, *The Whole World's Goin' Crazy*, with the larger-than-life

Mad Hatter depicted on the cover. Eventually, we stopped using the cannon; we put it in storage and I never saw it again.

Around this time, we started using fog machines on stage. It wasn't the good, safe kind of fog used today; it was the old-fashioned kind of fog that made you choke and your eyes water. We also used traces of gun powder around the stage on metal rails that we would ignite at certain dramatic moments in the show. Those days were a hoot.

We signed in the U.S. with London Records, and *Stand Back* was theirs to break in the States. London Records was a label with an identity crisis at this time, known primarily in the rock world in America for issuing the pre-1971 recordings of the Rolling Stones and an early single by the Texas-based band ZZ Top. The rationale for the move to London was explained to us by our management team. "Yes, they are in trouble, but that's *good* for us because they'll put all of their energy into working our record." So we signed with the label, and you guessed it, we were fucked from the start. We handed this gem of an album, which was making sales history in Canada, to a sinking ship, and the record, in the States, went down with it. Rock and roll is a vicious game.

14

With the success of *Stand Back* and the fun we had making it, you would assume that life was great and the band never stronger. Wrong.

You may remember there were personality problems between band members when the Henmans were still in the group. Unfortunately, there were serious problems between Jimmy Clench and the rest of the band, problems that made the *Stand Back* tour difficult for everyone. It was reported back then that there were brawls and fist fights, but that was not true. As I say, Jimmy was complicated, so I'll make an attempt to explain the man as I knew him as best as I can.

Some parts of this book are difficult for me to write. This is one of those parts. Let me say first of all that Jim was a friend of mine. We spent a lot of time together over the years, and I knew the man about as well as anyone who ever worked with him.

Jim was one of the most generous people I ever met. He would give of his time happily, if it was needed. He would roll up his sleeves and get his hands dirty without thinking twice if he thought you needed a hand. He was loyal, and he was a kind and honest man.

Jimmy was also sharp as a tack. You'd want him to be your partner in a game of Trivial Pursuit or Scrabble. He knew a lot of stuff. His intelligence was never in doubt by those who knew him. And Jim was extremely funny with a great sense of humour, a great smile, and a contagious laugh. But sadly there was the other side of Jim that was dark, angry, and self-destructive.

I will not go into examples here, but at times Jim was his own worst enemy. His temper and tantrums were well known by those close to him. It was a real pity. I have no idea what Jim's formative years were like and what made him so chronically unsatisfied in life, but that was the way he was. It got worse as he got older.

Touring the *Stand Back* record was when the problems started. The thing is, it's hard to say what the disagreements were about, really. It was just a lot of little stuff, the kind of petty crap that can survive and thrive when people are disagreeable. The arguments were becoming more common and more out of control. Jim started with the physical stuff, like throwing things backstage again, the same problem we had back when David and Ritchie were in the band. Dressing room arguments were now frequent and getting nastier. Things were being thrown or destroyed, and there were arguments and lots of bad vibes on stage, not between Jimmy and me, although we definitely had our moments, folks, but more between him and one of the other guys. It got to the point where something had to change. I was fed up and threatened to leave. Jim was warned many times about his behaviour and to cool it, but it made no difference until eventually I had enough. I said that if things were going to continue like this, then Jim had to go or I was taking a walk. Jim was replaced with Steve Lang. When Jim left the band, the problems disappeared.

The following quote is from an interview I did for a Canadian publication called *Music Express*:

"It was not a great time for anyone to be out of the deal but there were bad feelings between Jim and all the other members in the band. I had feelings of guilt about it for a long time because I was one of the people who decided he'd have to go. It's hard to sit back in relative comfort after the success we were having as a band and think of Jim, who had played and sang so well on our records, and now was no longer there but instead trying to find a new gig and make his way. Of course, I felt bad."

I was delighted to hear that Jim joined BTO after April Wine, and I hoped he would find peace and happiness in his life.

Steve Lang was a friend of Brian Greenway's. In fact, they were in the last version of Mashmakhan together, the same band for which Jerry Mercer drummed and of which he was a founding member. Steve joined Mashmakhan right after Jerry left to join guitarist Roy Buchanan.

By late 1975, we had sold more albums than ever before, and with the *Stand Back* tour behind us and Steve Lang our new bass player, it was time to write and record a new album. We called this new record *The Whole World's Goin' Crazy*.

For this recording, we went back to Tempo Studio in Montreal. Ian Terry, who was the recording and mixing engineer on *Stand Back*, was at the controls once again. I had been working on writing some new ditties and it went well. I even collaborated on a few tunes.

The song "Gimme Love," which opens the album, was co-written by me and Johnny Hagopian, who played guitar in a Montreal-based group called Moonquake. They did some opening dates with AW in the Maritimes when we toured *Stand Back*.

It was a straight-ahead rock song inspired by a great main guitar riff that Johnny Hagopian and I jammed out. I moulded a song arrangement out of it and added lyrics. I remember singing this song and hitting those high notes in the chorus. I had never sung falsetto before, and I freaked a bit.

The second song on that first side is "So Bad," a rock song that has a sort of Jimi Hendrix feel to it. The riff reminded me so much of Hendrix that I called Frank Marino of Mahogany Rush and asked him play on the song. Frank has this style that draws very heavily from the Jimi Hendrix Experience. Frank was awesome in the studio and made the guitar tracks rock. He has that processed, flanged sound and it worked great on this tune. His solo killed.

Now that I realized I had a falsetto at my disposal, I was using it all over the place. Someone should have slapped me and said, "Myles, enough of this high falsetto, already!" (Come to think of it, somebody should have slapped David Lee Roth of Van Halen a long time ago for that falsetto squeak he makes. I find that annoying as hell because it's in nearly every song he sings.)

The next song, "Wings of Love," was an ambitious piece of music for me at the time. The arrangement was already elaborate, but the song became even more sophisticated when we added the ondes Martenot, an electronic musical instrument invented in 1928 that's similar to a theremin in that it's controlled without physical contact by the performer. The Beach Boys used the similar-sounding electro-theremin on their hit song "Good Vibrations." The ondes Martenot, which can be played either by depressing keys on the six-octave keyboard or by sliding a metal ring worn on the right-hand ring finger in front of the keyboard, has been heard on the soundtracks of a number of major films including *Lawrence of Arabia, Heavy Metal, Ghostbusters, My Left Foot,* and *Hugo.* It was also featured in the *Star Trek* theme.

The instrument we had was a very fine example and quite rare. A lady named Marie Bernard, a friend of one of the engineers at Tempo, suggested we try adding a track of this wonderful instrument to the song. I'd never heard one before, so I was played a tape recording that featured the ondes Martenot's sound. I found the sound intriguing and unique so I said sure, let's give it a try. The only complication was that the instrument belonged to the music department of one of the universities in Montreal and they wouldn't loan it out. Since we couldn't go there to record, we had a problem. She had an idea. We'd borrow it without the university knowing.

Marie and a friend went to the university that night, "borrowed" the instrument, and brought it to the studio, where she figured out some wonderful parts that we recorded, and then she returned it before it was even missed. She had a lot of *chutzpah* doing that. Good for her. What she played that night, under pressure because of the time constraint of returning the instrument to the university, was very impressive indeed. I am forever grateful to Marie for introducing me to the ondes Martenot and for a wonderful track.

I played the Fender Rhodes parts. The Rhodes piano has a kind of a bell-like sound. It was a very popular instrument at the time even though the tuning with the Rhodes was always finicky.

There is a low Moog track on the song. I played the guitar solos on my white 1961 Gibson SG Special through a Marshall. I'm not sure what effects are on the guitar, but the sound is very cool and the high notes soar. I still have the guitar, and it still sounds great.

The next track, "We Can Be More Than We Are," is based on a jam I had with Jim Henman some years previously. We started jamming on it at Tempo Studio, and it developed into a section of music that faded in and then out. We recorded a phone conversation between Gary and me and laid that onto the track. The call is from a guy called Ivan, who is actually calling me for some musical advice. In the middle of the call, I start singing, "We can be someone, we can be more than we are." Just a fun piece of music.

"Rock N' Roll Woman" is a straight-ahead rock track with up-tempo acoustic guitar rhythms, power chords, and some of my new-found falsetto cries at the end for good measure.

"Shotdown" is a great rock and roll song. It was a big hit and still a favourite in St. Louis, Missouri. The power slides played on guitar in the choruses are the hooks in the song. They're good lyrics about a guy who doesn't want to be shot down by a girl he likes. It's juvenile, but I like it.

"Like a Lover, Like a Song" is a love song I wrote on piano, but in the studio I had Dwayne Ford play it because he could do it better than I could. The mellotron track on this song was played by Serge Locas.

I came up with the song title "Kick Willy Road" because of a road sign that caught my attention while I was travelling with the band in rural B.C. I went back and took the sign off the post, threw it into the trunk of the car, and brought it home. I don't know whatever happened to it.

The last track on the album is the title song, "The Whole World's Goin' Crazy." It's a fun, silly song, and the lyrics make absolutely no sense.

The fireman rushes over
He's got stretch marks on his hose
And he punched out the light
Under everybody's nose

You get the idea, folks.

In the chorus of the song we played with the speed of the recording tape. It's the very opposite effect we used on "Hard Times," in which my voice sounds much deeper than my normal voice. I sang the parts in a regular voice, so when we brought the tape speed back to normal, the vocals were very high, sounding like Alvin and the Chipmunks, which is kind of like what a person sounds like after sucking on helium.

The album cover for *The Whole World's Goin' Crazy* was designed by Bob Lemm of Promotivation, the in-house art department at Aquarius Records.

Because the image of a cannon on the cover of *Stand Back* was a big success in terms of marketing that album, we wanted to have something interesting and visual for *The Whole World's Goin' Crazy*. "Let's put something on the front of the album that we can take on the road" was the thinking. "What about the Mad Hatter?" I suggested. I liked that whole *Alice in Wonderland* kind of thing and the craziness of it. Bob said, "Okay, let's see what we can do."

They had an artist (actually it might have been Bob, but I'm not sure) draw the Mad Hatter, and the person did a terrific job. He's got the globe swinging on the end of a watch chain and everything. It looked right out of the book.

Then somebody suggested that we make a large *papier mâché* model of the Mad Hatter and take it on the road. We nicknamed him Henley, and because he was sixteen feet tall, he travelled in his own truck. It took two guys from the crew to make Henley run. They would get inside the thing, pulling levers so that Henley could move to the music. There was a lot of room inside Henley, and there were things that went on within the bowels of our Mad Hatter, stuff that I can't mention here, folks. I'm sure you understand.

As the follow-up to the multi-platinum album *Stand Back*, much was expected from *The Whole World's Goin' Crazy*, and I don't think we disappointed anyone. We had already racked up a number of firsts in the Canadian music industry during the '70s, and with this album we could now also lay claim to having had the first Canadian album to rack up pre-release orders of more than 100,000 copies. To quote *Music Express* at the time, "The Canadian tour is a killer and grosses a million in gate receipts, the largest grossing tour by a Canadian band to that point, 1976. The fans can't get enough of the band, though the critics across the country slaughter them, crying sellout, dinosaur, irrelevant and worse. When he returns to Montreal, Myles pays cash for his house and a new Cadillac. This time, the band itself refuses to tour the States, preferring the adulation of its Canadian fans to a cold, bottom-rung reception they know they'd get in the U.S. at this point."

An interesting note is that during this tour, the chamber of commerce in Moose Jaw, Saskatchewan, presented the band with the keys to the city as well as gifts. My gift was a seat cushion because they heard I had just bought a new car. After the show, which ended early enough to go out for a late supper, we enquired as to what was the best restaurant in town and went there for a bite to eat. It was a fancy place with one of those fake velvet ropes at the entrance to discourage patrons from just walking on in. The four of us went to the entrance, where we were told we couldn't come in because we were wearing jeans. We pulled out the key to the city, assuming it would get us a table for sure. No dice—we were turned away. That irked the bejeezus out of me, so when we got to the curb, I stopped, took off my jeans and placed them over my arm, and then turned and walked back in the restaurant, heading for the bar. I never made it to the bar.

By the way, our opening act for the *Whole World's Goin' Crazy* tour was Heart from Vancouver, who had just released their debut album on Mushroom Records.

In our box set from 1992, Martin Melhuish noted: "The success of the tour confirms the group's star status in their homeland. That success is sweet, but as 1976—the year of the Montreal Olympics—comes to a close, there is a growing frustration within the group about their lack of recognition in America. Heart, who a few months earlier had opened for them on their Canadian tour, is now topping the charts with their debut album. April Wine wants some of that action, too."

There is no question we were frustrated by the lack of success in the United States, and the rest of the world for that matter. We were also tired of being nominated for Junos and always being denied a win. The only folks who really appreciated our efforts in Canada were the fans. The Canadian music industry people and organizations were pretty much indifferent, despite the phenomenal sales we were generating, and that was also very frustrating for the band and the fans.

It was time to refocus, redefine the band, and find success outside of Canada. I had a plan.

15

After *The Whole World's Goin' Crazy*, I wanted to do a solo record. I decided it was time to make a musical statement outside of the context of the group, so I began to work on a solo project I was going to call *Goody Two Shoes*.

I started writing more personal songs, different styles of songs that were unlike what I was writing for April Wine. The writing was going well, and I was excited and happy.

I was halfway through the record when Aquarius Records decided it should become an April Wine album. The band was really on a roll, and they didn't want to take a break. That meant, in short order, I had to come up with a number of songs to balance off half of what had already been recorded. To admit that I was royally disappointed would be correct. But I succumbed to pressure and, being a team player, changed my course in midstream. Today, I regret that decision. I should have stuck to my guns, but it's all academic now.

Those new songs were written quickly with AW in mind. I really didn't have anything on the solo album that sounded like April Wine, so at the last minute, I very quickly wrote a song titled "Forever for Now." The band went back into Tempo Studio and started the recording process with engineers Ian Terry and Billy Szawlowski. The song "Forever for Now" is a simple, straight-ahead rock tune and the first song on the album. The record company liked it and decided that would be the name of the new AW album.

The second song on the first side of the album is "Child's Garden," a song I wrote for my dad that dealt with the time I was living at home. I was, like a lot of teenagers, confused and looking for answers. In my case, my mother was dead and life at home was a bitch.

I was acting out, I suppose, and getting into trouble, and this caused him some concern. I wasn't doing well in school. He was worried: He knew I was playing a lot of guitar and that I wanted to be in a band. He didn't want me to be a professional musician, though. He didn't think there was a lot of security in it. On that point, he was correct.

Besides the music and failing in school, I was doing other things that got me in trouble. I was doing some breaking and entering. I was stealing cars and drinking. He was losing a lot of sleep with all these concerns about me, obviously, as a loving father would. So this was written for my father in the hope that it would help explain the rebel spirit of a son who left home at eighteen, with an attitude and the reputation of being "trouble."

Luckily, my dad got to hear the song before he passed away. I called him and told him about the song and said some things that were on my mind, and I'm happy he got to hear the tune. He really appreciated that.

On the recording, Gary and I played the guitar parts, with Gary handling the solo and fills. This is the kind of playing that

Gary was so good at. I played all keyboard parts, including piano, with the Selena keyboard doing string parts. Jerry played glockenspiel, the instrument that has the chime-like sound in the intro and first verse.

The third song on the album, "Lovin' You," is a country tune. Because of the strong influence country music had on me growing up, with Dad being into country and western music as much as he was, I decided to try to write one. I wrote the tune on piano. I love the background vocals by "the Winettes," Judi Richards and Mary Lou Gauthier.

"Holly Would" is just a simple song with a play on words. For the main guitar part on this track, I ran my guitar through a Hammond Leslie so it sounded like an organ. I had to play specific chord formations to help get the right organ effect.

The last song on side one, "You Won't Dance with Me," the big hit from this album, was that song I wrote when I was playing in Woody's Termites. It's about a guy playing in a band and watching his girlfriend dancing and hanging out with everyone but him because he's on stage. Eventually he loses her to someone else because he can't give her the attention she needs.

While writing this ballad, I was reminded of some of the teenage drama that a young romance can lead to. The whole puppy love thing and the vulnerability issues that surface when in a "relationship" at such a tender age. How love treats a person during these years can greatly affect relationships in the future. Although romance as a teenager is more infatuation than true love, the pain of rejection can be brutal and leave some lifetime scarring on one's self-esteem, in my opinion.

I was also reflecting on the times back when guys didn't dance at social events, like sock hops and high-school dances and so forth, except for slow songs such as the waltz. The fear of rejection on the dance floor could be nerve-racking.

I tried to inject some humour in the song by speaking some lines, as Elvis would:

It's hard to say
What I have to say
And I hope you understand
But Jill told Fred
You wish I'd . . . drop dead
Now what am I going to do?

The musical influence in the song's style is obvious—the Everly Brothers. The two-part harmonies all the way through the tune are right out of their songbook. Gary Moffet's harmonized solo in this ditty is classic Moffet.

When we performed this song live, I'd bring a girl on stage from the audience and dance with her while the band continued to play. We had this big mirror ball that would light up so that it was refracting light everywhere, and it would rotate, creating this mood of an old dance hall/ballroom kind of thing. It was a big hit with the audience and really a nice part of the show. Obviously, it's a very personal song.

The next song, "Come Away," was written by Peter Jupp and George Bowser. George is half of a musical comedy team called Bowser and Blue with Rick Blue. I produced a single for George when he had a band called Bronze, which was before Bowser and Blue formed in 1978. I asked him recently about some recording we did all those years ago and the fact that he sounded exactly like me on one of the songs. It was the strangest thing.

"We recorded two singles back then," George said. First was 'Lady Lover'/'Superstar,' and the second was 'Easy Come, Easy Go'/'Don't Shoot Her Down.' You did a great job; they just weren't hit songs. You also recorded 'Come Away' on *Forever for Now*. The funniest session was when I sang a song called 'Joy Ride' and Ian Terry freaked out because I did an exact copy of your vocal." (Fast forward thirty-eight years, as I'm trying to find somebody to replace me in AW, as I've had enough touring, and we're auditioning singer-guitar players for the gig. After many auditions, the band and I gave up because we couldn't find someone who played guitar and sounded like me vocally. It worked out, though, as I decided to continue working with AW, with a reduced schedule, giving me time for other projects.)

The next song is "Mama Laye," which is one of my favourite songs on the record. I like the feel and the Caribbean vibe with a mystique and voodoo thing going on. It's great fun to play live, and I still perform it these days. Again, Gary does an outstanding job on guitar. Mary Lou Gauthier sang background vocals.

"I'd Rather Be Strong" is a tune about social concerns, an observation of the times:

> *It's a sad situation*
> *A lot of hopeless information*
> *On the news*
> *Nothin's gonna please you*
> *And nothin's gonna change*
> *Well that's your view*
> *So many hungry people*
> *It's a shame and is it legal?*
> *Well it's a sight*

There's something goin' on
Somethin' we can change
And it's our right

The background singers on this are Judi Richards, Tony Grant, and Gail Mezo.

The next track is "Hard Times," which is basically the music from "Big Bad John," a big hit in 1962 for Jimmy Dean. I had some funny lyrics that I wanted to put to the melody of "Big Bad John," and I thought it would be a hoot. I was able to get a hold of Jimmy Dean to tell him I had these lyrics and I wanted to sing them to his song. He said, "Maybe. Why don't you send it to me?" I typed the lyrics and mailed them, and he called me back and told me I could do it. He thought the lyrics were funny and that it would be a fun record. The only thing was, he wasn't sharing royalties of any kind on that song. "I get everything," he said. I said, "Okay, Mr. Dean. No problem. I thank you so much." Pam Marsh, my friend from the East Gate Sanctuary days, is on the album doing background vocals with Judi Richards and Mary Lou Gauthier. Barry Keane, who plays with Gordon Lightfoot, makes an appearance on percussion.

Photography is credited to Judi Cezar, the sister of Richard Cezar, the drummer for the group Coven, which Jim Clench was the bass player for right before he joined AW in 1971, as well as Graham Fowler and legendary photographer John Rowlands, who recently had his work with David Bowie honoured with gallery exhibits on both sides of the Atlantic.

"Marjorie," the last song, is one of my favourites from the album, a great big acoustic ballad. What's cool about this song, for me, is that I got to play the keyboard parts, which were a bit more complicated than anything I had tried to arrange and play before. (Remember, folks, I'm a guitar player not a keyboardist.) It was a challenge and it turned out well.

The keyboard I used for those string sounds is called a Solina, and I played it on several albums back then. I rented it from a music store called Jack's, owned by Jack Tepley. Jack was cool. He had a picture of himself with the Beatles hanging on the wall from when they performed in Montreal in 1964. When I was finished using the Solina on a record, I had to return it to Jack. Why I never bought the damn thing I'm not sure. I seem to recall he refused to sell it.

Music Express said of *Forever for Now*, "*Forever for Now*, which started its life as Myles' solo album and its one foot in the boat and one foot on the dock approach with its varied musical influences . . . produces a number of surprises. The title track, released as the first single, dies on the vine and causes widespread mourning until the release of "You Won't Dance with Me." Though it peaks just short of the Top Five in Canada, it is destined to become April Wine's bestselling Canadian single ever as it tops the 100,000 sales mark and then sweeps the album to platinum status in its wake."

16

T hat week was complete madness!"
That was Mick Jagger's take on that period in early
March of 1977 when the Rolling Stones and April Wine
shared the stage at Toronto club the El Mocambo for two historic shows, recorded by both bands for subsequent live albums.

It was a time in which the future of the Rolling Stones, "the World's Greatest Rock Band," hung in the balance as Keith Richards was charged with possession of heroin for the purpose of trafficking, following a raid by the Royal Canadian Mounted Police (RCMP) on his hotel room at the Harbour Castle Hilton (now the Westin Harbour Castle Hotel) on Toronto's waterfront. His passport was confiscated, and he faced the real prospect that, if found guilty, he was looking at a sentence of seven years to life under Canada's criminal code. He ultimately pleaded guilty to simple possession. This came days after his common-law wife, Italian-born actress and model Anita Pallenberg, was arrested at the airport by the RCMP for drug possession when she arrived in Toronto with Keith and their seven-year-old son, Marlon. Pallenberg later pleaded guilty to marijuana possession. It was that incident that led to the subsequent raid on the couple's hotel room.

If that wasn't enough of a circus to attract the attention of the world's tabloid press, twenty-eight-year-old Margaret Trudeau, the wife of Canadian prime minister Pierre Elliott Trudeau, showed up at the club on both nights, leading to a flurry of conjecture and innuendo under front-page banner headlines in British scandal sheets such as the *Daily Mirror* that shouted: "Premier's wife in Stones scandal."

Margaret Trudeau had been a surprise visitor to the club on Friday night, arriving in a Stones limo. She came back again the next night, reportedly at Ron Wood's invitation, and horror of horrors, she was seen leaving the club with the Stones and their entourage. The press hopped on the story quicker than you could hum two bars of "It's Only Rock and Roll (But I Like It)," and Maggie's sojourn with the Rolling Stones became fodder for gossip on two continents. Adding fuel to the fire was the fact that the night of the first concert was her sixth wedding anniversary.

But there she was, staying at a suite in the same hotel as the band. She also hosted a well-guarded party for the group.

We were not invited.

In an interview the following day, she expressed her annoyance about the innuendo and conjecture being made by the press.

"Look, it was like this: on Friday, I went to the Rolling Stones concert and on the Saturday, I went to work as a photographer. And I was pleased to get the chance to meet nice people, whose music I have loved for some time, and I'm not changing my taste in music to satisfy the people of Canada or anyone."

There was just so much going on over the few days when this infamous gig went down in Toronto the Good. But it wasn't all goody-goody.

Actually, it was more badass, but, hey, these were England's celebrated bad boys, the Rolling Stones, after all. That made it all the more sensational and, of course, newsworthy. It was conspicuous, not only for the fact that the Stones were performing in a small Canadian rock club, but also because of Keith Richards' drug bust for possession of heroin.

As well, there was the controversy that surrounded Canada's first lady, the hippie and childlike, free-spirited Maggie Trudeau, who was hanging out at a hot, sweaty, smoky bar—yes, you could smoke indoors in most public places back then—with the air reeking of tobacco, alcohol, and drugs, all mixed together.

The events leading up to the El Mocambo concerts had unfolded in great secrecy. In winter 1976, the phone rang at the Old Montreal offices of Aquarius Records, our recording home, and promoter Donald Tarlton's Donald K Donald Productions, two formidable organizations in the Canadian music industry. Skippy Snair, a promotion representative for Aquarius, answered the call. Peter Rudge, former American manager of the Who and manager of Lynyrd Skynyrd at the time and who was also handling the business affairs of the Rolling Stones, wanted to know if Skippy could suggest any good clubs in Toronto.

Rudge had confided in Snair that Mick Jagger wanted to record part of their new live album at a club in Toronto but that info needed to be kept quiet. The Stones needed the live recording to complete a double-album set of live concert performances.

A few days later, Rudge, who had been doing a little investigating himself, asked about a club that kept coming up in conversations called the El Mocambo.

Rudge took Skippy Snair into his confidence because of a well-established relationship. On July 17, 1972, the Rolling Stones were in Montreal to play a date at the Forum, a concert at which some maniac planted a bomb under one of the band's trucks parked on the street next to the venue. When the bomb went off, it blew a hole in the bottom of one of the trailers containing fifty-two speaker cabinets that were to be unloaded for the night's show. Fortunately, nobody was hurt, but the pressure popped all of the speakers, and it looked as if the show would have to be cancelled. They were all JBL fifteen-inch speakers—104 in all—and the only place it was possible to get that number of speakers was Los Angeles.

Skippy was one of the first people from the Donald K Donald organization on the scene, and he and Rudge put their heads together on how to save the show. When Donald Tarlton arrived, he and Skippy got on the phone to Los Angeles and found out they could get the speakers. The problem lay in transporting them to Montreal. All available cargo space on the planes arriving in Montreal in time for the show was filled.

Luckily they found an Air Canada flight that had a shipment of lobsters, traced the cargo's consignee in Montreal, bought the space, bumped the lobsters off the flight, and had the speakers put on the plane. The speakers made it in time, the show went on as planned, and Peter Rudge and the band were impressed. That established the DKD organization's relationship with Rudge and the Rolling Stones.

Although the El Mocambo looked as if it were the likeliest site for the projected Stones club concerts, Mick Jagger and Peter Rudge wanted to check things out in person. They also wanted a band to be a smokescreen for the concert. In other words, they wanted a band to be scheduled as the headliner, a band that could sell out the venue on its own, when in fact, it would be the Stones appearing.

As it happens, April Wine was looking for a site to record a live album. Skippy saw the opportunity and pounced: "How about having April Wine go into the club with you in Toronto?" Rudge agreed. The stage was now set for the Canadian rock event of the decade.

The Stones came to Toronto towards the end of February and set up headquarters on the upper floors of the Harbour Castle Hilton. As far as the public was concerned, April Wine was playing for a week starting February 28 at the El Mocambo and the Stones were in for a recording date at one of the local studios. It was even arranged with the local radio stations to hold two separate contests involving the Rolling Stones and April Wine.

CHUM-AM ran a contest that offered tickets to April Wine's recording session at the El Mocambo, and CHUM-FM had a contest in which twenty-five winners would get a chance to party with the Stones. No location for the party was announced, and little did the listeners know that approximately six hundred winners would eventually form the audience for the band's live recording session.

Needless to say, Richards' drug arrest put a real damper on the Stones' Toronto activities, and most of the members of the band stayed at the hotel just waiting for rehearsals and the two live gigs at the club.

On the day of April Wine's first show, the Stones were supposed to do a sound check at the club, but they couldn't make it and so we were left to our own devices.

The next day, Tuesday, the first day we and the Stones, who for the sake of secrecy were being billed as "the Cockroaches," were supposed to play together, there were still hassles and we played the night ourselves. It was nerve-racking, waiting to meet and work with the Stones up close and personal.

Finally, on Friday night, March 4, the Stones were ready to go. That afternoon we did a sound check after the Stones were finished theirs, so we got to meet them finally, and it was a great experience.

To say that it was intimidating opening for the Rolling Stones would be an understatement. But we played and sang well.

I was introduced to Margaret Trudeau the first night, just before the Stones' performance and not long after April Wine's set. She had what appeared to be two large bodyguards standing just behind the table where she was seated. She was friendly and seemed happily in awe of the whole event, which was certain to become history.

I had been chillin' with the band after our set when a man came out of nowhere, looking out of place in a suit and tie, found me backstage, and insisted that I come out—through the audience—and say hello to a VIP guest in attendance who wanted to meet me. "Sure," I said. It didn't seem like I had an option. He led me to a large wooden table that was really three or four tables pushed together. The suit made the introductions.

"Mrs. Trudeau, this is the lead singer for April Wine that you wanted to say hello to, Myles Goodwyn. Mr. Goodwyn, this is Mrs. Margaret Trudeau." I bet he was at the top of his class when he graduated finishing school. Mr. Goodwyn, indeed.

"Hello, Myles. I loved your set tonight. I'm an April Wine fan."

"Thank you, Mrs. Trudeau. I enjoyed the—"

"Call me Maggie, Myles! By the way, I love your voice." She was still smiling at me. I liked her. A lot.

She was seated with several unremarkable people, at least to my mind.

"Will Mr. Trudeau be coming tonight?" I asked innocently while smiling my best I-hope-you-like-me-in-person smile.

She looked at me with amusement in her lovely brown eyes and answered a simple, soft but firm, "No."

"Really?" I pushed on. "Tomorrow night perhaps?"

I was hopeful. I'd seen Pierre Trudeau speak on his famous campaign tour a decade earlier in the spring of 1968 in Brantford, Ontario, and I was a fan. The man was classy and brilliant.

Her reply was again a soft and now flirtatious "no." Now I was thinking, *Pierre, buddy, you've got your hands full*.

She took a sip of her bevy and then proceeded to light up a smoke. Then it was like a light switch was turned off. She was clearly trying to ignore me now by starting up a frivolous chinwag with a hanger-on at her table. I took stock.

"Right," I replied. Surely, I had something more important I should be doing.

"Well, Maggie, when you see him, remind him that he still owes me twenty bucks, okay?" I quipped. A guy dressed all in black came to the table and said that Ron Wood would like to speak with her privately. Backstage.

She immediately butted her fag and gamely followed the minion in black through the crowded room towards the private backstage area.

From the moment the Stones hit the stage at the El Mocambo, the whole event was unreal. The audience didn't sit down for the duration of the two-hour show.

The two shows went off without a hitch, with four songs from the two nights becoming the third side of the Stones' *Love You Live* double album, which was released in September 1977.

The experience of working with the Rolling Stones for a few

nights gave me a chance to get a peek into the complexities and the craziness of being so incredibly famous and being constantly observed and scrutinized by the press, the authorities, and fans alike. It's not everyone's cup of tea, that's certain. My respect for the guys only increased because of our chance meeting in 1977.

In a remote truck parked outside the club, producer extraordinaire Eddie Kramer was recording everything musical both nights for both bands. Ours would be released later that year and be called *April Wine Live at the El Mocambo*. Catchy title. No flies on us.

A few months after the club dates, I would be in New York City mixing this record with Eddie in Jimi Hendrix's Electric Lady Studios. When I arrived at the studio that day, there was a group of long-haired musician types checking in ahead of me. They looked like a band, for sure. I waited patiently for them to be finished, and then it would be my turn to sign in for my session. After they were done at the reception counter, they stood off to one side as I checked in.

"Hi!" I said to the receptionist. "My name is Myles Goodwyn. I'm with April Wine, and I have a mixing session with Eddie Kramer."

I had no sooner said this when I heard one of the long-hairs laughingly say that April Wine was a silly name for a band. I felt put off immediately. They quickly forgot all about me and walked off. Welcome to New York City! I turned back to the lovely young receptionist and asked her who they were.

She told me they were a new band called KISS.

I chuckled and thought to myself, "Now *that* is a silly name for a band!"

Because this gig with the Stones in Toronto came out of

nowhere, we weren't really prepared with any new material. Of course, we all wanted to have something new on the live recording, and so we needed new material. Fast.

I quickly wrote one song called "She's No Angel." I got the title from an old black-and-white Mickey Rooney movie. We recorded the song in the studio. We added the sound of a live audience and tried to make it sound like it was part of the evening or at least a live track. I don't think we fooled anybody for a second.

There wasn't enough time to write more original material, so I went looking for some good tunes to cover. We found the material we needed, rehearsed it, and headed for Toronto.

Live at the El Mocambo opens up with a couple of cover songs written by Bob Segarini. Bob is an American musician and writer who moved up to Montreal from California back in the early '70s. He had a band called the Wackers, and I liked some of the songs he wrote back in the day. The two songs of his that we covered, "Teenage Love" and "Juvenile Delinquent," hadn't really done anything much airplay-wise, so we thought these two songs would be good to cover. "Teenage Love" is about what you'd expect it to be, teenage lust. It has a great rock feel to it. "Juvenile Delinquent" has pretty much the same purpose as "Teenage Love." A classic theme repeated.

There was nothing else new on the album. That was it. The rest of the songs were just live versions of earlier studio tracks including "Tonite Is a Wonderful Time to Fall in Love," "Don't Push Me Around," "Oowatanite," "Drop Your Guns," "Slow Poke," "She's No Angel," and "You Could Have Been a Lady."

In the midst of all the madness of the El Mocambo dates, the Stones still took the time to write us a note: "To April Wine.

Thanks for helping us out this week and the best of luck tonight! With love, The Rolling Stones." Thank you!

Shortly after the El Mocambo gig, we were invited to open for them at their Rich Stadium date in Buffalo, New York, and played to 40,000 people.

If you had asked when I was a teenager who I'd like to share a stage with, I would have said the Beatles and the Rolling Stones. One out of two ain't bad!

17

A fter the last studio album, April Wine needed to refocus. *Forever for Now* had a lot of diversity—too much in my opinion. To be honest, as a solo record as it was originally intended to be, it was cool, but as an AW record, not so much as far as I was concerned. If we were to break out of Canada and find success internationally, we needed to make some changes.

I'd been thinking about adding another guitar player for a while. All the work that Gary and I did in the studio was great on our recordings, but on stage we were unable to cover all the guitar parts. A third guitar would pretty much take care of that problem. The guys in the band agreed.

Even more important, the material we were writing needed to be more specific and not as diversified. If we wanted to rock, we needed rock songs. I started writing with this in mind.

One of the first songs I wrote for the record was inspired by a vacation trip to Las Vegas. It was a song about a woman who loved to gamble. It was called "Roller." A great start.

"Get Ready for Love" and a rock ballad called "Rock and Roll Is a Vicious Game" followed. So far so good. It was time to find our new fifth band member.

Brian Greenway first saw April Wine in Quebec City in the early '70s. "I was in the band Mashmakhan at the time. It was an all-night, indoor, winter carnival–style festival with all kinds of bands, and there was a snowstorm outside. Nobody could really get in or out. It was at a CEGEP so it was like a gymnasium. The schedule was hours behind, and April Wine went on at five o'clock in the morning. Nobody had cigarettes but there were garbage bags full of dope, and you got so sick of smoking dope. Every now and then, this guy, who was probably a [stoned] dope dealer, got up on stage, held up hundred dollar bills, and lit them on fire. A number of bands at the time, including April Wine and Mashmakhan, went up to Rouyn-Noranda, which is about 640 kilometres north of Montreal, by bus as part of a visit arranged by Aquarius Records. I was in contact with Myles and the guys in the band at that point as well.

"I auditioned for the band in 1973. I had a meeting with Myles right after the Henmans had left. Myles lived in an apartment building in Westmount [Montreal] at that point and we had a meeting, but eventually Gary Moffet got the job. In hindsight, he was probably the better choice. I wasn't as good as Gary was then. Listen to the albums that he played on. He's very efficient, and it would have been a different April Wine had it been me instead of Gary at that point. It wasn't my time. I don't know the reason I didn't get in.

"Prior to April Wine, I was just working from gig to gig as a musician and not making much money. I had been in the Dudes, which formed in 1975. I only knew Myles on the road. We never hung out socially. He had a different set of people. He golfed a lot, and I was not in the same league and not in the same group of people and did not do the same things.

"When I finally joined April Wine in the summer of 1977, there were three guitars: me, Myles, and Gary. We called it 'Three Guitars, No Waiting.' We all had very different styles. The closest in style were probably me and Myles. Gary had a style all his own and was very meticulous. My first shows with the band were in the Maritimes and Place des Nations in Montreal in the summer of 1977 as we were just finishing off the recording of *First Glance*. (I actually named that album. When I first saw the picture, I said, 'Ah, first glance!') I was on trial for three months. I wasn't immediately accepted into the band. I remember them telling me, 'We'll go out on the summer tour and we'll see how it goes.' So, I had to wait until the fall before I was officially brought into the band.

"They had started recording the album *First Glance* before I joined. It was half done. That was at Tempo Studio, and with me as the third guitar player, we went back in and recorded some new stuff and then we moved it up to Le Studio in Morin-Heights, just north of Montreal in the Laurentians, to finish it. I actually had a song on the album titled 'Right Down to It,' which I used to do with the Dudes. I remember doing 'Roller' and 'Rock and Roll Is a Vicious Game,' because I played keyboards on that. Myles told me to go and learn a string part. I'm not that great a player. I just came up with something that worked. I think one of the reasons I got hired by the band was that I could sing and write, play a little keyboards along with harmonica and guitar. Jim Zeller played the harp on 'Rock and Roll Is a Vicious Game' and then I copied it live. I'm a chameleon when I play. I'm a good copier of anything."

When we had enough songs to go into the studio, we went back to the familiar Tempo Studio in Montreal with engineers

Ian Terry and Billy Szawlowski. Another important change at this time was moving the project from Tempo to a studio in the Laurentians, north of Montreal, called Le Studio, which was gaining an international reputation as a major recording facility. But first the recording started at Tempo.

The first track on *First Glance* is called "Hot on the Wheels of Love," a song I wrote about a guy stealing a car one rainy night to get to his girlfriend. I know a lot more about stealing cars than I should, folks, but the good side of my bad behaviour, as it turns out, was the inspiration for this tune. The bass part is so damn cool and important to the feel of the song that Steve Lang and I shared the writing credit on this one. With most rock songs I write, the song starts with a guitar riff, or lick. This composition was no different. Jerry did a great job on the drums, and the tune really rocks.

The slide guitar solo is played by Brian. He's also the voice of the highway patrol officer calling in an APB (all-points bulletin).

I see him sheriff, mercy sakes he's coming up fast
I only have half a mile left to catch that boy
He's heading for the border . . .
Damn, he's gone!

"Get Ready for Love" has a sexy rock and roll attitude to it, and the lyrics are suggestive, of course.

Throw your coat on the floor baby, come on in
It's good to see you again, now how ya'll been?

The question I'm always asked about this song is, "What's that barking sound on the song?" It's the sound of two quick, short scrapes with a guitar pick on the low E string on the guitar. It sounds like a dog barking. It's a catchy hook at the beginning of the song and each verse. Brian and I share the soloing duties, me first with a *wah-wah* guitar solo, then a slide solo by Brian.

The first of the two ballads on the record is "Rock and Roll Is a Vicious Game." When I wrote this, I was thinking of all the musicians who didn't realize their dream of becoming a rock star, or the musicians who wanted to make an honest living in the music business but never made it, which is the case for the majority of those who try. It can be a tough, heartbreaking, shitty business.

> *He rocked his way through yesterday, lord he thought he*
>   *had a chance*
> *He played guitar and wrote some songs of love and*
>   *romance*
> *He did his share of travelling, like a dog without a home*
> *A fugitive who would rather give*
> *A star that never shone*
> *Isn't it a pity*
> *Isn't it a shame*
> *No one ever warned the boy, rock and roll is a vicious game*

As I was working the lyrics, I thought of those who did succeed but sadly, tragically, self-destructed: Elvis, Jimi, and Janis, to name a few.

The featured instrument on the tune is the harmonica, played by Montreal psychobilly blues harmonica player and friend Jim Zeller. I played the Fender Rhodes piano track.

"Right Down to It" is a Brian Greenway song. This is the first time Brian sang lead on the record, and he did a great job. This is the only song I did not write on *First Glance*.

"Roller" finishes off side one. As I mentioned, I wrote it after my first trip to Las Vegas. This song started off being a busy tune with lots of chord changes, but over time, it got simpler and more dynamic as we learned the song. It is one of the few original songs that we played live a few times before we recorded it. That really helped the arrangement ideas. The structured guitar parts are definitely an element that make the song unique. Gary, Brian, and I jammed the parts until we had something exciting and interesting. With the high "bye bye byes" at the end, it makes for a killer last song of the night live. (These days I refuse to perform an unrecorded original song in public. There are too many people out there illegally taping the concerts and recording videos. It's simply not safe anymore. And that sucks big time.)

Side two of *First Glance* opens with "Comin' Right Down on Top of Me." I wrote this tune on the piano.

Is the sky really falling, or does it just seem that way?
Where's my reasons for living, have they all slipped away?
It's coming right down on top of me
It's getting so I can hardly breath

I know I'm not the only person to feel like this at one time or another.

The ending on this song—the "false ending"—happened because we were cutting it live in the studio at Tempo and we were distracted when the lads in Nazareth dropped by to say hello. I looked up from the piano in anticipation of the ending and saw them making faces from the control room. We fucked up the arranged ending and improvised the one that's on the album. Boys will be boys.

"I'm Alive" is track two, and it's a simple upbeat rock song.

"Let Yourself Go" is next. I wrote it and asked Brian to try singing it. I liked the way he sang it. We doubled the lead vocal with slide guitar, and it sounds cool.

The final song on *First Glance* is "Silver Dollar," an interesting composition. Okay, it's not a rock song, so sue me! When writing this piece, I was thinking of Sergio Leone and the spaghetti westerns he made in the '60s and the haunting music he used in his soundtracks. The theme from *The Good, the Bad and the Ugly* is one of my favourites. My song "Silver Dollar" is a kind of theme for the story of a man who is about to die. His killer is going to end his life, take his horse and his money. Even his "brown-eyed daughter."

> *You won't need that drink of water, no more*
> *And you won't need that fine young stallion, not any more*
> *You won't see your brown-eyed daughter, not any more*
> *And you won't need that silver dollar, no more, not any more*

The harmonized guitar theme that reoccurs is very reminiscent of a Sergio Leone movie with its minor-key western sound. Writing the guitar lines in the theme, I was imagining the guitar notes as trumpet notes. I played the guitar solo at the end.

The title of the album was apropos as it was America's first real look—or first glance, if you will—at April Wine.

18

The 1970s was a strange, interesting (and dangerous) decade. The U.S. pulled out of Vietnam, Margaret Thatcher became England's prime minister, and here in Canada, the '70s gave birth to Quebec nationalist and Marxist militant group the FLQ and Bill 101. Richard Nixon resigned as president of the United States in 1974. There was an oil crisis for the first time in North America, and cars were lined up at the pumps. In the U.S., for a time, gas station customers with a licence plate ending in an odd number were only allowed to buy gasoline on odd-numbered days, while even-numbered plate-holders could only purchase gasoline on even-numbered days.

Muscle cars fell from favour during the early '70s. I read that it was believed the 1976 Cadillac Eldorado would be the last American-built convertible, ending the open-body style once so popular in the auto industry.

Technology introduced several exciting discoveries during this decade. There was the invention of fibre optics, which transformed the communications industry. The Apple Computer Company was officially founded in a garage in Los Altos in 1977.

Microwave ovens and VCRs became commercially available. The Sony Walkman arrived in 1978.

The '70s introduced the world to disco "music." I DO NOT LIKE DISCO. (And that's stating it nicely.) There was just so much not to like about it. For example, lyrics were usually mindless, about shaking your booty.

How about tunes and groups like "YMCA" by the Village People? Or "Super Freak" by Ricky James? Disco was blatantly and shamelessly formulated, like the "pea-soup-pea-soup" of the high hat and the 4-4 *thump thump, thump thump* of the "programmed" bass drum. Most of that genre used one beat and one tempo only. It was repetitive and boring. Every kind of tune could be turned disco, and was. Christmas songs, country songs, rock songs, gospel—nothing was sacred.

But it did save lives, the Bee Gees in particular. Ha ha ha . . .

Thankfully, there was great popular music in the '70s, too. Yes, Pink Floyd, Queen, AC/DC, the Clash, Van Halen, and many more.

But as a friend of mine once said, "Life's about adding and subtracting," and we lost some important artists that decade. Elvis, Janis, and Jim Morrison, to name a few.

Great movies were being made, classics such as *The Godfather, One Flew Over the Cuckoo's Nest, Star Wars*, and *Jaws*. Fashion in the '70s brought us bell-bottoms and platform shoes—lava lamps and mirror balls became hip again.

A white powder called cocaine hit big time. It messed up a lot of people during the '70s. Good, smart people lost their businesses, their families, and even their lives. It was a phenomenon that boggles the mind in retrospect. And it was not a cheap way to kill oneself. Cocaine was not a poor man's drug: "It's God's way of saying you make too much money," quipped the late comedian Robin Williams, who had been a reformed addict.

Musicians, of course, used cocaine freely. Who else? Everybody, that's who. David Bowie was well known as a cocaine user during the '70s but later gave it up and said he wished he had never gotten into it because drugs took over his life.

I used cocaine. I used it more than most, believe me. I seriously overdosed once and was carried out of my home on a stretcher, put in an ambulance, and rushed to a hospital. I took that as a wake-up call and quit cold turkey.

Alcohol and drugs started affecting the fate of the band. So far it hadn't been a real problem within the band, but that time was not far off.

Harder . . . Faster was recorded at Le Studio with engineers Nick Blagona and Paul Northfield. This would be our first complete recording project at Le Studio, *First Glance* having been started at Tempo and then finished here. This time we'd be taking full advantage of all the facility had to offer.

Andre Perry and his partner, Yael Brandeis, had built an amazing environment for artists to be creative. Besides the state-of-the-art recording studio, there was a lovely band house and a large private lake. The first band house was burned down accidently by Roy Thomas Baker and Ian Hunter, according to Nick Blagona. We stayed in the new house during our visits to Le Studio, which was two storeys with a large eat-in kitchen and oversized living room with a fireplace. A grand piano and a seriously nice hi-fi system were at our disposal for our listening pleasure. There were bedrooms on the main floor as well as on the second. Each bedroom had its own unique décor. Mine was nice and comfortable and traditional in style. The whole shebang was situated on acres of private property, so it was peaceful and conducive for work or relaxation.

All this came to an end in the late '80s. Andre and Yael sold Le Studio and moved from Morin-Heights, Quebec, to Nassau in the Bahamas. In fact they were moving in as I was leaving the Bahamas in 1989.

We rehearsed the new material for *Harder . . . Faster* until we were comfortable and familiar with the tunes and the arrangements were solid. I wrote six of the eight songs, and one I co-wrote with Gary. Brian wrote a song, and we did a cover version of a King Crimson tune.

Harder . . . Faster starts off with "I Like to Rock." Gee, Myles, what's that song about?

Well, folks, I like to rock, and besides, it was written with a specific idea in mind. I felt we could use a new song to start a live concert set. In the same way "Roller" with the "bye bye byes" at the end of the tune worked as a last song of the night, having a rocker that kicked off the show would be terrific.

The intro with the peddled low E string on the guitars creates a nice tension, perfect for setting up a dramatic entrance for the band and the start of the night.

Brian Greenway recalls that during the recording of *Harder . . . Faster*, a BBC TV crew, with director Derek Burbidge from *The Old Grey Whistle Test*, came over and shot a video, the famous one for "I Like to Rock." It was shot at Le Studio. "We were working on the song at the time," says Brian, "and one of the solos that was on the video is actually not on the record. I was playing live."

Gary, Brian, and I jammed the main guitar riff on the outro. "Day Tripper" and "Satisfaction" just came out of the jamming at rehearsals. It made for a neat fade-out on the record.

The video for "I Like to Rock," which was pre-MTV, was fun to make. It's cool now to watch the video and remember the studio in its prime. There are some scenes of us playing table hockey that bring back memories of the rivalries that kept us entertained many an hour. My team was called the Lobsters. I took it seriously. I cut the fingers and thumbs off of rubber wash gloves for better grip on the player control knobs. I spent a lot of downtime practising puck passing technics and defence moves. Maybe you have to be Canadian to appreciate the game. The competitions got intense at times, but it was all in good fun.

"Say Hello" is a song I wrote because of a drum beat I developed playing the drums at some point. I was a drummer briefly as a kid, and the rhythms and tempo of a new piece of music are crucial in composing something worthwhile. This particular beat I'd been playing for years before I wrote a tune to use it in. The song starts with the beat, and that drum beat has become a hook for the song in the same way a guitar riff in the intro of a song is a hook.

It's one of those tunes that has the same chords repeating, while the melody of the vocals change. "Enough Is Enough" is like that. It's a simple idea that can really work well.

Nick Blagona created a real interesting "bubbly" guitar rhythm sound for the song. He had me play the chord progression, note by note, string by string. In other words, the notes that would normally be played as a chord became instead a dancing series of individual notes. He added some kind of chorus and delay to that, and to get the bubbly sound all the notes were "triggered" to a high hat playing a sixteenth pattern. Nick also did some wonderful editing on the original bass part that Steve played. He created "holes" in the bass pattern that are really fantastic. People who try to play that part like the record are in for a treat.

"Tonite" is the third song on the album, an acoustic/electric guitar–inspired track that changes tempo completely in the middle of the tune, rocks out, and then drops back to the slower, kind of spaced-out last verse, chorus, and ending. The lyrics are about a guy who finds the courage to face uncertainty. Once he decides to face his self-doubts and insecurities and live his life on his terms, he is saved.

> *Anxious thoughts, filter through the haze*
> *His mind's confused and he just can't find his way, yeah*
> *He knows he just can't fake it, how will he ever make it*
> *His life before him to unfold*
>
> *Tonite's the night, tonite's the night*
> *Tonite's the night he'll go out and find a way*

"Ladies Man" is one of those upbeat rockers that has egotistical lyrics about sexual prowess and nothing more. It's fun to play live, though.

Track five is "Before the Dawn," the second song that Brian wrote for an AW album. He also sings the song and plays lead guitar. It's a great tune with a clever arrangement and has always been a popular stage number.

Brian Greenway remembers that prior to *Harder . . . Faster*, April Wine had done a lot of travelling. "It was a fun album because, once again, I had a song on an April Wine album. It was titled 'Before the Dawn.' We were also doing a cover of the King Crimson song '21st Century Schizoid Man.' We were doing a lot of rehearsing because we found that rehearsing songs and then taking them out on the road before we recorded them really worked in the studio, and it was easy and fast."

Again, taking a new, unpublished song on the road these days is no longer a viable option because of the portable hand-held recording devices that everyone carries with them at all times these days. A shame, really . . . oh, well.

"Babes in Arms" is a simple pop tune with handclaps and power chords. Group handclaps are difficult to make work in the studio. It's challenging, even for people with great timing, to clap perfectly in sync. Today we use taped handclaps, which has solved the problem but has also ended the fun of being in a group of people standing around a single live mike trying not to flam but instead making each clap crisp and in sync with each other. It's not easy, trust me. It's also a challenge not to get giddy and laugh at times.

I find that doubling a vocal in unison is the most difficult of voice overdubs. To make two or more vocals work in singing the same part takes a lot of practice.

When I double-track my own voice, I have an unusual approach, so I've been told. Doubling a vocal track means singing the same vocal part again exactly the same way, repeating every note and nuance in pitch and in sync. Most singers like to hear the original vocal while they sing along. I prefer to listen to what I did on the original take and then repeat it without hearing what I'm trying to repeat. I find it less constricting somehow. Multi-layered vocal harmonies have a great, full sound. Think Queen and "Bohemian Rhapsody."

"Better Do It Well" is a collaboration with Gary Moffet and another straight-ahead rock song. "21st Century Schizoid Man" is a song I waited ten years to record. King Crimson's debut album, *In the Court of the Crimson King*, captivated my imagination the first time I heard it back in 1969. I've played it too many times to remember. It was one of only a couple records I brought with me from Halifax when AW left for Montreal in 1970. Finally AW worked out the arrangement for three guitars, bass, and drums, and it was well worth it. Obviously, the fast instrumental that kicks in halfway through the song is where the fun really begins. Figuring out the notes, the phrasing, and the timing took a while. It's not easy to play, but it came together and we had a ball with it. The record company didn't appreciate it as much as we did, and they placed it last on the album. I asked Brian to sing the song because it didn't fit the sound of my voice, and Brian did an admiral job indeed.

Jerry was very helpful in figuring out the parts from the original version. The training he got from back in the days when he sang in a church choir helped him hear the proper notes, and it was a great help to us at-times-confused guitar stranglers. Engineer Nick Blagona deserves much credit in helping to create the track with his expertise in editing and overall production.

"We were very much a band as a unit—the five of us—and that was never achieved again," Brian Greenway related in an interview. "It was multi-platinum so it did very well. It was the second album, as five guys, after *First Glance*, which had a lot of interest shown in it by the U.S. and the rest of the world. We were a very good support band. We did the Nazareth tour and Rush and Foreigner and Styx for months at a time. We were climbing the charts. We were the flavour of the month. Everything was new. We were doing what we had tried to achieve, so yeah, it was fun. Everybody was sort of together on this. There was no friction because everyone was having fun. We were all doing the same things."

Here's how we got the title for *Harder . . . Faster*.

There was a lounge at Le Studio where you could relax when not actually recording, with a kitchen area with a great cappuccino machine. There were chairs and a large sofa, tables, and so forth. And there was a TV and VCR player. Andre had a large selection of movies available to his clients to watch and enjoy when time permitted. I was always too busy singing or playing and co-producing with Nick to spend time watching videos.

There was a double-paned window in the thick, sound-proofed door that separated the control room from the lounge. From time to time, I would look through that window while working to see what was going on in the other room.

One day the boys were watching a porno film called *Behind the Green Door* starring Marilyn Chambers. When I opened the door to say something to the guys, I heard Miss Chambers yelling, "Harder! Faster!" I laughed and said, "Fellas, I believe we have a title for the new record."

If you listen very, very closely to the big flourish at the end of "21st Century Schizoid Man" (headphones will help), you'll hear Miss Chambers calling out for our album.

19

April Wine was travelling outside of Canada more often as time went on. It was a lot easier back then to fly gear and a good deal less expensive. After 9/11, all the rules for international and domestic travel changed forever, as we all know. But during the years when we started touring outside our homeland, we experienced the freedom to come and go as we wished. I've flown on the Concorde twice. I flew on the large-bodied 747 when there was a first-class lounge on the upper deck with an electric piano for first-class passengers to play if they wished. Smoking cigarettes, and even cigars, was permitted. There were ashtrays in the toilets and in the arm rests of the seats. The seats in first class were real leather, over-sized, and extremely comfortable, far more comfortable than any first-class seat of today. It was also possible to visit the cockpit and chat with the pilots if you wished.

For a while, April Wine leased a brown Lear that we were told was from the fleet of golf legend Arnold Palmer.

In my personal life, I was vacationing more and more, with at least one trip a year. My first real vacation was to Cuba in 1977 after the success of the *Stand Back* album.

My longtime girlfriend Phyllis and I travelled to southern destinations during the winter months, typical snowbirds escaping the cold Canadian winters. Our first trip to Hawaii was for two weeks. We had no reservations after the first week so we travelled footloose and fancy free, as they say, and it was quite the adventure. We stayed at the best places and a few times in crappy joints with the guest phone being a phone booth on the street corner. We even spent a night or two sleeping in the rental car. (If you do this kind of travel, folks, it helps if you're young.) Most of our experiences were good, but there were a few snags, like getting ripped off in Honolulu. I gave a guy some cash to buy some pot and he disappeared in the front of a building and out the back with the money, never to be seen again. I know, I deserved it.

Las Vegas was a great destination back then. Not so much today, although I still like to visit from time to time. In 1975, Phyllis and I went to Vegas for the first time and I ended up writing the song "Roller," so that trip was well worth the cost. The City of Sin was so cool back then. All the great hotels—the Sands, the Desert Inn, the Dunes, the Riviera, and others—are gone now, and the city has gone from being an exciting adult-only destination to a family resort.

My first stay was at the now-demolished Thunderbird Hotel and Casino, with its pastel colours and arched doorways. It had an art deco styling and was my first choice of a place to stay when in town, until it was no more.

I used to play blackjack when I gambled. I loved the game, and I learned the rules and studied strategies from books I bought. I became a decent player and usually did well, as long as I knew when to walk away. My gambling allowance was US$5,000 per trip. I never lost it all, although I did leave a lot of it at the tables a few times, but as a rule I made a few grand at the end of a trip and was happy. It was hours of fun and entertainment, and what the hell, it was Las Vegas and gambling's the name of the game.

Speaking of entertainment, the best part of Vegas was, and still is, the live shows. I may have made and lost money over the years, but I still have great memories of seeing some wonderful Vegas shows. I saw Bob Newhart and he was great, with his dry sense of humour and laid-back delivery. Gladys Knight and the Pips were awesome. I saw Wayne Newton's last performance at the Aladdin and had front-row centre seats for Frank Sinatra. These days, I still take in a show or two when in Vegas. The Cirque du Soleil has been a good ticket in recent years.

I've spotted a few celebrities, too. I once watched movie star Tony Curtis pull up in front of Caesar's Palace in a grey Mercedes SL convertible. He parked the car and dashed up the stairs of the casino. He was wearing a rumpled suit, sans tie, and looked like he was up on an all-nighter. He returned to the car a few minutes later in a hurry and sped off. Ann-Margret was performing at the hotel at the time, and I always figured that he ran in to leave a message at the desk for her and then fucked off. Who knows?

One time, Telly Savalas, who was best known for his TV role as Kojak and for movies such as *The Dirty Dozen*, *Kelly's Heroes*, and *Birdman of Alcatraz*, in which he played opposite Burt Lancaster and was nominated for an Academy Award for best supporting actor, was involved in an exciting game of craps that Phyllis was the star of. Telly was at a craps table when Phyllis was rolling the dice, and folks, she was on a *roll*. Her winning streak went on and on. People were gathering around the table cheering her on, including Savalas.

Finally, she told the dealer she had to stop because she needed to go to the bathroom. No one wanted her to stop playing, as they were all winning money, so the dealer held play while she relieved herself. Everyone waited patiently for her return to the table, including Telly Savalas.

After her luck ran out, Telly came up to Phyllis carrying his winnings, thanked her kindly, and gave her a quick kiss on the hand. That was cool, and Phyllis got a kick out of it.

Phyllis and I had met in Montreal in 1970. We had been together nine years, and she wanted to get married. I did not. Why ruin a good thing, right? Finally she said to me, the next time we're in Vegas, we're going to get married or else. Fine.

Our next trip to Vegas was when AW was performing at the Aladdin Theater. Phyllis and I got married at the famous Candlelight Wedding Chapel on the strip. Michael Caine, Bette Midler, Whoopi Goldberg, and Barry White are just a few of the people who have also been hitched there. The ceremony took about fifteen minutes, in and out. Our manager, Terry Flood, and Gary Moffet were witnesses. The nine years as boyfriend/girlfriend were over.

After *Harder . . . Faster* and months of touring, it was time to record another album. It was the same old routine. The record company wanted a new record, as soon as possible.

So it was writing time again. I had a name in mind for the new album. It was taken from the common phrase "the nature of the beast."

For this project, I wanted to record with a new co-producer. I enjoyed working with Nick Blagona, but I wanted a change. I started looking.

I was a big fan of Queen and I had several of their albums,

so I started reading the liner notes and realized the same name appeared a few times, although he was just an assistant. Over those few albums, Mike Stone went from a tea boy—which is what they call an errand boy over there in England—to co-producing and engineering Queen albums. I wanted to see if he wanted to do an album together, so I got a hold of him. He was in the hospital at the time. He had a problem with one of his vertebrae and they had fused it together, so he was having a hard time. He was bedridden for quite a while, and then he had to walk with a cane and was very stiff. He was going through rehab when I reached him to see if he was interested in coming over to Montreal to talk about doing a record together.

I sent him *Harder . . . Faster* and *First Glance*. He became familiar with the sound and the growth and the success we had at that point. He got back to me and said, yes, he was interested in my offer, so he came over to see me in Hudson, Quebec, where I was living at the time. He stayed at my house and we listened to a lot of music together over a period of a few days. It was soon apparent that we liked each other and we were comfortable together. We enjoyed the same kinds of music, and we were respectful of each other's accomplishments. We drank Scotch and discussed the next AW record. I played him songs I had written for the record, concentrating on whether or not he liked what he heard, and if he'd like to co-produce it with me. He said yes, we shook hands, and that was that.

Mike suggested we go to England and work at the Manor Studio, a nineteenth-century stone mansion in the village of Shipton-on-Cherwell just north of the city of Oxford that Richard Branson, head of the Virgin Group of companies, which included Virgin Records, had converted into the U.K.'s first ever residential recording studio. Mike Oldfield had recorded his classic *Tubular Bells* album there in the early '70s. Mike Stone convinced me to record at the Manor. The record company agreed to the budget Mike and I had put together, and AW was off to England.

There was a lawn party going on the night we arrived at the studio. The country estate is situated on many acres of pasture-like greenery, with some trees about and a large sprawling lawn with a long driveway cutting through it from the highway to the Manor entrance. A large tent was set up near the main house. The sides of the tent were open and surrounded by lots of people milling about carrying food and drink, while a band played on a stage inside the tent. Branson was having a Virgin Records company party, and the Stray Cats with Brian Setzer were performing.

We checked into the main house, which was a grand stone manor with something like ten bedrooms, many bathrooms, and too many fireplaces. There was a staff of domestics who arrived in the morning and disappeared at the end of each day. There was a cooking staff to prepare meals for us long-haired musoids.

After being shown around the place and assigned our individual rooms, we joined the party outside. We met Mr. Branson, indulged in food and drink, and then trundled off to bed, each of us knackered from the five-hour time difference. Sleep was a welcomed friend. *In the morning we'll be making history*, I thought, before I slipped into a deep sleep. "Making history" is a term I like and use in the studio. As in, "Okay, guys, tape's rolling, let's make history!"

Days at the Manor started with a hearty English breakfast, usually fried eggs, bacon, sausages, pan-fried potatoes with onions, tomatoes, beans, and toast. It was a lot of food before work, but that was what we ate many mornings before waddling into the recording studio adjacent to the main house.

The studio was filled with great equipment and had a nice live room. It was a comfortable environment to work in.

The Nature of the Beast contains eleven songs, and I wrote all but one of them, which I co-wrote with Lorence Hud. All the songs on this album are true rock songs. Yes, we wanted to rock out—and we did.

The Beast starts off with "All Over Town." The main guitar riff was inspired by the guitar riff in the Knack's one hit, "My Sharona." We met the Knack in England in 1979 when the song was a hit and again in L.A. when we were performing there. We were both with Capitol Records at the time.

"Telling Me Lies" is another rocker with a sustainable guitar riff at its core. "Sign of the Gypsy Queen" is the third song on *The Beast,* and it was an FM radio hit for the band. The original song was written and recorded by fellow Canadian Lorence Hud. It was a medium-sized hit for Hud in Canada in 1972 but relatively unknown outside the country. I liked the song, and so I contacted Hud and told him I wanted AW to do a version, but it needed another verse, and I had written one that worked perfectly. He agreed about the additional lyrics working well, so that was that.

AW's arrangement of the song was worked out in jamming in pre-production. Our version has a lot of dynamics that served the tune well. Brian played the guitar solo.

Brian has explained that the Lorence Hud song, "Sign of the Gypsy Queen," had a hook and chord structure that is haunting and was good for the times . . . E minor, D, A minor, C.

"Every generation has a chord structure that they work off of. Nowadays, it's reversed from that. When I found out we were doing the song I said, 'I want that solo!' I was going to get that solo. I could hear it. I knew I could do justice to it. Myles said, sure, give it a try."

It was cool that Brian wanted the solo and I said sure. After spending a long time trying to play a great solo, what he was coming up with wasn't that great, and I told him so. "I'm going for lunch, and when I get back from lunch, if you haven't got something great, then Gary or I will take a shot at it." I knew I had set a fire under Brian's ass right then and there. I did that to motivate him, of course, and Mike knew exactly what I was up to. So I left Brian and Mike to it and went for a bite to eat.

When I got back a few hours later I was in a good mood, and I stuck some silly-looking fake plastic grapes in the lapel of my jacket to bring some levity to the moment and walked into the control room. "So, guys, let's hear it." I listened to the playback and was delighted to hear an awesome solo. Brian nailed it. I rattled him a bit to get him going, and the result was, as they say, history.

"Wanna Rock" was barely two minutes long and it served its purpose. These days we sometimes perform the tune on stage, but instead of me playing guitar, I play the song on piano. It works great.

"Caught in the Crossfire" is a sci-fi song about "new age war," and the sound of laser fire was added to the track for effect. Why not?

Track seven is "Future Tense." I wrote this after reading Alvin Toffler's book *Future Shock*. Toffler's point is that the tactics of the past will not be successful in the future. If future shock is to be avoided, society must control the accelerating thrust and must make plans for the future and the changes it will bring.

"Big City Girls" was written about an experience AW had at a hotel in Saskatoon, Saskatchewan. Some girls were invited back to the hotel after a gig. We partied until things got weird when we realized these girls were hookers. We wanted no part of that, and we asked them to leave, which they did but not before they literally carved "FUCK YOU" with a knife on the hotel room door. Outside, they destroyed the roof of a convertible parked in front of the hotel. It was a real nice car, and they might have thought it belonged to us. Crazy.

"Just Between You and Me" is the album's only ballad. This song had a guitar solo (I don't remember who recorded it), but when it came time to mix the tune, I didn't like the solo that much. I decided to replace it and then finish the mix. The problem was, all of AW's gear was back in Montreal along with the other fellas in the band. I had no guitar or amp to record with. So without a guitar or amp, and the need to replace the solo, I found a decent guitar that belonged to the studio and went direct into the recording console and through a distortion box called a RAT. The sound that Mike dialed up worked beautifully, and we rolled tape and made history.

A taxi driver Mike and I called Oh Henry ran drugs for Mike and me from London to the studio. He was *the* guy that delivered drugs to the Manor. Mike and I got to know him quite well. I'm not sure Jerry did. He preferred the kind of stimulant that you smoke. Gary, Brian, and Steve were not big users, while Mike and I were. Mike and I also drank a fair share at the time.

There was cocaine on the tour as well, and Mike and I had these sayings like "No blow, no show" and "No zap, no rap." We were half-serious. Mike and I used blow on and off stage for a few years. Drug abuse started way before the *Beast* project. We were using during the recording of *Harder . . . Faster*.

I remember once we were arriving at an airport, and Mike and I had a lot of coke on us and needed to get rid of it. As we approached the airport, we snorted as much as we could without throwing up. It was crazy.

There was always some dope around the studio. When the supply was low, or God forbid Mike and I ran out before Oh Henry showed up with a new supply, we would become desperate. We'd be looking between the console faders for rocks of coke that might have been carelessly handled and dropped on the console, or perhaps some that had ended up on the floor, which was covered in a wall-to-wall carpet. Yes, we were stupid to be using this insidious drug, but everybody was using it in the late '70s, remember. Mike and I were no different. I don't like to think about these things, so let's move on, shall we?

Mike and I stayed in England to finish recording the album and mix it. Besides using the Manor Studio for *The Beast*, we did a few overdubs at a classic recording studio that was part of Mike's old stomping grounds, Trident Studios, in the Soho district of London. Mike had recorded there with Queen a lot, and it was a real thrill to be inside the hallowed walls of a legendary facility. I sat at the very piano the Beatles used for some of the recordings on the *White Album*. The same piano that Elton John recorded "Candle in the Wind" on. The piano where Mike recorded Freddie Mercury playing "Bohemian Rhapsody." Here I was playing that very same piano. It was surreal. The list of artists and groups that recorded at Trident was a who's who of the best coming out of England between 1968 and 1981. To be there with Mike was an honour and a privilege. Mike and I finished the album together and went our separate ways.

Nature of the Beast was mastered in New York by the great George Marino at Sterling Sound. On my way from Sterling to LaGuardia airport, Geddy Lee and I shared a cab. He had been at Sterling mastering Rush's *Moving Pictures* album.

20

With another album under our belts, it was time to tour. Once again we embarked on a long tour in support of the album in the U.K. and the States. We recorded *Live in London* at the Hammersmith Odeon during that tour. It was probably the height of the band's career.

The *Live in London* recording was an interesting experience. First of all, just being in London was fantastic. Anyone who's been knows what I mean. Piccadilly Circus, Trafalgar Square, Soho, Big Ben, the Tower of London—we were tourists loving it all. The fact that we recorded a live, sold-out show at the Hammersmith Odeon was icing on the cake.

There are fifteen songs on the regular CD and thirteen on the laser disc. The video of the band's performance and the footage out and about in London were filmed by Derek Burbidge. It was released in 1981, the same year as the *Nature of the Beast* album.

The rest of the time we toured Canada and the U.S. We had hot and cold spots in the States. Some areas never took to the band. New York was one. One time we opened there for blues man John Mayall. We came on stage with the energy of the Tasmanian Devil himself: long haired, wearing satin pants and platform shoes, ready to conquer the night with some hard-ass rock. It was a ridiculous billing and they hated us. Who could blame them?

Another time, we opened for Sha Na Na, which was a group that performed a song and dance repertoire of classic '50s-style rock and roll. We did our thing as a warm-up band the first night. Again the pairing was ridiculous, and we were fired after one performance.

All of a sudden we had a hit with "Just Between You and Me" in the U.S. and Canada, and we were touring like crazy and playing to some of the biggest crowds of our career. We had done some major dates the year previous including the Texxas Jam at the Cotton Bowl in Dallas in the summer on a bill with the Eagles, Cheap Trick, Foreigner, Sammy Hagar, and, believe it or not, Christopher Cross, who got booed off the stage, and we were on the bill with Rainbow, Judas Priest, and Scorpions later that summer as part of the first Monsters of Rock music festival in Castle Donington, England.

This 1981 excursion was the largest in our history. We were touring in the U.S. and Europe as well as Canada. When we crossed the Atlantic, we played England, Germany, Sweden, and a number of other places we had never been before. We were on a TV show in Rome, we performed a few shows in the Netherlands (we got to meet Xaviera Hollander, a.k.a. the Happy Hooker, in Amsterdam), and of course we toured around England. Back on this side of the pond, we played more extensively in the United States with bigger shows, like the California Jam and those kinds of major events. These dates were so interesting and intriguing that the memories from those times are almost dream-like now.

The video for "Just Between You and Me," which was taken from the subsequent *Live in London* video, recorded at the Hammersmith Odeon in London, England, on January 27, 1981, was actually the fourteenth video played on the first day that MTV went on the air on August 1, 1981, which meant we were the first Canadian artists to be seen on the network.

What's even more remarkable, in retrospect, is that on that first day the video was played five times. Only the Who ("You Better You Bet") and Phil Collins ("In the Air Tonight") shared that honour. We also had two plays of "Sign of the Gypsy Queen," also from our *Live in London* video, which was officially the longest song at 6:26 played on MTV's first day.

The constant touring meant there was a lot longer time between albums. Finally, we were able to get off the road, and I had the time to write some more songs for our tenth studio album, *Power Play*. Mike Stone was engineering, and he and I were sharing the production duties back at Le Studio in Morin-Heights, Quebec. We certainly never took a hiatus to go fishing or lie on a beach somewhere—we were working all of the time. When I wasn't touring, I was busy writing the next record.

There was a lot of pressure at the time because *First Glance* did so well, as did *Harder . . . Faster* and *The Nature of the Beast*. *Power Play* didn't do as well, and some people look back and say that was difficult for the group and for the record company because suddenly we were selling fewer records—which is not the end of the world, by the way. When you think about it, even bands like the Rolling Stones, arguably the best rock 'n' roll band in the world, have had albums that didn't sell as well as the previous one. Elton John went through it. This was our little bit of a letdown. It was still a decent album, and I'm proud of it.

"Anything You Want, You Got It" is another example of me writing for a purpose, saying, "Okay, we've been opening the concerts with 'I Like to Rock' for a while, and then we opened up with 'The Band Has Just Begun' for a few tours. We need a new opening song—let's get something fresh." So I wrote this song that now everybody knows. We've opened with it many times, and it's a cool rock 'n' roll song. It served its purpose well.

The next song is another example of a phrase that everybody uses, "Enough Is Enough." We shot a video for it, which was played a lot on MTV in America. As a matter of fact, it was one of the first videos played by MTV in their inaugural year of broadcasting. British video director Derek Burbidge, the same guy who filmed *Live in London*, shot it, and it was perfect for that song.

"Enough Is Enough" is one of those songs like "Say Hello" in two respects. One, "Say Hello" is a common phrase, and second, it uses the same chord progression over and over. Essentially, I just changed the timing of the melody around so it kind of sounds like the chords are changing all the time, but it's really the same basic chord structure.

It's nice to take a phrase that's really common and find a nice melody and a great beat and then take something as simple as three or four chords and make it interesting. The same chords are on the bridge, the same chorus, solos, and verses, and yet it all sounds different. It can be a bit of a challenge for a songwriter, but these two songs worked very well.

Somebody brought our attention to a song called "If You See Kay," written by David Freeland. I liked it and the record company liked it, though not everybody in the band was partial to it. Steve Lang, for one, didn't care for it. He thought it was cheap and gimmicky, you know, "'If You See Kay' . . . F-U-C-K. That's not very tasteful!" He was right, I guess, but I replied, "You know, it's a good tune, and it's kind of cute and kind of clever, too. Let's see what we can do with it!" So I convinced them to do it. It turned out great. It's a fun song and it is what it is. We made a video for it as well, and it got lots of airplay.

The fourth track on the album is a ballad titled "What If We Fall in Love," which is a really fine song about the dangers of falling in love. It's a well-crafted song, and the solo in the tune is another example of Gary Moffet's wonderful guitar playing. The thing with Gary is that when he was the designated guy for a solo, he would take it home and work on it, unlike Brian and me, who would typically strap on the guitar, "man up," play it on the fly, and hope for the best. Gary would come in with his solos worked out, and he would show up at the studio with at least two versions, and they were always wonderful solos.

"Waiting for a Miracle" is about a relationship gone wrong, and nothing less than a miracle will make any difference.

A prima donna or a debutante, you say
A first offender, you had your chance, and you threw it away
So why don't you just get on your pony
And ride out somewhere where you can be lonely
All by yourself, instead of tellin' me
Here we are, and we never get very far
Things are never as you say they are
And you'd rather be somewhere else in time
Anywhere, well you don't mind.
Waiting on a miracle, wasting all our time

"Doin' It Right," the sixth song on the album, was written by Tom Lavin of Powder Blues from Vancouver. This was a Canadian hit for them and I always liked it. AW did their thing with the tune, and it's a solid version. We also did a video for the song with Derek Burbidge.

The next song, "Ain't Got Your Love," is a Marshall-driven guitar rock tune. I played the guitar solo on my '62 Stratocaster, which I used a lot on this record. (The guitar pictured on the album cover is my 1975 Gibson Artisan.)

The next one is called "Blood Money." There was a Canadian mass murderer by the name of Clifford Olson who killed a lot of innocent people, mostly children, and the police couldn't find the bodies. Olson told police he would show them where the bodies were if they paid him $100,000. I couldn't believe how crazy and sick this guy was, and I wrote this song. Normally, I don't write about politics and I don't write about religion and I certainly don't preach to anyone about anything, but in this case, I had something to say.

One thing about April Wine songs, at least the ones I write, is they are just rock 'n' roll songs with nothing heavy or disturbing in the lyrics. It's typically girl/boy stuff. Occasionally, a topic will arise and I'll sugarcoat a serious issue, as I did with "Lady Run, Lady Hide," which is about the frailty of our environment. "Blood Money" is as angry as I had ever been on a record.

The next track is our take on the Beatles' song "Tell Me Why." I had been working in my home studio all night and into the morning on some new song ideas, and I was tired. It was time to pack it up. So I turned on radio station CHOM-FM in Montreal and was listening to some music while I shut things down. I heard the Beatles doing "Tell Me Why," a really bubbly, happy kind of pop song. I was sitting there listening to the song—I'm a big Beatles fan—and I started to get into its structure with its minor changes. I picked up my guitar and did a soulful, slow version, and I thought it sounded great. We recorded it that way and it worked beautifully. We've had many comments over the years from people saying most artists don't redo Beatles songs in such a unique and interesting way. It's really nice that people liked our version so much.

For anyone who wants to know about the guitar, the one that plays constantly through the song, it's my 1962 Fender Strat played through a Marshall and a chorus effect. I played fills from the beginning of the song to the end, with a bluesy rock feel.

The last song on the album is called "Runners in the Night." I played the same '62 Strat with the Marshall, only there's a little more dirt on it, again with a delay and some sort of chorus pedal. On this tune I also play from the beginning to the end. We don't do it live, but it's a song I'm really proud of. It's the kind of song the record company didn't get at all, and that's why they placed it as the last track.

There are videos for almost every song on the album, including "Enough Is Enough," "If You See Kay," "Waiting on a Miracle," "Doin' It Right," and "Tell Me Why." That's quite something. Derek Burbidge was the director on these videos.

At this point, there was a lot more partying going on. We were in America a lot, and it's a different culture. Things are different down there. It's more about partying, sex and drugs, and rock 'n' roll. That's a phrase that came out of the States, and they live by it. It's a way of life for bands and a lot of concert-goers down there as well. There are lots of groupies, and they take it seriously, folks. We were still young and we got caught up in all that. The debauchery became more evident with the band in that we drank more and there were more drugs around. The whole idea back then was that it was a party. We were all on the same page here, so you have the drinks beforehand, you get loose, you go and have a lot of fun, then you go to the parties afterwards, and that's when it really gets crazy. Then of course you get up and do it all again. We were part of that, and there weren't too many bands out there—our style of band—that weren't living the lifestyle.

In some of the bigger cities in Canada, you'd go into the popular nightclubs in Toronto and Montreal and Vancouver, and that whole Studio 54 scene from New York was there, too. While AW was enjoying the fame that was coming our way, we were victims of some of the same traps that snared everybody else, from Elvis on. There was nothing unique in the fact that we were indulging in alcohol and drugs while we were out there. You start getting into that, and after a while, things can start getting messed up. It could be said that perhaps some individual performances would suffer on any given night because of one cocktail too many before the show. Or you're going on the next day just dragging your sorry butt on stage because you had over-indulged the night before.

The pressures of that era of the band were neatly summed up in the essay that accompanied our CD box set: "Whether writing the songs, producing them, or promoting them, Myles Goodwyn had been working against some kind of 'deadline' for the last three years with no significant time off. He needed a break . . . so he took one. After a hiatus of 18 months, during which the band recorded *Power Play* with such cutting-edge hits as 'Anything You Want You Got It' and 'Enough Is Enough,' the band was ready to tour again. The 1982 *Power Play* tour was the largest tour April Wine had ever attempted. It incorporated the most elaborate stage the band had ever used. Their return to Canada, after two years away, saw them sell out shows across the country. Yes, the band was welcomed home with open arms, but *Power Play*, even though successful, did not meet with the critical international acclaim that the group's previous two albums enjoyed. Both 'Enough Is Enough' and 'If You See Kay' charted on Billboard's Album Rock Tracks and remained there for a number of weeks, but 'Enough Is Enough' only remained on Billboard's Hot 100 Singles chart for 8 weeks. However, the album itself peaked on Billboard's 200 Album chart at 37 and remained on the chart for a strong 20 weeks, still a phenomenal accomplishment, but perhaps not enough for this perfectionist band from Canada."

21

April Wine's *Power Play* album had been a disappointment for some folks, I get it. I did the best I could. But then, I always do. Personally, I liked most of the songs on that record, and I'm proud that it sold well. But as they say, you can't please all the people, all the time. My fellow band members were not pleased with the record, and the fact that it did not sell as many copies as *The Nature of the Beast* didn't sit well with the record label. I can't hit a home run every time at bat. But my batting average didn't suck either. Some of the best bands in the world have ups and downs in their careers. That's how it is. The reality is, when our records sold well, I got a pat on the back. When they didn't, it was all my fault and I got shit. Maybe not to my face, but I got it nonetheless.

When I look back at what I've done over the years as a singer, guitar player, songwriter, and producer, I'm pleased. Mostly. At the risk of sounding vainglorious and self-serving, no one in AW ever wrote a hit song but me. And I've written more than one, thank heavens. I know that and they know that. As far as I'm concerned, that's okay. I worked damn hard, year after year, always trying to be better at what I do, a better singer and a better guitarist. And I did get better as time went on. I worked diligently and tenaciously on becoming a good, consistent song-writer. To me it is the most important part of what I do. Always has been.

When the other guys were doing whatever it was they were doing between records all those years, I was writing. Year after year after year. If I did not write a winner, we were kind of fucked. We all knew that.

I'm so grateful for the inspiration that came my way, all the times it did. Many a time I sat staring at a blank piece of paper while my guitar stared at me waiting to be played. To be picked up and led down a brand-new trail. To make history.

And so here I was again, feeling the pressure of writing a hit album. It was harder to be motivated this time. I kept thinking, *I'm tired of this do-or-die pressure; maybe I should pack it up.* I was a thirty-five-year-old rocker in a kids' game. I was twenty when I started playing to keep the lights on and food in the cup-board. It was always hard work, mind you, but a lot of fun, too. I loved writing and recording, but now it wasn't as much fun any-more. I realize now that I should have taken a good hiatus from the band and the pressures in order to rejuvenate the love of the art. I guess I didn't have the *chutzpah* to challenge the powers that be.

The feelings between me and the other guys were not warm and fuzzy anymore. I liked the guys, I always did and I still do, but things were changing. Priorities were changing. Respect is essential in a healthy relationship, and whatever respect we had for each other was being tested. Anyhow, this is my version of that moment in the life of AW. Their version may be at odds with mine, I don't know. And it makes no never mind to me anymore anyway.

For the record, I have great appreciation for Jerry, Gary, Steve, and Brian for the unique value they brought to each and every studio recording and live performance over the years. The sound of AW was only possible with this combination of players. We were a team, and we worked hard for the success we achieved. Sharing the stage with these guys over the years was a pleasure and an honour for me. The exceptional musical ability of the guys is clearly evident on our recordings and our live performances. I know I was lucky to have this band to interpret my songs and to help make them as good as they could be by giving of their talents, unselfishly, time after time. I owe them much, and I hope they know that.

One of the issues that seemed to be part of the discontent of others around this time was the period between records.

Apparently, I took too much time between *The Nature of the Beast* and *Power Play* and between *Power Play* and *Animal Grace*.

Let me point out something here. AW turned out eleven studio albums and two live albums between 1971 and 1984. That's thirteen records in thirteen years. Gee, excuse me for being lackadaisical.

My personal life was blessed on January 15, 1982, when Phyllis gave birth to our beautiful daughter, Amber Roberta Ann Goodwyn. I was fortunate to be home at the time she was born. When Brian's first daughter was born, he was on the road with AW.

The year before, I had bought a new home and did some renovations, and that was a big deal. It took my attention away from AW for a short while. I spent some quality time at home without being locked up in a room somewhere, writing. To say there's a lot more to life than being in a band and making the next deadline is an understatement.

Unfortunately, over the years, I did not take enough time off from my work to be with my family. My wife—make that two wives—and children suffered for it. I was selfish. That's the biggest regret I have in this life. I wish I had made more time for family during those years. I'm paying the price now.

Seventeen months after Amber was born, while preparing for *Animal Grace*, Phyllis and I had a son. His name is Aaron Myles Francis Goodwyn, born July 16, 1983.

I now had a happy wife, two beautiful, healthy children, and a wonderful new home in the country. My personal life did not suck.

Meanwhile, back at the office . . .

Animal Grace was a difficult album to do for a number of reasons, and it took some time to squeeze out some decent songs. I looked for inspiration, and luckily, I was inspired.

I found a direction for the album, which led me to a few new places musically. Again, I was grateful and relieved, for the umpteenth time, to be writing quality material again.

Brian Greenway recalls this period in AW's career: "*Animal Grace* was next, which had the song 'This Could Be the Right One' and the accompanying long video that we did in the U.S. The sound was changing. Everything was well recorded, but it just wasn't April Wine anymore. It was difficult because, back in those days, you couldn't be like your last album but you couldn't be too different, so it was a very fine line. It still happens today. Record companies were changing, and video was also making things change. What should have happened, in hindsight, was the artist should have stayed true to himself and kept writing what he was writing instead of trying to write what he antici- pated the market wanted or the record company wanted. That's what made you happen in the first place."

Brian's comments are telling statements. In all fairness, I'm sure Brian wasn't the only one having these thoughts at the time. The irony is that I was being true to myself at that moment in my life, but that was not where others wanted me to be.

The wheels were coming off, folks. I was now a disappoint- ment to everybody because the previous album didn't do as well as hoped and my leadership was being questioned. For the first time in my career with AW, I was thinking maybe it was time to pack it in. But first I had a record to make.

As usual, AW toured with the release of every new album. After *Power Play* came out in 1982, we spent a long time on the road promoting it. We were never home.

For *Animal Grace,* the band went back to Le Studio, and Mike Stone once again was engineer and co-producer. We all hunkered down at the band house and started recording. When I could, I drove home from the studio and back the next day. The trip was a long drive and involved taking a ferry across Lac des Deux Montagnes, and I could not get home as much as I would have liked. The police stopped me one time doing about 160 kilometres an hour.

The first track on *Animal Grace* is "This Could Be the Right One." The background vocals on this song are, for AW, very ambitious, and it took a lot of arranging and layering of parts to make it perfect. It was well done and I was pleased. The song itself is about the doubts a person can have going into a new relationship. One can feel an attraction towards another, can get involved emotionally and physically with this person, and yet worry about the consequences of the relationship. It's natural to not want to be hurt, or to not make a mistake.

Derek Burbidge, who shot our *Live in London* video, shot the video for this song. The video makes no sense to me as it has nothing to do with the subject matter. To be honest, I didn't press the issue as I do not like making videos to start with.

In terms of refined vocal work, with "This Could Be the Right One" rating a 10, then "Sons of the Pioneers" is a 15. I enjoyed working on the multi-layered vocals, and who better to record extensive vocals with than Mike Stone, famous for "Bohemian Rhapsody." The vocal work was more than what AW was used to doing. It was exciting for me as a writer, and let's face it, this was my eleventh rodeo and I needed to do something different musically.

"Sons" is a nod to all the pioneers who opened the doors to knowledge and discovery in medicine, space, our oceans, technology, and so forth, and that includes the early frontiersmen and -women adventuring into unknown territories despite the hardships and the danger.

> *You were the ones, there is no doubt*
> *You ate it up and spit it out*
> *You were the ones, you made it clear, you could take it*
> *And now it's time, our fate is surely here now*
> *There is no doubt about it, it's time we thought about it*
> *We are the ones, the way is clear, for the sons of the pioneers*
> *Sons of the pioneers (sons of the pioneers)*
> *Men not afraid to try (men not afraid to try)*
> *Sons of the pioneers (sons of the pioneers)*
> *Men not afraid of fear*

The third track is where I really start straying from the mould. Let's face it, the fans who liked to party hard to "Crash and Burn" off *Nature of the Beast* were not going to love the shit out of the next number.

"Without Your Love" is a different kind of pop song that featured some keyboard playing by Dan Barbe. I wrote and played the tune on a keyboard. I liked the long, floating instrumental passages that haunt a major part of the composition.

"Let's Rock Tonight" and "Hard Rock Kid" are straight-ahead rockers. "Let's Rock Tonight" I wrote; the latter is by Canadian writer Tom Lang.

"Gimme That Thing Called Love" and "Too Hot to Handle" were pop songs, which was different for AW.

"Last Time I'll Ever Sing the Blues" closes the record, and it's a cool, bluesy rock song. I wasn't sure about including it, but Mike really liked it and it made the album. I'm glad it did. I recently recut the tune with American guitar great Rick Derringer as a guest on a blues record I'm recording called *Myles Goodwyn and Friends of the Blues*.

22

Animal Grace turned out to be our last studio album. The vibes were so bad in the studio that there was no way the group could continue. Why did the band break up is a question that has been asked of me many times, and it's a question I've never really addressed publicly until now.

Recording *Animal Grace* during the spring and summer of 1983 at Le Studio was very difficult. There was a lot of tension in the studio between members. There was substance abuse by Mike and me at this time, and that certainly did not help matters. The discontent was also palpable because of the poor sales of the previous album, *Power Play*, and other problems I have already alluded to. So there were a lot of reasons why the wheels came off when they did and why it all came to an abrupt end. It was a *great relief* as far as I was concerned. After more than fourteen years of constant recording and touring with April Wine, I was ready for a new challenge. "Cleaning up my act" was at the top of my agenda.

One day during the recording of *Animal Grace*, I showed up at the studio and was told by Mike Stone that the other guys had been writing and recording new songs while I was away on a few weeks' break from the studio. I guess their faith in me at this time was next to nil, and if the sinking boat was to be saved, then they'd be the ones to "man the rescue." I understand it was kind of an act of desperation on their part and I'm sorry it got to this point between us, but I was furious nonetheless and walked out of the studio.

These guys didn't have the ability to write and sing for AW, and they should have realized that instead of trying to do it without me. An intervention might have helped, although I'm not certain it would have. But they were determined in their own way to carry on and chose to use the studio as they wished. Regardless, I empathize with their choice as I reflect on the situation these many years later. They are good guys all, and I wished things had ended differently.

Brian remembers, in a recent interview for this book, that there was a lot of tension within the band and morale was zero. He says it got to the point where I didn't want anybody around the studio unless they were working. Brian went up there one day and everything just changed. "The door slammed shut, and April Wine was over right there on that day," he recalls. "This is where Myles put his foot down and said, 'Okay, it's just me and Mike Stone, and no one's to be here unless they are playing and once they've played, they leave.'"

Clearly, it wasn't a pleasant time, and when it was all over, nobody gave a shit about the record. We owed it to the record company. Brian continues: "I don't remember playing a lot on the album." What he does remember is a lot of substance abuse going on in the studio and that vodka and orange juice were prevalent.

As far as the decision to record without me present, Brian

explained it this way: "Myles left for a few weeks while the studio was still booked. There was nobody in it. Aquarius Records was still paying at whatever it was a day for that studio. Gary and Jerry and I and Steve went there, and I suggested that I should take over lead vocals and they said, 'No!' They didn't want that so I said, 'Okay.' Vote of non-confidence there. We didn't know if Myles was ever coming back at that point. I remember us saying to each other, 'I think Myles has quit the band.' We didn't know what we were going to do. We didn't know if there was an April Wine anymore."

Trying to be creative while finishing this album was hard enough, but with everybody hanging out, it made the recording session even more difficult and awkward. Brian continues: "Finally, Myles did come back and laid down the law and said, 'You're only here when you are working, guys, and then leave!'"

Harsh, I agree, but it was what it was, and it was time for us all to move on. We finished the album despite all the turmoil and conflict, and as they say, that was that. History.

I really do wish we had taken a few steps back and examined what was right and what was wrong with the band in those final years and that we had tried to work things out between us. Perhaps a year or two off would have done the trick. Oh, well. Unfortunately, that didn't happen.

Ending the band wasn't something that happened suddenly, folks. I saw it coming from miles off, and so when it finally did happen, I felt a freedom I had craved for a long, long time.

PART THREE

The Bahamas

23

After April Wine broke up, I decided I wanted to semi-retire. I had no interest in recording or performing with April Wine or as a solo artist. I had my fill of the endless cycle of creating new material, of recording studios and international touring. To quote the title of one of my songs, I felt that "Enough Is Enough." After sixteen years as a professional musician working constantly, I was tired and I needed a break. I went for it.

Besides wanting to escape the endless work ethic of April Wine, the lifestyle I was living at that time was not a healthy one, and I needed to clean up my act. I felt I had to get away from all the influences and routines that were part of my existence in Montreal, and ending the band and moving away was the option I chose to take. As I reflect now, I wish the band had stayed together and we had taken a year or two off and then gotten back to work, refreshed, but that didn't happen. It was my fault.

So I left Canada, choosing the island of New Providence in the Bahamas as a Shangri-la for me and my family. I had visions of sunshine, beaches, warm weather, great fishing, and no taxes. It sounds great, does it not? Damn straight. I was now thirty-six years old with a young family, and I was ready for a Caribbean adventure to last a lifetime.

Our first trip to Nassau was not without drama. I had rented a small villa on Paradise Island for a place to hang our flip-flops while I shopped for our new home. That first night, at about 3:00 in the morning, Phyllis awoke from a deep sleep to go to the bathroom and found a person going through our personal stuff in the living room. She screamed and I woke up. I quickly realized what was going on, saw the intruder, and yelled at him, and he took off out the door, which I left unlocked when we'd retired for the night. I didn't think we had to lock the door to keep bad guys out in such a beautiful place as this Caribbean paradise. I couldn't be more wrong, as I would learn after living there for a while.

I chased this guy out the door, barefoot and in my underwear, and fearless as to the consequences for both of us if I'd caught him. Luckily, I didn't catch him. I watched him leap over a stone wall and disappear into the darkness. When I returned to the villa, I discovered the thief had gotten away with several thousand dollars in cash. Thankfully, no one got hurt. Live and learn.

I ended up buying a cottage on the ocean facing Paradise Island. It was situated on Eastern Road in Nassau, New Providence, and although it wasn't a big place, it was very nice, in an ideal location, and we loved it. The cottage was appropriately named Sea Cottage.

I bought Sea Cottage from a very nice-looking, successful man of about my age with a lovely, small but shapely blonde wife. I'll call him Roy; her name I forget now. Roy and I became friends, and his wife and Phyllis got along well. She was very nice, and she would eventually leave him and the scary lifestyle she was subjected to with Roy.

Roy helped me buy a car and then a boat during the year I knew him. We boated the local waters off New Providence together, fished, and generally had a lot of laughs that first year I lived at Sea Cottage. And then it went to shit when he moved back to the States and turned his evil, conning eyes my way in an effort to intimidate and extort money from me.

Ironically, Roy came from money. He was tanned, well groomed, and always dressed impeccably. He sported a gold Rolex and wore monogramed shirts and fashionable Ray-Ban sunglasses and so forth. He was well spoken, obviously, and he was always charming. The best cons are. Roy was a brilliant, cunning individual who was unable to accept the normal challenges of life but instead was driven by the desire to con. I believe he lived this way just for the thrill of it, and he was damned good at it.

We were friends for a while, and I was oblivious to his dark alter ego.

When I bought Roy's house, the legal paperwork of transferring ownership was all completed properly, and practical issues such as utilities and so forth were signed off to me as well. Roy and his wife moved out of Sea Cottage and into a deserted house formerly owned by late bad guy Robert L. Vesco, the fugitive financier who spent most of his life eluding American justice. He was sentenced to a lengthy prison term in Cuba in 1996 while still being wanted in the U.S. on federal charges for alleged crimes that ran the gamut from securities fraud and drug trafficking to political bribery.

The Vesco house was creepy, and it sat alone on a small tongue of land that jutted out in the water off the eastern end of the island. I visited it a few times, but I was not comfortable there. Was Vesco's spirit to be found there?

I found out Roy was doing a bit of drug dealing at this time, selling cocaine. It was scary stuff, and I wanted no part of this. Besides, Roy was becoming more distant, and unbeknownst to me, he was planning to leave the Bahamas soon without saying a word to me about it.

And so Roy didn't stick around the Bahamas much longer after he moved in to Vesco's house. About six months later, he moved back to the United States. From there, he set about making my life hell. He had my power and water services turned off, claiming I was living there illegally and that the house still belonged to him, and he was taking me to court. Here I was, living in a faraway country with a wife and two young children in a house with no services, trying to convince the local establishments I was the victim of a crazed con artist. I was getting nowhere, and I realized it would take a long time and a lot of money in legal fees to straighten this mess up. Roy knew this, of course, and he gave me an easier way out. And so I wired US$5,000 to a bank somewhere in the U.S., and he disappeared from my life for good.

24

Now I'll tell you about some of the good times in the Bahamas, and there were many.

The best part of living in the Bahamas was the ocean. I love the sea. Growing up in Nova Scotia, I was always near the ocean, and the love of salt water is in my blood. Now that I was living in the Caribbean, I was all set to enjoy world-class fishing and boating of a different kind in the Bahamas, a place that has some of the best water in the world. I needed a boat.

I bought the wrong kind of boat, though. It was a good boat, made by a reputable company, but it was a twenty-two-foot cuddy cabin boat with twin gas-powered inboard engines. It was kind of a sturdy, fair-weather, all-purpose vessel when what I should have bought was a dedicated fishing boat that I could use to take the family to a close-by "family island" beach.

My boat was great for cruising around, but that was about it, really. It was not designed for fishing. Luckily, I didn't need to buy another boat as I soon became friends with folks who did have the proper boats and gear, and I'm happy to say they were very generous in sharing.

My new neighbours next door to Sea Cottage, John and

Linda Sands, are great people and they became dear friends. They have two wonderful daughters about the same age as Amber and Aaron.

The Sands family owned the largest liquor distribution company in the Bahamas, Butler and Sands. The Butlers were no longer involved in the company when I met the family. They were the main supplier of booze for New Providence and the family islands as well, and that, folks, was a big deal. The family consisted of John's parents, Evert and Trish Sands, and John's brother Jimmy.

Another neighbour of ours who lived two doors down, in the opposite direction, was a fellow Canadian, pianist Frank Mills. I'll never forget the first time we met. Because Sea Cottage was right on the water, I could walk right into the ocean from the back of my property. Actually, the waterside of a house is always the front of the house. On one of my first occasions to swim in the ocean in front of the cottage, I ran into Frank. We introduced ourselves as we stood up to our tits in water and chatted amicably for a while about life and such.

What I found odd and amusing in talking to Frank that day was his constant use of the word *frankly*. As in "Frankly, Myles, the fishing is great here." Or "Frankly, I'm getting hungry." Frankly this, frankly that. Frankly, Frank, I found that whole *frankly* thingy kind of weird, buddy.

Frank had a great older-model boat, a Bertram I believe it was. He was a good captain of his vessel, and we had a couple of great days fishing off New Providence. About a twenty-minute boat ride straight out of the harbour is a black hole on the ocean floor. It's hard to find, and you need to read the shoreline and use other bits of local info to locate it. On clear, sunny days, you can see from the boat right down to this pit in the bottom of the ocean. Frank knew how to find it, and it was a real treat to go there and fish. We could see all kinds of fish swimming over and around the black hole. There were sharks, barracuda, and so much more. It was kind of like visiting the aquarium at Atlantis, Paradise Island, but bigger and better and all natural. We would troll back and forth over this hole in the ocean. A few hours spent fishing there was always well worth it. Frankly, I feel very lucky to have had the chance to fish in that spot. Thanks, Frank.

Another neighbour in Nassau was Claudette Nihon, of the super-rich Alexis Nihon family of Montreal and the Bahamas. Her children and mine went to the Montessori school in Nassau and were friends, and so we spent time with them travelling to a beach on one of their two forty-foot Hatteras boats, complete with a captain and crew. It was totally decadent and great fun.

The Sands family had several boats and a float plane, as well as a private island. Despite their wealth, they are salt-of-the-earth people and a real pleasure to know.

The largest of the Sands' boats was a unique old, refurbished creature of some kind (wooden, I think), about forty feet long and powered by a noisy inboard gas engine. It was a lovely, dependable craft and could have been hired as an uncommon sightseeing vessel for tourists to cruise around the waters off Nassau. The smallest boat was an open eighteen-foot fibreglass boat powered by a single outboard engine.

One afternoon, John and I and a friend of ours, named George, decided to take the eighteen-foot runner to their island and spend the night. It's about a two-hour trip or so on the ocean with no land in sight the entire way, and we needed to be on our way before darkness set in.

John had no problem getting there. He knew the way and we got there with our cargo of spirits, no problem. Our first duty upon arriving was to start the generator. It was a large, greasy, growling mass that gave us power for the house. It was housed in a solid wooden shed up back and away from the house so you couldn't hear the rumbling noise it made constantly. When John tended to a chore, such as starting the generator or shutting it down eventually, he took great care in doing so, and he was deliberate in all aspects of the job. It was serious business.

We had a great evening having drinks and chilling together. It was fantastic to just be with the guys in a very special place on earth.

Unfortunately, the next morning, I got out of bed sideways, moving like a spastic sand crab, my back aching from sitting on a wooden plank seat and the two-hour pounding it got coming to the island from Nassau. It didn't bother the other two. The ride was something I wasn't used to, not yet.

We returned the same way the next evening, and all three of us got shit from our wives for disappearing on Valentine's Day.

On another trip to the island, Frank Mills and his girlfriend at the time, Trudy, were visiting while I was there with my family. We all travelled there on the big boat. It was only my second trip to the island cottage, and I did something incredible. Incredibly dumb that is.

The first evening of our arrival, I wanted to do some fishing just before the sun went down. The Sands built a long cement dock that created a safe, calm haven for the boats when they're moored in the lee of it. It is L-shaped and runs about twenty feet out from the shore and then maybe forty feet across at a right angle, forming the L-shape. It's approximately twelve feet wide, so there's lots of room to stand and cast a fishing line. The sea wall stands about five feet above the water line, more or less, and that water level's not affected too much by tides. The water in front of the dock is always deep.

John's father, Evert Sands, loaned me a spool of strong monofilament fishing line. It was excellent quality line and a lot of it. For bait, I got a big piece of fish head that we brought with us from Nassau and a good-sized single-barbed fish hook and trotted off to the dock to test my luck. The sun was just going down. I baited the large hook by pushing six inches of steel through the severed fish head and out the other side. Fine, nice and secure. This was not going to come off the hook when I tossed it out to sea.

After a couple attempts at casting and hoping for the best, no luck. I brought the bait back to the dock by drawing in the line hand over hand and rewinding it around the large plastic spool. The third try's the charm, I was thinking. Again I let out about thirty feet of line from the spool, and then I started swinging the baited line back and forth, gaining speed until I had all the momentum I needed to hurl the bait far from the dock. Unfortunately, I forgot to keep a foot pressed on the spool that lay on the dock as I had the other two times, and the bait, the hook, and the spool of expensive monofilament, which belonged to Evert Sands himself, all ended up about thirty feet from the dock. I was dumbfounded.

There was only one thing I could do. I stripped down to my skivvies and dove into the ocean. Did I mention that it was now dark out and the water black and menacing?

There was enough light coming from shore for me to see the shiny spool floating on the surface of the water. I swam out and grabbed it and then turned towards the shore to get my bearings. I was close to thirty feet from the dock in a straight line, but I needed to swim to the dock first and then along the longer arm of the dock, and then around the end of it and into the safety of the calm waters near shore. There was no other way to get back, so off I went, swimming and pulling a shiny object and the shark bait behind me. I was not going to lose Mr. Sands' stuff, no matter what.

When I walked into the house sometime later, wet, with the spool of fishing line neatly wrapped and ready for return, I was asked what happened and why I was so wet with my clothes under my arm. Did I catch anything? I told them the truth.

They were all floored. Frank Mills couldn't stop shaking his head in either amazement or disbelief. They all said I was foolish, that those waters were full of sharks and I could have easily been attacked. Mr. Sands told me the damn line wasn't worth the risk I took, but then again, he was smiling. I think I done good. But never again.

On one visit we caught a shark from the shore. We used a large fish head for bait, like the one I used when I almost lost the spool of fishing line, only this time the heavy line was baited with a badass hook at one end and the other end was tied to the dock. We attached tin cans close together on the line so there would be a clanging noise when the line was disturbed and we'd hear if there was a fish on the line. Once all that was in place, we retired to the patio to enjoy the spectacular views of the sea spreading out before us, seemingly to infinity, while the adults drank and chatted and the kids played together. There was always island music playing in the background, the air sweet with flowers and a slight taste of salt. Although the Sands had done this before, it was certainly new to me, and so when the cans started clanging, I was the first on my feet ready to rush to the dock and see what was up.

We all went to the dock, and John grabbed the line with both hands, gloves on, and gave it a good pull. It pulled back. Hard. "It's a shark!" he shouted. I then grabbed hold and we started pulling that baby into shore.

But the shark had different ideas and took off. John yelled out, "Here we go!" And off he went, holding on to the fishing line for dear life and following the shoreline with the shark fighting for its life at the other end. I followed as the others cheered.

We got that seven-foot nurse shark through sheer tenacity and brute force, pulling the fishing line with all our might. Finally the shark was too tired to fight anymore, and we pulled it to the dock, where a series of solid whacks with a club to the head put an end to the grey shark's stubborn attitude. If that's disturbing to some of you, sorry, wait until you hear what happened next. We cut its head off.

After surrendering the remains back to the ocean, we carried the head up to the house, where we put it into a very large metal cauldron over a roaring fire and boiled it for several hours. When the boiling was finished and the remains of the head were examined, we collected the teeth and made bracelets and necklaces for the children.

I was lucky to see some of the family islands by float plane when I lived there. Butler and Sands had a Beaver-brand seaplane that had been refurbished to better than new condition. Jimmy Sands, John's younger brother, got his pilot's licence, and the plane was used to do business around the family islands. I tagged along several times. I was nervous the first trip, but as

Jimmy said, it's runway all the way. That made me feel better. I soon got comfortable being a passenger, and it was a great thrill to see the islands this way.

Jim would fly the plane to an island, land on the water and run her up onto the beach, take care of business, have lunch or a snack, get back on the plane, and fly to the next destination. Flying low over the crystal-clear water, we saw many schools of different species of fish—stingrays, dolphins, and even whales. It was breathtaking stuff to witness firsthand. I miss the Bahamas because of memories like this.

Speaking of stingrays, John once showed me how to catch one of these unique creatures. Folks in the Caribbean have been catching and eating many different varieties of ocean wildlife for generations.

One day while visiting the Sands' island retreat, John and I took one of the small boats that belonged there and was used only when people were visiting. It was a narrow boat made of wood and about sixteen feet long. There was a small outboard motor . . . a kicker-size motor. We took this boat near the beach in shallow water where we could see the rays partially buried in the sand. When we spotted the ray we wanted, we turned off the motor and paddled along until we were in striking distance. At this point, John took out a wooden spear that had a pointed hook at one end and a rope tied to the other end that was tethered to the pointed bow of the boat. When he was over the targeted ray, he harpooned it and off we went, the large stingray pulling us across that water at a surprising speed.

Rays are large and they are powerful. I've stepped on one or two without getting hurt as all they want to do is get out of the way, really. It's unfortunate that Australian personality Steve

Irwin was accidently killed when he was stabbed multiple times by a large ray while filming a segment for his television reality show. He must have been causing the ray distress because they are typically docile creatures. Once the ray was exhausted, we towed it back to the house where it was then prepared for eating. Like skates, they are delicious.

I became a member of the Royal Nassau Sailing Club not long after I arrived in Nassau. It was a place frequented by John and other new friends of mine so, of course, I joined the club.

The club was founded in 1924 by Admiral Sir Francis Bridgeman and members of the New York Yacht Club. It obtained its first royal patronage in 1926 from King George V and its second in 1936 by King George VI. The club's current royal patronage was granted by Queen Elizabeth II in 1952.

The club had a nice social agenda for members that included a swimming pool. We spent a lot of time there enjoying the luxury of a large pool, with snacks and brunches available seven days a week. I was recording my solo album in Philadelphia, a year after moving to Nassau, when I got a call from my wife saying our son Aaron fell out of a tree near the pool and split his forehead open. It was a very nasty gash that required many stiches; the scar is still visible today.

Sunday brunches at the club were especially great. My favourite meal there was the boiled fish with grits and biscuits. I visited Nassau recently and had to have boiled fish during my stay. It's brilliant when prepared properly.

There was always a group of interesting people at the club at lunchtime during the week, sipping and eating local delicacies with lively, interesting conversations on the go more often than not. Hemingway would have enjoyed the place, I think.

If found it interesting that many of the Bahamian business-men I knew went to work in the morning and then went to a club or a restaurant at noon, had several drinks with lunch, and then went home for a siesta. They'd go back to work towards the end of the day, spend a bit of time, lock up around four-thirty, and then head to a bar for happy hour. This was normal behaviour for many locals, and no wonder there were a lot of folks with drinking problems.

The life of leisure has its challenges, and living in a Caribbean country is not for everyone—it takes a lot of discipline to maintain a healthy lifestyle. Some handle it well, and others have a party lifestyle that invites overindulgence. I was always crossing the line between handling day-to-day issues and dealing with life in a nor-mal, responsible way and partying like I was on a constant vaca-tion. Alcohol was always my Achilles' heel in terms of abuse, so I was living in a place that would slowly kill me if I wasn't careful.

Sitting on the outside deck at the Royal overlooking the har-bour was nice at any time, but especially when you were settled in a comfy chair, a drink in hand, enjoying the harbour views and the activities that animated the busy waterfront—cruise ships coming and going, fishing boats heading out or returning from a half day or a full day of fishing, some chartered, others private. And, of course, a large variety of pleasure boats to admire and, in some cases, to criticize, usually in good humour.

Large private yachts owned by business tycoons, movie stars, musical superstars, and the like were constantly visiting Nassau. My Chris-Craft fair-weather boat would not have been noticed unless it was on fire . . . ha ha.

The Bahamian Angling Club is part of the Royal Nassau. Trish and Linda Sands were longtime members of the club, and I became a member as soon as I could. Trish held many club records and rightly so—she is a brilliant fisherwoman. I've fished with her several times, and it's a treat to watch her bait a hook, her hair tied back, wearing a man's shirt with the sleeves rolled up, a cigarette dangling between her lipstick-free pursed lips, and her skin dark and weathered after years of fishing. Trish might be playing with fish guts during the day, but at night she cleaned up real good. She was a very attractive woman by anyone's standards. Trish is very knowledgeable when it comes to fishing the waters of the Bahamas, and I learned a lot from her. She is a great, classy lady.

I earned an angling club all-time record myself during my stay in Nassau. It may still stand today. Trish was with me that day, and it was a thrilling experience. In the novel I've written, called *Elvis and Tiger*, I used that experience as an inspiration for a fishing tale about how Elvis lands a large fish during a storm at sea.

Not all my fun was had fishing. I played a lot of golf in Nassau. I was a member of the Paradise Island Golf Club. I got my first of three holes-in-one playing that course.

It was in Nassau, while taking part in a celebrity golf tournament, that I met the great Canadian Hall of Fame golf legend George Knudson. We hit it off and became good friends. My *Elvis and Tiger* book is dedicated to George.

George was a great golfer, Canada's best ever in my opinion—no offense to Mike Weir, who is also a great golfer.

George and I played a lot of golf together, and he never offered a lick of advice. My swing is homemade, and despite hours of private lessons and countless golf instruction books read and reread, it's vulnerable and always unpredictable. But then such is the fickle game of golf. But with all my flailing about, George never intimidated me by criticizing my game. He was a very classy individual.

Once I asked George to hit a ball with a club of mine, a new-style club I had won in a tournament. It was made by Spalding, and the club heads on these irons were all large and bulbous, the idea being that, if they were more like woods, they'd be easier to hit with. Every pitching wedge had a fat head on it! Obviously the clubs were quite silly to look at, and I ended up retiring them after being laughed at one time too many. Anyway, George humoured me and accepted the 3 iron I passed him, a club he'd never laid hands on before. He proceeded to hit a long, beautiful, straight shot after delivering that wonderful, effortless, classic swing of his. A great moment. What a golfer!

In Nassau, we preferred to play golf alone, just him and me.

One time I was in the Toronto area, near Oakville, close to where George lived, and I called him at home and asked if he'd like to play a round, just the two of us. I wanted to play the Jack Nicklaus–designed Glen Abbey Golf Course. This renowned golf facility is home to the Canadian Golf Hall of Fame, to which Mr. Knudson has been inducted, and the Royal Canadian Golf Association, and it has been the host of many Canadian Open Championships over the years. At that point, I'd never played the course.

His lovely wife, Shirley, answered the phone. After a few pleasantries between us, she called out to George, "It's Myles. He wants to know if you wanna play the Abbey today; just the two of you. He has a tee time.

"He says, 'Okay, Myles!'"

With my children Aaron and Amber.

Having lunch with Sheldon Dingwall (left) of Dingwall Guitars and Glenn McDougall (right) of Fury Guitars, in Saskatoon, 2008. Glenn started Fury Guitars, Canada's oldest surviving guitar company, in 1962. I have a collection of Fury guitars.

Backstage with blues guitar legend Hubert Sumlin at the Dutch Blues Festival in Nova Scotia, in 2008. Sumlin was most noted for his guitar work with Howlin' Wolf.

On the red carpet at the 2010 Junos with Brian Greenway, when we received a lifetime Juno Award on behalf of April Wine members, past and present.

Playing with Brian Greenway and April Wine, circa 2010.

At the airport with Eddie Money and two tickets to paradise, circa 2011.

With Red Robinson (centre) and April Wine at the Red Robinson showroom
in Vancouver, in 2012. A real pleasure to meet and work with this incredible
pioneer of rock radio in Canada several times over the years.

With my friend Canadian rocker Kim Mitchell in 2014.

With George
Thorogood
in 2016.

The first guitar I ever owned (left) and the Gibson I wrote all my hit tunes on.

Enjoying some oysters in Halifax with Dr. Stan Van Duyse, my partner in Soleful Caring, a charity that provides shoes for the homeless. We'd just had our first successful day together, after our inaugural campaign in 2014.

(From left) Aunt Lola, Uncle Gerald, Aunt Carrie, my brother Allan (standing), me, and Uncle Bob, 2013.

My son Cary's high school graduation picture, 2014. Today, he is about to start his third year at Carleton University. He was diagnosed with type 1 diabetes a few days before his tenth birthday, but the disease has not slowed him down.

My girlfriend, Kim, and me in Florida, in 2014.

On the beach in Wreck Cove, Cape Breton, not too far from where it all began for me and April Wine back in 1969. Some people say you can't go home again, but I disagree. The Maritimes is where I belong.

I was delighted and told Shirley to tell George I'd meet him there. Imagine, my first time at the Abbey and I'd be playing with George Knudson!

Five minutes later, the phone rings. It's the man himself.

"Myles, do you know what day it is?"

"Yes?" I managed.

"It's Saturday and I don't play golf on the weekends. It's too busy."

"Okay, I understand." Bummer.

"Come on over for a swim instead and stay for supper!"

And so that's as close as I came to playing Glen Abbey until many years later when I played a round in a foursome with Jim Clench, Brian Greenway, and good friend Gil Moore, drummer for the rock group Triumph.

In the '80s, George released a golf instruction video on DVD called *The Swing Motion*. He also penned a book called *The Natural Golf Swing*. Both are excellent.

In 1988, George told me he was going to make a second golf video. I told him I'd love to write the background soundtrack for it. He was delighted.

That year he made plans to return to playing professional golf in the now popular PGA Seniors Tour. George had a lot of plans; unfortunately, he became ill and, shortly after, succumbed to cancer.

When he told me he was going on tour, I was excited and offered to caddy for him whenever I could. It's not as if I didn't have experience as a caddy. I carried the bag for Jeff Sluman in 1987. He went on to win the 1988 PGA Championship. I caddied thirty-six holes for a lady pro in the women's Futures Tour. If that's not enough credentials, I was caddy master at the Oakfield

Golf and Country Club, where I'm presently a member, way back in 1961.

Of course, it didn't matter a lick whether I'd caddied before or not. I offered and he said sure. I didn't ask about financial compensation—I'd do it for free. Duh!

Not long after that, George was diagnosed with lung cancer, and he underwent treatment. The treatment was deemed a success, and I met him for supper when he was feeling good. We ate at a Japanese restaurant. It was him, his wife Shirley, and me. His face was fuller, more round, and his hair thin. This was from chemo, but he was in good spirits. He loved Japanese food, and he told me that sake made him feel "high." We talked about his return to pro golf. He was a wonderful person to talk with. Anyone who knew George knows what I mean. He was very special. It was a good evening. It was the last time I'd see him alive.

In 1988, after his bout with cancer, he set off to play in the Liberty Mutual Legends of Golf senior tournament. I did not attend this event. I called Shirley to see how it was going for George, and she told me he was tired, too tired to compete. He came home and was told a short time later that the cancer had spread.

He died on January 24, 1989, at the age of 51.

25

———

During my years in the Bahamas, it wasn't all play. There were two projects I undertook at that time. One was to write and record an April Wine album. On that I had no choice. The other was a solo recording.

When April Wine broke up in 1984, it wasn't a friendly, wish-you-well kind of ending. There was much disappointment, and there was a lot of soul-changing anger. Not from me—after all, it had been my idea—but from the other guys. Gary Moffet, in particular, was angry, and sadly, to this day, Gary will have nothing to do with me. Too bad for him, too bad for me, and too bad for the fans. But that's just my opinion.

I did not want to do another AW album after the breakup. I was through with the group, and I wanted out of all contracts and obligations to the record company for more product and any touring obligations. The record company, Aquarius Records, said they were owed another AW album, and after delivering that, I would be free to pursue a solo career. To avoid expensive and lengthy legal action and risk not being able to record anything for anyone else, I decided it was easier just to give them a record. It was to be called *Walking Through*

Fire. I never promoted or toured this album. I delivered the product and walked away.

Brian Greenway was interested in being part of the *Walking* album. He understood the mission and was cool. He was the only one from the group whom I asked to be part of the recording. I would have asked the other guys, but that was not an option, for obvious reasons.

I needed a band, so we found Marty Simon on drums, Daniel Barbe on keyboards, and Jean Pellerin on bass. Of course, my buddy Brian was on guitar and vocals.

I decided to record at Compass Point Studios in Nassau, the studio founded in 1977 by Chris Blackwell, the owner of Island Records. AC/DC recorded their mega-selling album *Back in Black* there, and in the late '70s into the mid-'80s, it was the recording home of some of the biggest names in rock and pop music including Emerson, Lake & Palmer, the Rolling Stones, Celine Dion, U2, Dire Straits, Bob Marley, Eric Clapton, David Bowie, and Talking Heads.

The producer on the project was Lance Quinn, who prior to this had worked with artists such as Bon Jovi and Talking Heads.

I needed songs, so I put pen to paper and wrote six of the ten on the record. I also started looking for additional tunes.

I came up with four more songs, written by established songsmiths. "Rock Myself to Sleep" was written by Kimberley Rew and Vince de la Cruz of Katrina and the Waves fame. This is a great pop tune, perhaps the only tune I really like on the project that was not my own. It ended up on the soundtrack for the classic 1985 scary movie *Fright Night*.

"Wanted Dead or Alive" was a song brought to me by Lance, and I liked the feel very much. I had never played this groove before, and so it was included. It was written by Jeff Cannata and Michael Soldan. In retrospect, I didn't really fancy "Beg for Your Love"—at least not our version. It was written by fellow Canadian Eddie Schwartz. The fourth cover is a song called "Open Soul Surgery" by another Canadian songsmith, Jim Vallance, who co-wrote many of Bryan Adams' hits over the years.

Although this record was a labour of necessity and not of love, I still tried to sing and play as well as I could at the time. I always take songwriting seriously, so all the tunes of mine on this piece of vinyl are serious attempts at good songwriting, musically and lyrically. The first of my songs on this album is "Love Has Remembered Me," a straightforward love ballad. I like this tune very much, and it turned out well.

The second tune of mine is "Añejo." *Añejo* is Spanish for "aged" and it is also a kind of rum. The tune is about rum running or bootlegging and was inspired by my partiality for Añejo and water with ice, a drink I discovered in the Bahamas. The main guitar theme riff is very haunting and catchy, and I quite like it. The bass lines are great. I like the song okay, but overall, I missed the mark slightly, in my opinion.

"You Don't Have to Act That Way" is a light pop tune that has its place, like "Let Yourself Go" from April Wine's *First Glance* album. Sometimes simple and catchy is cool enough for me.

"Hold On" came out quite different from the way I had envisioned it. It was slower and more deliberate. I don't even remember anymore where I was going to go with it. I had gone home early after a day in the studio, and the guys in the band, along with Lance, rearranged and recorded the song that night. The result is pretty much as it is on the album. When I came in the next day, the guys were eager for me to hear their version. At first I was upset. I'm not sure if it showed as I tried to suppress my feelings. I did not like the fact that my tune was done without me. (Did I mention that I'm a control freak?)

Anyway, I listened a few more times and it grew on me. The guys were happy when I said, "Well done, lads, let's move on!"

"All It Will Ever Be" is a tip of the hat to Led Zeppelin. It must be obvious. That song rocks in a staggering, mid-tempo kind of way. I played it live on a solo tour to support my solo record released the following year. It's a fun song to play live.

The final song on *Walking Through Fire* is "Wait Anymore," a catchy up-tempo tune that has that singalong quality about it. To me, it's in the same musical vein as "One More Time" from *Nature of the Beast*.

The main differences between this AW record and previous ones are obviously the production and the use of keyboards and sampling. That was partly because there was no real band. It's a studio record, period. Drummer Marty Simon is into triggers and such, and that's what we hear. Danny Barbe, although a gifted keyboardist and able to play different styles well, was obliged to play '80s-style pop rock synths with the sounds of the day. I was okay pretty much with the approach and results, as I was not trying to fool anyone by pretending to be what AW had been. Besides, I only wanted it done and that it didn't stink. We accomplished our mission, although there are fans and critics who would disagree with me on that.

The album was released in 1985 to mixed reviews, which was not a surprise to me. Despite everything, the record did well because of its two singles, "Rock Myself to Sleep" and "Love Has Remembered Me."

Robert Palmer, with his wife at the time, Sue, lived with a son in a condo in the west end of New Providence, not far from Compass Point. There were a few Brits living in Nassau when I was there. Husband and wife rhythm section for Talking Heads, Chris Frantz and Tina Weymouth, had a place in the west end as well. There were three studio rooms at Compass Point, and all three were booked. Robert was recording *Riptide* in one studio, I was in another, and Spanish sensation Julio Iglesias was in the third. Yes, it was interesting.

Julio was amusing to me for a few reasons. One day there was a mother and daughter sitting in the reception area of the building waiting for him to show up for work. The mother looked cross, and the daughter was crying. I took this in and assumed Julio might have a lot of explaining to do when he arrived.

One day, I was playing pool with Julio in a common room adjacent to the recording area, and he, as always, was wearing a white cotton shirt, white cotton slacks, no socks, and white ballet-like shoes. He wore the same thing every single day. Of course, it wasn't the very same clothes, but everything he wore looked the same.

"Julio, I noticed that you wear the same thing every day. What's up with that?"

He explained to me that his wardrobe was all the same so he didn't have to think about what to wear each day.

I liked that; it made sense to me. Boring, perhaps, but practical.

He was a cool guy. One day we had lunch together at the studio. That morning he walked in and said to me, "Myles, I've got a guy bringing in some fresh fish. It's all prepared and ready to eat. You in?" It was delicious.

He said to me once that he liked what he heard, referring to the record I was making. "I like your voice."

I replied, "Thank you, you're sounding good too, man. You sell a lot of records."

He said to me, in all seriousness, "I don't sing well, but I sing in many languages. I sing the same songs over and over, but in different languages." He had a few guys with him that coached him on pronunciation of the song lyrics in different languages.

Robert Palmer was working with bass player, songwriter, and record producer Bernard Edwards, making a record that was different from what he was used to. He was exploiting, under the direction of Bernard, the synth sounds and sampled sounds and rhythms that were popular at the time. The result was fantastic.

I was sitting with him at his seaside condo after we had just been for a dip in the ocean. We were having a bevy together in his living room when he mentioned that he was travelling to New York the next day.

"I have to do a video." He didn't sound excited.

We talked at length about the fact that neither of us liked doing videos. "We're musicians, not bloody actors. I never cared for lip-syncing; we're not fooling anyone. It's phony." That kind of talk.

Well, the next morning, with his record finished and a dark suit packed in his suitcase, Robert flew to New York City to reluctantly make his video.

In the video for the song "Addicted to Love," five female models are dressed in sexy black outfits, wearing heavy makeup and seductive looks, all the while "playing" instruments in a band. Robert looks suave in his dark suit, lip-syncing the words. He nailed it. The total effect is hypnotic.

Riptide was a bestselling album, and the song "Addicted to Love" was a major hit for Robert. The video became the most iconic video of its era. It changed his life.

I never saw Robert again. The success of *Riptide* had him appearing internationally, and he was rarely home after that. I ran into Sue in Nassau one day and she told me they were leaving the Bahamas. I wished her and Robert the best.

I heard some years later that they divorced. That was not good news. The news of his sudden death in a Paris hotel room of a heart attack in September 2003 was even worse. He was only fifty-four.

26

___

The first time I attempted to do a solo record was in 1977. I wrote songs that were different from the ones I wrote for April Wine, like "Mama Laye," for example. I wanted to write tunes that were less rock and roll. I wrote a country song called "Lovin' You" and a silly song inspired by the music and feel of Jimmy Dean's country crossover hit from the '60s, "Big Bad John." My song was called "Hard Times." I even resurrected a song I wrote as a teenager called "You Won't Dance with Me." I was having fun.

Well, here I was, almost a decade later, preparing to write for another solo recording, and again, I wanted to have fun with it.

It was the late '80s, and the sounds of the day were a far cry from what I was used to in April Wine in the '70s and even the early '80s. For starters, synthesizers were now a big deal. Sampling was new and exciting. Even syndrums and other electronic drums were popular. I had been writing for guitar, bass, and drums for years, and I wanted to try something different. I was interested in creating grooves that were not like the straight-ahead rock feels that AW typically did. I went for it.

I needed a studio and, more important, a co-producer. I liked

Lance Quinn and the work we did on *Walking Through Fire*, although the circumstances were less than ideal. On that record, I got a taste of using triggers and sampling, from the drums mostly, and synths. I wanted to explore these new sounds available to me and learn a bit about the technology being applied to music to see where it would lead me. I started to write new material with that in mind.

I contacted Lance, who was into it, and he suggested I visit him in Philadelphia, where he lived, to check out a studio in which he'd like to do the project. I agreed and made the trip. The studio was called the Warehouse Recording Studio.

Working in Philly meant commuting from Nassau, and that meant a lot of time away from home and away from the family. My daughter, Amber, was five, and Aaron was four. I missed them and they missed me. As far as my wife was concerned, some distance might not be a bad thing as our relationship after seventeen years was showing signs of wear and tear. There was something wrong between us, but I was unsure what exactly. I brought it up a few times, but the conversations went nowhere. I thought she might be happy if I decided to spend some time away. We had missed each other when I was on the road touring, and as they say, absence makes the heart grow fonder. Now I was around all the time. Was that it? Or were we simply growing apart spiritually and physically? A break might be the best thing at that moment in time. Also, the distractions of home life would be a non-issue, and I would be able to concentrate 100 percent on the business at hand. I decided to go to Philly and work with Lance in a studio he knew and was familiar with. The plan was solid.

When I moved into Sea Cottage, I did some renovations right

away that included an extra bedroom/work area at the "front" with a view of the water. It was private and away from the rest of the house so I wouldn't bother the family with the noise of my songwriting. I had a small Alesis MMT-8 digital recording set-up, an Oberheim DX drum machine, a Casio CZ-101 keyboard with basic samples, a small amplifier—a Pignose, or some such thing, and an original Rockman—and, of course, a few guitars and a microphone for vocals.

I know this equipment is basic and simple, and if I told you how I used it you would laugh. I minimized everything about the way I used the stuff to create a new song in its simplest form. It's kind of like having the latest and greatest iPhone and knowing only how to make phone calls. I have always believed the simplest way to write and record a new idea is the very best way. Every other method is distracting and gets in the way of the writing and the spontaneity of the moment. For most of the writing I've done over all the years, I relied on an old Sony cassette player. I still use it to this day. I have piles of old, used tapes full of rough idea for tunes. The trouble I have these days is getting high-biased cassette tapes. But I find them. When recording new material, my motto is to keep it simple, stupid.

I spent a few months writing new material until I had enough songs that I liked to do a full LP. Then I packed my bags and headed for the City of Brotherly Love. Philadelphia is a great city with a great history. The studio was nice, not too big or too small. The live room was spacious, and the control room was comfortable. I played less guitar and keyboards than I normally would on an April Wine record and concentrated mostly on vocals and co-producing the project with Lance.

Lance chose the players on the album, a fine group of local

musicians. On guitars we had Doug Gordon; Lance, who is a great guitarist and was once in the *Tonight Show* band out of New York; and Joe (Snake) Hinchcliffe. On sax, we had Jay Davidson, and on harmonica, Rick Valente. Background vocals were performed by Rudy and Ritchie Rubini, Carol and Jeannie Brooks, and me. Lance, Jon Carin, Gerry Cohen, Kitten and the Cat, Rob Rizzo, and triple Grammy nominee Dave Rosenthal, known for his work with Billy Joel but who also has toured and recorded with Bruce Springsteen, Robert Palmer, and Cyndi Lauper, among others, performed on the keyboards and did the extensive programming. The live drum track on "Caviar" was performed by Andy Newmark, the former drummer with Sly and the Family Stone, who has also played with artists such as John Lennon, Pink Floyd, David Bowie, and Roxy Music.

Kitten and the Cat was a lounge act working in the Philadelphia area. I was lounging in some establishment one evening and they were playing there. We started talking during one of their breaks, and I offered them the opportunity to play on one of the songs I was going to record. They were excited, and so the next night I dropped by with a rough demo of a song called "Are You Still Loving Me," my personal favourite of all the new tunes. I suggested they do the track however they wished, arrangement, everything. The song is a love ballad about forgiveness. I don't know what I was expecting, but when they delivered me their finished result, I was amazed; they had done a terrific job. The entire track that you hear on the record was done by those two talented people.

The engineer on the recording was Obie O'Brien. Obie's a great guy, and he and Lance are friends of the band Bon Jovi, who were from just up the 95 from Philly in Sayreville, New Jersey.

One day they invited me to have lunch with Jon and his drummer, Tico Torres. I noticed right off that Jon was quite pretty. He and Tico were both nice guys.

Lance had produced Bon Jovi's sophomore album, *7800 Fahrenheit*, in 1985. It was the record just before their breakout album, *Slippery When Wet*, in 1986. Obie did some live work with the band and is still on the road with them.

The recording sessions went well and it was fun. The only part of the process I didn't enjoy was the programming. It took a long time to get it just right. I had so much downtime on my hands that I couldn't wait for my chance to sing. Other than that it was a good experience.

I was having fun hearing my simple demos become real. My vision of the songs having lots of groove and feel, with synthesized parts expertly played, colourful arrangements, and lush, chic background vocals, along with some cool guitar work, was all now a reality. Once the tracks were mostly finished, I got to sing, and I had a great time.

The record starts off with a tune called "Veil of Tears." It was an expression I hadn't heard of until a fellow named Murray Delahey said it in conversation one time. Murray was long retired from business when I met him in Nassau, a real old-fashioned gentleman, a class act who dressed in a suit and tie if he went out for dinner. He had travelled the world and had wonderful stories to share.

Murray taught me a golf lesson one time. We played golf together once or twice a month for a few years, just the two of us. We enjoyed each other's company. I had the bad habit of swearing after a bad golf shot back then, and I hit a lot of bad golf shots, folks. He finally had enough of that childishness, and on the drive back home after a round, he was very quiet. Typically there was always conversation between us.

"You okay, Murray? Anything wrong?" I asked.

He proceeded to give me shit about my bad behaviour on the course, and he told me he would not play with me again. I was stunned and said I was sorry and it wouldn't happen again. It was at least a month before he would have a game with me. I have never complained about a poor golf shot since. Thanks, Murray. May you rest in peace.

The second track is called "Do You Know What I Mean," the classic Lee Michaels tune. I did the song because I like the groove. In Canada, the release of this album featured a duet on this song with female singer Lee Aaron. She's awesome.

"Caviar" is the third track and the first single release, and it's the only tune to have a video. Andy Newmark flew in from Bermuda, where he was living at the time, to cut the drum track.

"Face the Storm" is a song about getting back into the music business after the breakup of AW. It's a powerful song, and I still perform it today in the Myles Goodwyn Band.

"My Girl" was written by Jeff Paris and Lenna Svajian. Because the title is the same as a number one song by the Temptations in 1965, and to avoid any kind of confusion, the title was changed to "Sonya" in Canada.

"Givin' It Up for Your Love" and "Mama Won't Say" are good tunes and were great fun to sing. I love the female background vocals. The arrangements are inspired and spot on.

The seventh track, "Frank Sinatra Can't Sing," is one of those fun songs for me, but with a serious message. It's fun in the sense that the feel is upbeat and the rhythm really moves along. I used the syndrums and deliberately repeated the drum fill going into each chorus. Loud and proud. It makes me smile every time I hear it. When I wrote this song, there was lots in the news about HIV/AIDS, the use of crack cocaine being popular in the drug culture, and I wanted to say "What a pity." I liked the title, figuring it was intriguing. People would say to me, "Aren't you afraid that Frank will have you whacked?" Let's face it, Frank was great singer, no doubt about that, but the years of drinking and smoking cigarettes did his voice no favours. The fact is, Ol' Blues Eyes couldn't sing too good at the end of his career.

While I was making this record, I was travelling home to see the family every few weeks. It was wonderful being with my kids; I really missed them. I missed my wife, too, but there was something very wrong going on. Socially, Phyllis and I had different friends. Some were mutual, like the Sands family, but there were other people my wife was close to and I wasn't. If I was on the golf course or fishing, she was visiting and hanging out with these other friends. I knew these people and I hung out with them from time to time; they were good people, but not folks I wanted to get close to. The whole issue was slowly dividing us, and I didn't really pick up on the significance of it. I guess I was too busy with my own shit.

While I was in Philly, I was starting to look at beautiful women a little more than I should have. I was having improper thoughts, thoughts of adultery. I was slowly losing it.

Meanwhile, the record got finished and was released worldwide in 1988. April Wine fans did not embrace the record, and the critics either disliked it or, worse, ignored it. Too bad—it's a good record if I do say so myself, and I'm very proud of it. It's the kind of recording I wanted to make at the time and I'm glad I did.

It's not the style of recording I would do again because I'm more of a rock guy at heart.

My one and only disappointment with this record was the cover artwork. It *sucked!* My idea for the cover was for me to be dressed in a white sport coat and tie, like I was on the cover of the reissued version, with a picture of a hard rock band with tats and leather behind me in the alleyway. I wanted this to look like a rock album but with a slight twist. I liked the idea of the contrast of my straight look versus that of the dangerous-looking band members. But my fucking record company fucked it up big time. All I got for an excuse was that there was a glitch, things got messed up, and it's too late to correct it, sorry. What a bunch of dickheads, my management included. That whole "electric jewels in the hands of fools" reality slapped me in the face again. The album came out with the cover unfinished. The graphics on the final album, without the dangerous, leather-clad band members, didn't look like a rock album.

There was a silver lining to that late '80s cloud. Avacost was a Nova Scotian band that I had first heard on a music industry show I was invited to attend back in 1989. I was impressed with their virtuosity, and I helped them out by recording some demos for the purpose of finding them a record deal. Grunge, the "Seattle Sound," had just emerged on the scene, and unfortunately, that's all record companies could hear at the time. Their loss.

Warren Robert was the leader of Avacost. Later he recalled: "You went to bat for us at a club in Montreal once. After the show the manager paid us way less than what was negotiated. When we told you, you would have none of it and tore him a new one on our behalf. We got paid. I'll never forget that you stood up for us as young, naive musicians and didn't let the manager take advantage of us. We played some pretty whacked-out music, so having someone like yourself, who was successful in music, believe in what we were doing gave us a boost and confidence that I have carried with me in life as I tackle music projects."

Twenty-seven years later, Warren Robert and Chris Mitchell from Avacost are now members of the Myles Goodwyn Band. The guys are still awesome musicians, and I'm proud to share the stage with them.

27

This part of the book was not easy to write.

Phyllis decided that she and I should take a break from each other, a trial separation you could call it. I reluctantly agreed to return to Canada for the summer of 1989, but I loved Phyllis and I wanted to make the marriage work, and if it meant living apart for three or four months to make things good again, so be it. I returned to Montreal and rented a place and lived the bachelor life that I didn't want. I had friends in Montreal, but I was lonely and missed my family big time.

I did a quick solo tour during this period. It was okay being on the road with some good guys, but I would not do so again until many years later with the Myles Goodwyn Band.

I kept busy writing songs, visiting friends, going to the gym, and getting some golfing in. Things like that helped keep my mind from dwelling on the negative thoughts that would creep into my psyche if I let them. It was a long summer. But, finally, I got word that Phyllis wanted to get together in Montreal. I was over the moon.

Now the story I'm about to tell you is my version of what happened that day. I have told the story to certain friends of mine over the years, and it always gets a good laugh. I hope you enjoy it. I usually set the story up by saying, "How do you know your marriage is over? Well, let me tell you!"

There was an Italian restaurant on the west island of Montreal that Phyllis and I enjoyed very much. We had eaten there many times over the years. This is where she wanted to meet that fateful day for lunch. I said, "Okay, sure!" and we decided on a time. The restaurant was nearly empty, the perfect chance for us to talk privately. She looked great. At that moment, a single negative thought crept into my vulnerable psyche: "Single life agrees with her."

We ordered martinis. I nursed mine; she drank hers in three swallows. I ordered her another. The talk was light and friendly. I told her that I loved her and Amber and Aaron and that I missed them terribly. The waiter returned.

We ordered food. I was feeling good and I was hungry, and so was she. We both ordered pasta.

She ordered a third drink and I a second. Then everything took a major shift in a real shitty direction.

She told me she wanted a divorce.

"What?"

"You heard me." She took another swig. I felt punched. I asked her if she was sure.

"Yes, I'm sure." Her reply was firm.

I was speechless, lost in thought.

Then the food came out of nowhere, two big plates of pasta and some fresh garlic bread on a cutting board. I looked at the large serrated knife next to the bread, transfixed.

So, folks, here's how you know your marriage is over.

Your marriage is over when, after your wife announces that

she wants a divorce, you feel like you're going to barf and she proceeds to eat every last fucking thing they put in front of her, and then she flags the waiter and enquires about dessert choices.

That's how it went down. She went back to Nassau and the kids and Sea Cottage; I went back to an apartment in Little Burgundy in Montreal.

Now that my marriage was over, I was seriously depressed. I was alone for the first time since I first met Phyllis back in 1970, nineteen years before. We had a lot of good times and very few bad ones. She had put up with years of me not being at home to handle situations as I toured year after year, town to town. There were birthdays missed. Easters and Valentine's Days absent. Too many New Year's Eves spent on a stage somewhere other than where I really wanted to be, which was home with her. The life of a musician is not an easy one, not for the artists or for those who miss them when they're off doing their jobs somewhere else.

I was lucky to have been home when Amber and Aaron were born, but then again, I was never around for long.

As I mentioned earlier in the book, my family life growing up was tough, with my mother dying so young and my dad falling into an abyss of sorrow. We were without a dad, in a way. Now my kids were without a father. Not one who was there when they woke up in the morning or when they went to bed every night. Not one who would always be there, but rather a father who came and went. A visitor. I didn't even live in the same country anymore.

I thought of moving back to Nassau, but I knew that would have been a big mistake for several reasons. No, there would be no moving back. I would have to be content with visiting.

***

Back in Montreal, the sadness I was feeling was beating me up, and I starting acting up. I was drinking to get drunk. I was going out at night so I wouldn't be alone. I was known as "Brownie," as I was always pulling out $100 bills and buying rounds for everyone. C-notes were brown back then, and the new ones, introduced in 2011, are also brown.

I had a circuit of bars that were all within walking distance of each other. Downtown Montreal can be a great place to party and meet beautiful women. After a while, I was picking up a woman every night. I seldom went back to my apartment alone.

I was not happy. I felt sorry for myself. I felt betrayed. And I was angry. Booze numbed everything. I was able to sleep after lots of alcohol, although pass out was more like it.

I was becoming more and more depressed, and I started thinking of suicide.

I was lost and scared. I needed help. I had a lot to live for—I believed that—and I knew that if I wanted to survive I needed to get off this insane path of getting fucked up, of being hungover and suicidal.

So I did what all rock "stars" do when the going gets out of control. I checked into rehab. I was there twenty-eight days.

I was okay again when I walked out of the Bellwood Health Services addiction centre in Toronto a month later. I was off booze.

I now needed to see my kids, and I needed something to do for the rest of my life, in that order.

It was early 1990, and I would be turning forty-two years old in June as a has-been.

I had no idea what to do. April Wine's career had ended years before; my solo career was brief and finished. One needs a record company to make records, and I had no record deal. The last two records I made cost a great deal of money and sold poorly. No one was asking me to "Sign here!" The future looked bleak, and I had to adjust my head around that.

At Bellwood, it was suggested I go to Alcoholics Anonymous meetings when I got out. This is what alcoholics do to stay sober. I didn't consider myself an alcoholic, and I wasn't worried about having trouble maintaining my sobriety. Common sense told me it would be best if I didn't drink anytime soon. I had to take it easy for now. I was still a bit of a mess emotionally, and I was afraid of ending up in the bars looking for companionship, and of course, that could easily get me in trouble again. No, I needed to focus on getting my shit together first.

I was not craving alcohol, or "white-knuckling it," meaning not drinking but still having a constant craving to do so and therefore never truly sober and happy in my sobriety.

Nonetheless, I started going to AA meetings in Montreal. I was lonely and I was often sad. I missed my children in Nassau. Besides, I was without work and I needed to keep busy, evenings in particular.

I arrived early at the meetings and helped put out chairs; I helped set out the paper materials such as the *Big Book* and pamphlets and so forth. I was a greeter at the door, welcoming newcomers and "lifers" as well. I volunteered to stick around and clean up after a meeting. I did it all. I had to stay busy because it helped keep the negative, destructive thoughts at bay.

Eventually, I met a guy who had been in the business as a songwriter, piano player, and record producer but was not active. I don't know how he fell from grace and I didn't ask. His name was George Lagios, and he was best known for his work with Quebec singer Michel Pagliaro. Pag, as his friends call him, had a number of regional hits in Canada. Great songs such as "Some Sing Some Dance," "Rain Showers," "What the Hell I Got," and "Loving You Ain't Easy."

I had decided to try to find some new talent and produce demo tapes to see if I could land the artists a recording contract with an established record label. George was happy to work with me on this project. He needed work, and I needed more ways to keep busy. We ended up producing some artists, but nothing came of it. No deals were made. The only good part of the venture was finding two new songs: "If You Believe in Me" and "Voice in My Heart." Both would end up on April Wine's comeback album, *Attitude*, in 1993, a year later.

George was a good guy. We hung out, and I kinda looked after him. He was broke and living with his mother, a sweet old lady who would make lunch for us from time to time. George and I became friends, and when this venture petered out, we maintained the friendship.

A year or so after I left Bellwood, I was in much better shape mentally and allowed myself a drink from time to time. Drinking didn't become a problem for me again until about ten years later, but I'm getting ahead of myself.

Not long after I started drinking casually again, I met a lovely barmaid and one thing slowly led to the next. She was someone who took my mind off of Phyllis entirely. Well, not at first, but eventually. But the relationship was doomed. She was on the rebound from an abusive relationship. Her stupidly rich ex-boyfriend even followed us around for a while, but he got the picture finally and had his pilot fly him back to the Caribbean on his private Lear Jet.

I was still visiting my kids in the Bahamas, of course. Sometimes as often as once a month I would fly to Nassau for several days and then back to Montreal. I started taking the new girlfriend with me. It quickly became apparent that she didn't like me spending as much time with my kids as I did. She acted jealous of all the attention I would give Amber and Aaron when I was with them. There was no way we would remain together. She was a good person, I think, but some folks don't want a relationship that includes the other person's children. It's that simple and that's the way it was. The problem for me was I had become quite fond of her, so when the relationship ended, I was hurt. It was a long, long time before I dated again.

So now I was without a job *and* a companion and desperate to do something worthwhile to end these woebegone days before I "lost it" again.

I'd like to say to those of you who might be thinking, *Hey, Myles, you must have had lots of friends to reach out to if you were lonely and depressed*. Well, I could have, but I am a proud and private individual to a fault. I could not bring myself to reach out to those around me. That was a mistake, of course; I realize that now. That's the wonderful thing about having true friends: They are there to lend a helping hand with compassion and without judging. Sure, I did have friends I could have turned to, I knew that, but with the exception of one couple—and they know who they are—I remained a rock. An island.

One day in 1990, I got a call from California. The fella's last name was Brown. He said he was a big April Wine fan and that Wayne Gretzky was his neighbour. He wanted to know if I was interested in putting April Wine back together and doing an album. Well, not an album exactly, but a CD.

I was interested. I had not considered it until then.

I told George Lagios about the phone call and that I was interested. He wanted to be involved. I said sure. We were disappointed with our search for unsigned talent in the Montreal area, and he deserved a good break should Brown's offer pan out. There was lots to do.

I decided to rent a rehearsal hall in Montreal and set up a recording situation in order to write and demo new material for a new AW CD. I was no longer interested in looking for new artists; I was going to do what I do best. This composing process is one I had to do alone. I can't write with another person in the same room. I never wanted to, to be truthful.

And so I rented a room, set up a simple tape recorder and small mixer, and went to work.

Every day I was in the room working, and the evenings were spent writing at the apartment. No more AA meetings. No bars. Just work.

In my apartment, I would make a fire in the evenings after working on music during the day, have a glass of wine perhaps, and relax. I had *real* focus then, and that was what had been missing in my life for too long. I had the right attitude, finally.

The new material was coming along, and it was time to contact a fellow ex-April Wine member to see if he was interested in getting together to jam some ideas. I did not mention Brown's offer to record the band.

Jerry Mercer badmouthed me to anyone who would listen

after the band broke up in 1984. I knew that and he admits it. I, on the other hand, never talked about why the band broke up until now. And I never talked bad about anyone, ever.

"Musical differences" sufficed as an explanation as far as I was concerned, until now.

It's important to know why I'm writing this book. Perhaps I should have stated this earlier.

I'm writing this for my family, first of all. I want them to know what really happened to me in my lifetime. Putting it on paper has not been easy at times, but I feel it needs to be said. I want them to know the truth.

I also want friends of mine, and fans of my music and the music of April Wine, to know what really happened over the years. For the same reason. Truth.

For decades my official statement about the breakup of AW, or the changes that took place within the band, was always simplified as musical differences, and although some of the other ex-bandmates expressed their version on these issues to anyone who would listen, the reality and the real truth, as far as I know, has never been told. I was there for all of it, the highs and the lows, through the thick and thin of it, and it's finally time I spoke out. Not in a nasty, hurtful, vindictive way—that does not interest me and serves no good purpose. I prefer to take the high road.

I also prefer the high road when it comes to my personal life. My two failed marriages, for example. In both cases, the divorces were very unpleasant, drawn out, and expensive, but the details will not be told here. I will not badmouth the women who have been in my life. There was a time when I was so angry at the way a relationship ended that I wanted to strike back physically and verbally, but I came to my senses; I'm better than that.

Jerry and I talked about the past, but more important, we discussed the future. We were both into letting bygones be bygones and getting to work.

We started rehearsing together in my makeshift studio/ rehearsal room, and it was working. It was fun and productive. We demoed all the songs I had written and prepared for the record. Hours and hours were spent arranging and working on the details of each and every song. I wanted it perfect. For months we went at it, and it was sounding good. Unlike my solo record, it ROCKED. Jerry's drumming was right on the money, and he was playing with confidence. What a treat it was to be able to do pre-production properly without a tight time schedule, the way it used to be. That tended to force quick decisions and hasty arrangements right before going into the studio. This time, we were going to be properly prepared to make history.

(BTW, I'll go on record as saying that *Attitude* is absolutely the best example of Jerry's studio drumming on tape. April Wine's *One for the Road* album and *Live From London* are the best ways to hear Jerry at his greatest live, aside from attending a live concert.)

When I felt the time was right, I placed calls to Gary Moffet, Steve Lang, and Brian Greenway in hopes that they'd be interested in joining Jerry and me. Gary was the only one who was not interested. Brian was excited and ready to go, so that was quickly settled. But in Steve's case, after we talked we weren't convinced his being part of the band was a great idea after all.

Steve's a smart cookie and a great bass player. After AW, he decided to get into the investment business and did very well. He was a businessman in Toronto with a family and a great life, with all the perks that come with it. Rock and roll is a full-time commitment and a difficult lifestyle to adapt to, and after some reflection we just didn't think it was in Steve's best interests to be part of the reunion. So I made a phone call to someone who I thought might be interested in the gig . . . Jim Clench.

Jimmy was in Montreal after returning from the Calgary area, where he had lived for years. After he left April Wine back in the '70s, Jim moved from Montreal to western Canada and joined BTO, the later reincarnation of Bachman-Turner Overdrive, which had disbanded when Randy Bachman went solo. BTO disbanded in 1979, and Jim went on to find employment in an oil-related business in the Calgary area but had moved back to Montreal recently, which was lucky for us all. It was great seeing him again, and our talks went well. He was in.

Because Gary Moffet was not available, we still needed a third guitar player. I called Steve Segal, a serious local musician. His reputation was well known to me. Steve is a Montreal-based guitarist who played with, or did session work for, Aldo Nova, Jon Bon Jovi, Alice Cooper, the Ramones, and Quebec sensation Celine Dion, along with many other artists. Steve's talents also include songwriting and studio production. He would make an excellent addition to the band.

Steve is a rocker through and through and obviously an awesome guitar player. When he said yes to my invitation to become a member of April Wine, I was delighted. It was a great moment.

We now had a band, and it was time to record.

PART FOUR

The Later Years

28

Before the new April Wine band went into the studio to record its new album, we wanted to do a tour. This would not only generate revenue but also tighten the group musically, considering that we'd never played live.

I arranged to meet with the people at Donald Tarlton's offices to discuss doing some dates in Canada. I met with Tarlton and longtime friend Lloyd Brault, one-time AW tour manager, now employed at DKD Productions handling the concert division. Lloyd went back a long time with AW, right up until we disbanded in 1984. His brothers Ken, Leslie, and Bruce all worked with AW through the years. They are great guys and very talented. Ken and Leslie are still in the business and doing well. Funny thing, Leslie has always called me "Neil." I don't know why really, but I like it. Sadly, in 2003, Lloyd died far too young at the age of fifty-three.

I was told at the meeting that they would have their people look into the viability of booking some tour dates. What that meant is they'd see if there was any interest in the band. About a week later the geniuses at DKD told us there wasn't much out there in terms of work because after a six-year hiatus, there was little demand.

"Well, okay, then, we'll take what you can give us." With only a handful of gigs, we hit the road.

Every one of the shows was sold out. In London, Ontario, we broke the attendance record at a large annual outdoor concert event. I remember the gig fondly. It was awesome. The geniuses couldn't have been more wrong. Fans wanted to see and hear the band, and we haven't stopped working since.

We needed a record company, but there wasn't a lot of interest in the band. Too much time had passed. Music had changed and we were "dinosaurs." Shit, we had been called dinosaurs by the Canadian press six years earlier. It was frustrating after all we had done over the years, but that's how it goes. We had our kick at the can. I get it. But still I wanted to make another record.

Of course, in 1992, it was no longer records they were making, it was CDs.

While I was looking for a label deal, I got a message to call Terry Flood at his home. He had heard AW was back together, and he wanted to talk about working together again. Terry and Derrick Ross had started a new record company, Flood Ross Entertainment (FRE). They formed the label after Terry left Aquarius Records and Derek left DMD Entertainment, a successful independent promotion and marketing company in Canada.

Why did I sign with Terry Flood with Flood Management and Aquarius Records? (Remember the tune "Electric Jewels"?) Perhaps, but without going into details, Terry assured me that the issues AW had with Aquarius had not been his fault.

Anyway, Terry convinced me that he and Derrick could get the job done. They told me, or rather Terry did, that they had serious backing. He said that between the two of them, they knew everybody in the industry, and we'd be in good hands if we signed with their new company. No one else was returning my calls. Terry and I worked out the details, and that was that. We had a signed record deal, and it was time to make history for the first time in almost a decade.

Gil Moore was the drummer for the Canadian rock band Triumph back in the late '70s and early '80s. Gil owns and manages a state-of-the-art recording studio in Mississauga, Ontario, called Metalworks. Since it first opened its doors back in 1978, Metalworks has been recognized as Canada's studio of the year for an unprecedented seventeen times at the prestigious CMW Canadian Music and Broadcast Industry Awards.

I called Gil and we had a chat. Gil was great and excited to have AW record in his studio. He's told me more than a few times how much he likes the band and that "Rock and Roll Is a Vicious Game" is a favourite song of his. Gil's a nice man, and I was eager to book the studio and start recording.

Gil recommended Noel Golden, who was a staff engineer at the studio. Working on the new album with Noel turned out to be a great choice and a great experience.

We recorded the drums in the warehouse section of the facility. It was a large ambient room with high ceilings and wired for recording. The feeds snaked back to a control room that had a beautiful vintage Neve console and Studer twenty-four-track tape machines. Noel got us wonderful-sounding drum tracks. Jerry never sounded better.

We stayed at a hotel in Mississauga while we made the record. We shuttled back and forth until the basis tracks were completed and then concentrated on the overdubs. Everything went smoothly, and all the pre-production back in Montreal really paid off.

My daughter, Amber, and my son Aaron had moved back to Montreal with their mother in 1992, so I wasn't travelling back and forth from Canada to the Bahamas anymore. When Phyllis got back from the Bahamas, she was having some personal problems and I was there for her.

During this time I had the kids with me, and I was doing vocals for the *Attitude* record. The vocal overdubs were being done in Montreal at a small studio owned by Maurice Applebaum. He had a modified Neumann vocal mike that I loved. (I have since bought one the same.) I had to work—sing—from nine in the morning until about 2:15 every weekday afternoon in order to drop off, or pick up, Amber and Aaron at school. Not the best time to sing rock songs like the ones on *Attitude* . . . but it was fine. I was glad to spend all that time with my kids after being separated for so long when they lived in another country.

Guitar player Steve Segal was brilliant on this record. His aggressive hard rock approach was perfect for this project. His tone was always amazing and his attention to details impressive. Nothing with Steve was finished until it was perfect. He's a great player, Steve Segal. Steve is also a guitar collector, and he always had killer guitars on hand. Typically it was a vintage Gibson Les Paul. He preferred Marshall and Soldano amps in the studio. Steve is a fun guy to be around, and that helped in the studio, too. Our road trips with AW were a hoot, with lots of laughs.

There are fourteen songs on the record. I wrote ten of them myself and collaborated on one with Steve. Brian co-write a song, and there were two outside tunes as well.

I won't go into detail on all fourteen songs, but I will say that we had a great time doing this record and you can hear it. It rocks like no other AW album ever did. It's different and it's solid, top to bottom. Noel Golden did a stellar job recording and mixing the record. After the overdubs were finished in Montreal, I headed back to Metalworks to mix. We had a great mixing room, no doubt about that, but there was a routine I incorporated that was curious, to say the least.

I owned a new 1992 Toyota Camry LE at the time that I drove up from Montreal. It had a factory-installed sound system with a great equalizer in it. I parked it in front of the studio every day we were mixing the songs. When we were close to finishing a mix, Noel would make me a cassette copy and I'd run out to my car and listen. If it sounded like it needed more bass, I'd run back in the studio and tell Noel, "More bass!" Anything I heard in the car I would report back to Noel, and he'd adjust things accordingly. At first he thought I was nuts, but he soon realized I was right. I did this with every song on the album. When the mix sounded right in the studio and in my Camry, I knew we had our final mix. The record ended up sounding fucking killer. For years, I thought of finding and buying a Camry just like the one I had at Metalworks during the recording of the album we would title *Attitude*, but I never did. I might get one yet because of that radio/cassette sound system.

George Lagios is credited with co-production on *Attitude*. George was there with me and the band but had nothing to do with the making of the record, to be honest. He was a friend and he and I hung out, working on other projects, before AW reunited in 1992. I thought it would be nice if he came along with me and enjoyed the session as a friend and as a kind of payback for the times we worked together as a production team but couldn't get anything going. Sadly, George passed away on December 26, 2012, at the age of seventy-three.

The artwork on the cover of *Attitude* is a picture of a young boy caught writing graffiti on a public wall with spray paint. The look on his face is one of insolence, with a punk attitude. The boy is my son Aaron, who was ten years old when the photo was taken.

Attitude was released in 1993, and it quickly achieved certified gold status in Canada. After seven years without a record release, we got our very first gold CD.

29

The title of our next album, *Frigate*, reflected those little tongue-in-cheek word things Myles loved to play with," Brian Greenway explained later. "In other words 'frigate' sounded like 'fuck it.'

"For the cover artwork, I had this little sailor doll off of the Empress of Canada that my aunt had when she had sailed in the late '50s/early '60s to the 'old country,' as they called it. I thought this doll would be perfect, so we took a picture of it and put it on the back cover. It ended up being the stage pass picture. For me, it was a pretty good memory."

Frigate was the follow-up album to *Attitude*. Unfortunately, we weren't as prepared for this record as we were for *Attitude*. Touring for us at the time meant the big tour buses and big crews and big shows. It was fun, of course, and nice to be back in action. Travelling in the States and Canada was a thrill after a long time off, and we were all grateful for the good success we were having. Touring kept us on the road a great deal in 1993, and I was already feeling the old pressure of getting a new record out right away, and I wasn't ready. I scrambled to write songs, but it wasn't *magic*. It was forced.

Around this time I met a woman named Lisa in a bar in downtown Montreal. I was single still and living on my own, not partying too hard but I wasn't a saint either. It seemed that Lisa and I always ended up in a bar somewhere whenever we went out, and we went out a lot. Booze was a big part of the relationship. (She would have loved the tour bus.)

Lisa and I moved in together. She was in love; I was in lust. I'll admit that I hate being single. I like to have a partner to share time and stuff with. My life as a celebrity, lightweight as it may be, and my private ways made me protective of my privacy. I have always been a very private person, and so I want the company and intimacy of another, without being social too much. It's the way I am.

Once again, booze and drugs were part of AW's makeup. This time there was no one doing cocaine, I don't think, but a couple of the guys liked to smoke dope. I didn't smoke; I preferred to drink. As a matter of interest, booze flowed constantly when we were on the road. The backstage dressing rooms were filled with alcohol. That was stipulated in our rider. There was so much booze backstage every night we couldn't possibly drink it all, and the crew kept filling the bus with it. The storage bays on our tour bus were *always* full of liquor: beer, red and white wine, Scotch, rum, gin, vodka, Baileys, and on and on.

One time, at a border crossing returning from the States to Canada, a customs official came on board our tour bus for a routine check. We were all loudly talking away, but when she asked if we were carrying any liquor, the bus went dead silent.

When it came time to work on new material, I faltered. For one thing, I was distracted because of trouble with the business side of things. I was also more involved with family matters. But I think the main reason was the realization that, as good as

Attitude was because of all the time and effort we put into it, AW's career looked no better, really, than it did before all the hard work. I also realized that the band was being booked in the wrong venues in the U.S. After a while we got the reputation of a bar band and an opener, at best, on a big stage. This was a major mistake on the part of our label/booking agents. Once you get a certain reputation in a country, it's hard, if not impossible, to turn folks around. That moment of clarity had a bite to it.

FRE was signing other groups in Canada, and these records weren't selling. The company was expanding too quickly, it seemed to me, and their overhead was too high. They were in trouble, and I was having to wait for money to record, money to cover pre-production costs, costs that are the responsibility of the record company and, in this case, FRE. All I was getting was a lot of excuses. Terry would tell me the money was forthcoming and to be patient. Finally, I was given enough money to start the process. (When FRE officially presented AW with a Gold Award for our CD *Attitude,* Derrick Ross addressed us as the Skydiggers, one of their other bands. I had to correct him.)

I didn't go back to Metalworks for *Frigate.* We didn't have the budget anymore. I suspected that this might not be a long-term record deal after all, so I started planning an escape route. By that I mean I decided to start a studio of my own so I didn't need to rely so much on FRE or anyone else to make a record. By the end of this project, the writing was on the wall.

I ended up building a home studio for the recording of *Frigate.* I did not want to have to worry if and when the money would come from FRE. It was in my ADAT (Alesis Digital Audio Tape) studio that we made this record. That was a disappointment after working at a class studio like Metalworks, but we made the most of it.

There are two classic cover songs on *Frigate*: "I Just Wanna Make Love to You," by Willie Dixon, and "I'm a Man," written by British artist Steve Winwood (Spencer Davis Group) and producer Jimmy Miller. Brian co-wrote a song on the album with Jeff Nystrom called "Can't Take Another Night." We also did a remake of "Tonite Is a Wonderful Time to Fall in Love" that missed the mark. The only single release from *Frigate* was "Drivin' with My Eyes Closed." "Mind Over Matter" was one of those oddball tunes that I really liked. It's the last track on the record.

Frigate was released in August 1994. It had been out for some months when I called Terry and reminded him I wasn't receiving royalties that were due to me. He agreed and said the money would be sent. It never was. I called a few times. Terry was more and more upset with my persistence.

After a while they stopped answering the phone. No one at FRE could be reached, at least not by me. Months went by. Finally it sunk in: FRE no longer existed, and we had not been notified. The company simply disappeared into the night, taking our recording with them. Officially, FRE declared bankruptcy in 1996, less than twenty-four months after the release of *Frigate*. It was a few years before I read that they sold the masters to *Attitude* and *Frigate* and a few more years before I found out what exactly happened to them and where they disappeared to. At the risk of sounding like a broken record, rock and roll is a vicious game, folks.

Our recording career was put on hold at this point, and it would be 2001 before another AW release.

From 1995 to 2000, April Wine continued to tour Canada and the U.S.A., doing eighty to one hundred shows a year. During this time I was investing in a studio and, eventually, my own production company and record label. A man has to do what a man has to do.

My personal life was rolling along, and in 1995, Lisa and I got married in Las Vegas. We decided we didn't want a traditional family wedding. Longtime personal issues with her divorced parents made her relationship with them difficult most of the time. Vegas was the answer for us.

We married at the Elvis Presley Chapel on Las Vegas Boulevard. Elvis was not invited. That would have cost an extra $100. No Elvis and no witnesses. Wham bam, thank you, ma'am.

On May 1, 1996, Lisa and I had a son named Cary David Goodwyn. I now have three children, and I love them all dearly.

Steve Segal had left the band in 1995, and AW were four again. The reason was a change in the direction of the music I was writing. I didn't want to rock hard anymore; it wasn't in me anymore to do so. *Attitude* was a high point for me, but *Frigate* was a letdown career-wise. We had no deal, only touring and playing the oldies. The whole FRE fiasco made me re-evaluate the future of AW. To go on pursuing the hard rock style, which Steve was so great at, was not what I wanted to do anymore. The songs I would be writing and recording from now on were so not his style of playing that his leaving the band made sense. Steve remains a good friend, and he's a big part of my bluesy recording, *Myles Goodwyn and Friends of the Blues*.

There are strong songs and good performances on *Frigate*, but the record was not as good or as successful as *Attitude*, and our ill-fated record company was quickly dying. And that was that.

Cheque, please!

30

After the release of *Frigate*, Jerry, Jim, Brian, and I were doing what so many bands from back in the day were doing: We toured endlessly. It was not all glamorous either, not by a long shot. Because we had been playing back and forth across Canada for decades, the supply and demand quotient was whacked. It's that "How can I miss you if you don't go away?" problem. We had offers in the U.S., but the gigs weren't great and the money wasn't enough anymore to make it feasible.

We had a crew of characters that needed work. Band members that needed work. So we started playing shit gigs to keep the AW thing alive. We started getting booked into clubs. I hate clubs. We'd be doing a headline set, which meant one ninety-minute set, often starting at ten or eleven at night, meaning we'd get to bed at three in the morning. These gigs were always sold out and full of people with too much to drink and a club manager who usually didn't give a fuck about the artist. Of course, there were some nice, respectful fans at these shows as well. Most of them didn't like the fact that if they wanted a Wine fix they had to come to a bar—albeit a large show bar—and not get home until early morning. I knew how they felt. Not all gigs were this type, mind you, but during these years, there were too many. One way to handle this disheartening situation was to drink. And drink I did. To quote Joe Walsh, "The smoker you drink, the player you get."

We needed to break this cycle. That's when I formed a production/label company called Civilian Records. I had a studio now that was better equipped than when I did *Frigate* on ADATs years earlier. The band and I wanted to make a record again.

I called Deane Cameron in Toronto. Deane is one of the pillars of the Canadian music industry who for twenty-four years was president and CEO of EMI Music Canada. He is currently the president and CEO of the Corporation of Massey Hall and Roy Thomson Hall in Toronto. I explained that I had started my own label and needed distribution. I also told him I needed an infusion of money to help get this venture off the ground. Deane listened patiently. He was respectful towards me and AW at a time when not too many were. Deane's such a class act. I'm truly honoured to know and have worked with him over the years. At the end of the conversation, he said he'd get back to me. Right before he hung up, he asked me what the label was called. I said, "Civilian Records." He said, "I like it."

It wasn't long before I got a call back from EMI. They had a deal and some money for me. Civilian was in business!

The first project was the April Wine CD *Back to the Mansion* in 2001. It was our fifteenth studio record and was recorded at my home studio, jokingly known as Mound Sound after the occasional missed mound, or "present," that my golden retriever, Archie, left on the lawn in front of the studio entrance. Ken Schultz, AW's front of house mixer and tour manager, was the recording engineer on *Mansion*. It was a tight ship, and the band guys were wonderful in accepting the studio. We created some history there.

Mansion has eleven songs. "Holiday" and "In Your World" were written by Brian. This was the first time he had more than one tune on a record, and that was good to see.

"Talk to Me" is a song I wrote for my son Aaron when he was going through some difficult times.

> *I always can't be beside you*
> *But know that I'm still there*
> *And I love you more and more*
> *I just want to make that clear*
> *When everything builds up*
> *And still you feel let down*
> *When you feel like you're goin' nowhere*
> *I'll be around*
> *When you can't go on*
> *When you can't get free*
> *When you think about giving up*
> *You talk to me*

I wrote "Looking for a Place (We've Never Been)" and "Falling Down" with Barry Stock. He also played guitar on the record. Barry was the guitar tech with AW for several years. He went on to have tremendous success as the guitarist with the band Three Days Grace. When we received a Canadian Music Hall of Fame award in 2010, he was one of the two presenters. Dave Cameron, a fan, was the other. They are great guys and good friends of mine still.

The rest of the songs are a mixture of pop rock tunes, some

on the light side, others smashing hard. It was nice to be creating again. Jerry did a great job and brought enthusiasm to each session. Brian, too. I was delighted to be making a record at Mound Sound, and Ken was always up and ready for any challenge.

The sessions were not without friction.

"I had two songs on the 2001 album *Back to the Mansion*," Brian Greenway later related. "I did all the playing on them except for bass and drums. The band was Jim Clench, me, Myles, and Jerry. It was painful at the end for Jimmy because we were trying to encourage him to write, and he would come in with stuff and say, 'Play a grunge chord!' Nobody knew what a grunge chord was, and he'd get so upset that nobody knew what he was talking about."

It's true, Jim wanted a song or two on the record, but he was bringing in inferior songs from decades ago that weren't accepted back then. We encouraged him to write *new* songs. He was very insecure about his ability to write a great song again. Remember, Jim wrote "Oowatanite" and "Cat's Claw." They are tough acts to follow was his thinking, I guess. He never brought in anything substantial, just vague ideas that we couldn't really work on.

As Brian said, Jim would get very angry at something as simple as not being understood about a guitar chord. That dark side of Jim was rearing its ugly head again, and that often caused unnecessary stress in the studio.

The recording was finished and mastered and the artwork completed. The cover is a picture of a gothic-looking fountain with a statue of an angel on top, a small shack, and a black limousine parked nearby.

Back to the Mansion was released on Civilian Records and distributed by EMI Canada in September 2001.

31

I n the early years of the new millennium we toured a lot, mostly in Canada but also in the U.S. Besides that, I now had an independent record label to look after. Although AW was the only act on the label, there was still some work to do to keep it functioning. EMI Canada was wonderful and always there for my small label, and hey, we even sold some records. We were never going to recapture the glory days, back when every record we made was certified gold and platinum and sometimes more. Those days are fond memories now. But the thing is, we have fans, and they want new material and we want to create, so it's a win-win. That's what Civilian was all about, making these things possible.

In February 2003, I received the East Coast Music Association's prestigious Dr. Helen Creighton Lifetime Achievement Award, which "recognizes an individual who has had a lasting and profound effect on the Atlantic Canadian music industry." It was a great moment for me and a highlight of my career. I am profoundly appreciative to be a recipient; being a Maritimer, this award is as good as it gets, in my opinion. The ceremony was held in Halifax, the city where AW started back in 1969. My friend Kim Mitchell presented the award, and there were great tribute performances from Crush, Julian Austin, Tara MacLean, the Ennis Sisters, and Charlie A'Court of AW songs "Oowatanite," "Cum Hear the Band," "Roller," "I Wouldn't Want to Lose Your Love," "I Like to Rock," "Tonite Is a Wonderful Time to Fall in Love," and "You Could Have Been a Lady."

I had met Julian Austin, who performed one of the tribute songs, in early 2002. Austin was a country singer from New Brunswick, but living in Calgary when our paths crossed. He had been signed with BMG but was no longer with them.

Austin showed up at an AW concert and got to come on the tour bus and meet the band. He said he was a big fan and knew our songs, singing a bunch of them on the bus that night. Julian is a charming guy and I liked him immediately. One thing led to another as we sat having drinks and talking for hours after the show. I told him I had started a record label, and he said he was looking for a deal. Well, you can guess where this story's going.

He explained to me that he was with BMG, but they didn't "get him" and they parted ways. One day, he called me and said he wanted to be on Civilian Records. Here was an established country star wanting to be on my little ol' label. What amazing luck! I said sure. He wanted me to produce it. I said no. He persisted. I said okay. I thought this was an exceptional opportunity in the development of Civilian. Julian was a relatively new artist who had a whole future ahead of him, and Civilian was going to be part of that future, at least for a time. My lawyer drew up the contract and we both signed it. It was real now, and it was time to make a country record.

Things turned sour right away. Julian had a band in Calgary who was supposed to make the record. I was behind this idea

100 percent because they were an established band already and good to go, or at least this was what I thought. This plan was ideal because the pre-production costs would be minimal. I had a tight, efficient budget prepared for the project and it was all good.

Then I got a phone call a few weeks before Julian and the band were to fly to Montreal and start work on the record. Julian told me he decided to fire his band and get a new one. I couldn't believe it. My budget just tripled, at least, right then and there.

That's how it started. It got worse—much worse—as the soap opera went on and on. That experience pretty much finished off my dreams of a successful record label. Financially, I never really recovered from that fiasco. The record was completed, but radio and the fans were not interested. That whole bad-guy-rebel shit is cool if it's not offensive and not burning bridges along the way. Anyway, financially the well was nearly dry by the time it was all said and done. Despite everything, I liked Julian. I liked his songs and I liked his voice. I hope things work out well for him.

AW continued to tour, but it was all becoming a rut for me. I no longer felt any spark of excitement on the road, playing the same songs over and over. I started thinking of adding another player again and learning some material we weren't playing as a four piece. I needed someone who could sing and play guitar and handle some basic keyboard parts.

Around this time, I reached out to Gary Moffet again but got no response.

One of the guys in the crew heard me talking about this idea on the tour bus and made a suggestion. Carl Dixon was not a name I was familiar with, but I had heard of Coney Hatch, a band he had been a part of. I was told he could sing and play guitar. I looked into it. Dixon became a hired hand in AW and began touring with the band.

A live recording was the next project for Civilian. Our last record had been *Back to the Mansion,* and it was time for something new. I suggested recording some shows, and the band was into it. So I set about putting together a basic mobile recording studio. Ken Shultz helped me choose the gear we needed, and I rented everything he suggested. We scheduled three shows, all in Ontario, and Ken was in charge of capturing the band on tape on those nights. There were no mishaps or problems with the recording equipment, and at the end of the trip, the band was happy and Civilian had a new product in the can.

When it came to mixing the live tapes, there was one problem. There was nothing we could use from Carl's performances except some background vocals. The performances just weren't up to par, and Brian and I had to replace all his guitar parts at Mound Sound. We got the project mixed and mastered and then released the CD *April Wine Live 2003.*

We kept touring, although we let Carl Dixon go. We were all shocked later when we heard he had been involved in a terrible car accident in Australia. Luckily he pulled through that ordeal and is doing well today.

In the summer of 2004, AW travelled to Sweden to be part of Sweden Rock 2004. We shared the stage with Heart, Foghat, UFO, and many others. It was a fun trip but not really practical as we travelled so far for a quick set and then straight back home. It was a blur, as if it never happened. A real tour, or at least a few weeks' work over there, would have made sense, but that's not what was offered. We have been asked back since, but I've no interest in doing that rush over, rush back thing again. These days I have even less desire to travel in Europe because of the constant threats of terrorism over there. What a world!

Previous trips to Europe were great fun, though. The first time AW went to Germany, the runner from Capitol Records who met us at the airport and drove us to the hotel was a cool guy, but his English wasn't that great. On the way to the hotel I told him I would like to visit a few pawn stores. I was, and am, a guitar collector, and I was eager to see what the pawn shops in Germany had to offer. I was thinking of the Beatles playing Rickenbacker (John Lennon) and Hofner (Paul McCartney) guitars, for example.

When we arrived at the hotel, I asked the driver to wait for me while I checked in, then we'd go check out some pawn shops. He said, "Okay, no problem."

Fifteen minutes later, we were on our way. He had a few stores in mind, and after a short drive he pulled up in front of one particular place. I quickly got out of the car and entered the store with him on my heels. He could sense my excitement. I looked about the place, and all I saw was porn magazines and sexual paraphernalia. I looked at buddy and said, "This is a porn shop! I want to go to a *pawn* shop, not a *porn* shop!" We both got a good laugh out of that. He must have thought I was some kind of pervert.

He told me he wasn't too put off because there were guys who wanted to visit porno shops when visiting Germany because the stuff that's readily available is super-hardcore and tough to get back home. Some folks are into that, but I wasn't. When we left there, he drove me straight to a used guitar shop, and I bought an old, blond Hofner six string, which I still have today.

Back in 1981, we did a television show in Italy in which

we lip-synced to the music of "Just Between You and Me." We were in and out of that station in about two hours. Instead of flying home right away, we turned that one show into a week's vacation, as planned. I stayed in Rome with Phyllis, and Jerry remained in the Italian capital as well. The other fellas rented a car and drove around neighbouring countries for a week.

As we sat on a 747 parked at the gate waiting for departure, we realized Jerry wasn't on the plane. He was late. Now we were hoping Jerry would miss the flight. It wouldn't be the first time. The last time he had to rent a prop plane to take him to our next stop on the tour.

"Oil-spotting" is a term for being left behind on purpose, for not being on the tour bus on time, one time too many. Once in Pittsburgh, I was kind of oil-spotted when I missed my drive to the airport. The guys thought I had already left for the airport on my own. Or so they said. The night before, I was in the lounge after a concert in town. I remember it was in the winter, and it was bitter cold outside.

While I was having a drink by myself, I heard a woman speaking in a loud voice. She sounded annoyed. I looked to see what was up, and I saw a big guy, obviously drunk, sitting at the bar hassling a pretty lady who was sitting near him. He said something to her again, and the lady was looking quite upset. No one seemed to care that the woman was being harassed, so I went over to have a word with the asshole. I told him to stop bothering the lady. He said *or what?* I said *try me.* I stared at him. He looked away, downed his drink, and walked out of the bar.

The damsel in distress was much obliged.

The next morning I woke up with a hangover and my wallet was gone. Money, credit cards, identification, all gone.

I went to the hotel lobby looking like shit on a stick and in need of a miracle. My miracle was in the form of the guys in Styx, who were about to head for the airport themselves. They took pity on me and gave me some travel money and a lift to the airport. I told them I'd repay them after the show. Luckily for me, the lady I rescued the night before didn't steal my passport.

Fast forward a few decades and AW's on a concert billing with Dennis DeYoung, former frontman for Styx, at an outdoor gig near Ottawa. I drove into the backstage area in a cloud of dust in a black Jaguar XK8. I got out of the car to see Dennis looking at me with amusement.

"You're still alive!" he said.

"It feels that way," I replied honestly.

32

On April 27, 2006, my son Cary was diagnosed with type 1 diabetes, just days before his tenth birthday.

This news was profound and life changing for the whole family. One of the symptoms of diabetes is thirst. I had noticed that Cary seemed to be more thirsty than normal. He would ask me for a drink of my water and then drink it all and want more. I mentioned it to his mother, and we decided to take him to the doctor. I was in the studio recording when I got the call from Lisa confirming he had diabetes. I hung up the phone and screamed so hard and long my throat hurt for days. I was at Mound Sound working on *Roughly Speaking*, a new record for AW with engineer Jeff Nystrom. I sent Jeff home. And I then had a long cry. I had been reading up on diabetes after I heard that extreme thirst was a symptom, and I knew how difficult dealing with the disease would be for Cary. The realization that my son was faced with this horrible, life-threatening condition was devastating.

The days, weeks, and months that followed the diagnosis brought a profound learning experience for the family, full of appointments with doctors, specialists, counsellors, and so on.

Cary was brave and wonderful through it all, a real champ. His mother was amazing in her ability to grab the bull by the horns and deal with everything that had to be done. One of the human qualities that really helps in understanding and treating the disease properly is intelligence and information. It helps to be smart. Lisa and Cary are both smart people.

I went to some of the appointments in the very beginning, but I was away on road trips all the time. Because the disease is so complicated to treat properly, especially when first diagnosed, it is daunting to deal with. It is overwhelming for many.

Diabetes is a chronic disease and a full-time challenge. I was so afraid back then of making mistakes. No sooner did I get a handle on something than I'd have to pack up and go back out on the road. When I got back from a road trip, I lacked confidence again, afraid of doing something wrong and causing my son harm. I was feeling a lot of guilt at home. On the road, I was extremely depressed. When I get depressed, I drink.

Some parts of this book are very difficult to write. This is one of those parts, folks.

The years of living the lifestyle I was living took its toll. Life in a rock band is a hard way to make a living—not too many would argue with that. Alcohol and drugs are the reality for many in this business. Ask Keith.

I've lived this way of life a long, long time. Thousands of late nights, countless cigarettes, rivers of booze, and my share of drugs. I've done it all, folks, and I'm not proud of it. Quite the opposite.

I was not a noisy, obnoxious drinker, I don't think. I didn't fall down. Much. I was functional and dependable, usually, but as the drinking increased my life became unmanageable. Drugs came and went. Booze was different. When I was happy, I drank.

When I was angry, I drank. When I was sad, I drank even more. I know this about myself.

I tried quitting a few times but it didn't stick. I am a stubborn man. It runs in the family. So does alcoholism. Am I an alcoholic? Maybe. I can't trust myself to drink responsibly anymore, so what does that tell us? I quit ten years ago, and thankfully I do not miss it one bit. I quit smoking at the same time, and I don't crave nicotine anymore either. I'm one of the lucky ones.

I drank and I smoked for more than forty years. People have said to me many times over the years, "How do you keep your voice sounding so good? You sound the same as you always did." Now you know.

Booze has been a constant through the best and worst of times in my career and life in general. A few years before Cary was diagnosed with diabetes, I spent a month at a rehab outside Montreal. It was my second treatment. After my first visit to a treatment facility—I did twenty-eight days in Bellwood after my first divorce—I quit drinking alcohol for about a year but then started drinking again when life was good and I figured I could handle it.

Life is good, but it's not perfect, is it? As Dr. M. Scott Peck wrote in *A Road Less Travelled*, "Life is difficult. This is a great truth, one of the greatest truths. It is a great truth because once we truly see this truth, we transcend it. Once we truly know that life is difficult—once we truly understand and accept it—then life is no longer difficult. Because once it is accepted, the fact that life is difficult no longer matters."

When Cary was diagnosed with diabetes, I became depressed. I was so down that I'd sit alone in the back of the tour bus or in a hotel room drinking to pass out. I felt sorry for myself. What a pathetic waste of skin I was. This selfish pattern of "poor Myles" lasted a season. Ninety days. The time it typically takes Stephen King to write a new novel.

Cary was diagnosed in late April, and it took until August for me to come to terms with it. I had help. After a gig one night I met a woman who heard that my son had diabetes. Her daughter had been living with diabetes for a few years. We started talking and I told her about my depression and how I was handling things poorly. She told me she went through the same thing herself. She explained that she was overwhelmed when she learned that her daughter was type 1. She was a mess and had a hell of a time just getting out of bed. She told me of the guilt she felt for not being there for her daughter in the moment. And then one morning, about three months after the depression hit, she was okay and finally accepted things for what they were. That night she told me she had just come back from a trip to Mount Kilimanjaro in Africa. She was part of an organization taking a group of kids with diabetes there to climb the Machame Route up the mountain. I thought that was brilliant. She was wonderful and an inspiration.

I decided I had to get in the moment myself and get active in helping my son. I wasn't home much, so I started raising money for the Canadian Diabetes Research Foundation. Each night I'd go on stage before AW performed, or before the encore, and I'd talk about diabetes a little bit and ask people to make a contribution to the CDRF. We would have a booth or table set up in the venue to accept contributions. People are generous at times like this, and I'm happy to say that AW has collected many thousands of dollars over the years. We still collect for the cause. I started doing personal appearances when I could, and I donated a guitar here and there at fundraising events.

Cary was doing well adapting to his new way of life, and his mom was there for him every step of the way. I'm so grateful for that. It certainly wasn't easy for him or her. I wrote a song for Cary back then called "Over the Moon," and I performed it live in the encore at AW shows for a while. It goes, in part, like this:

Carry on my son
Understand that you've done nothing wrong
It'll be better soon
You'll be over the moon

You're a prince among men
You're my pride and joy
And it will be better soon
You'll be over the moon

Unfortunately, home life between Lisa and me had become loveless and barely tolerable, but for now, and a little while longer, the beat went on.

The marriage was a mistake. Lisa and I should have dated until we squeezed all the sex out of it we possibly could and then gone our separate ways. Well, that's my take on it. Nevertheless, our marriage was doomed, and we both knew it. She was down with it and I wasn't. It would mean not living with Cary anymore. Our marriage might have been a mistake, but Cary wasn't.

33

My daughter, Amber, co-designed the CD cover for our new album *Roughly Speaking* with Montreal graphic artist J. Eberts. J. Eberts also did the artwork for the *Greatest Hits Live 2003* CD. Amber's a smart, beautiful woman with a great sense of humour. She is also the mother of my only granddaughter, Fiona. Her brother Aaron was on the cover of *Attitude*, as I've mentioned. Now, if I get Cary on a CD cover, that would be cool.

The *Roughly Speaking* CD cover is an artist's drawing (Anthony Lukban) of the squiggly lines a lie detector makes as it marks the reaction and response to questions asked to determine if the person is telling the truth or not. The squiggly lines spell out the title of the CD. It's a cool concept. The recording on this disc was done old school, using two-inch, twenty-four-track tape. Jeff Nystrom engineered the sessions.

This is the last studio recording made by AW to date. There are eight songs on this CD, which has a definite blues influence to it. It was recorded and mixed at Mound Sound. Jim Clench plays bass, Jerry was on drums, of course, and Brian and I were on guitars. Brian also played harmonica.

The first three tracks are all bluesy rock songs starting with "I Saw Someone (That Wasn't There)," followed by a slow piece called "I've Had Enough for Now (and I Wanna Go Home)" I wrote both tunes. Willie Nelson, Walter Breeland, and Paul Buskirk penned the next tune, "Night Life." I added some additional lyrics. It's a classic song that I always wanted to record. If you were to Google the lyrics for this song, I think you would find different words depending on who's singing.

"Sheila" is a pop song with a Beatles feel. Think "I Saw Her Standing There." It's about an overzealous fan named Sheila. The song recalls an experience I once had with a fan who became obsessed with me for some reason, and it got really weird. The police were involved, and she was banned from all AW concerts in Canada. She started showing up at gigs in the States, and that became a problem. It was freaky. Finally, she went away.

"You Don't Even Know" is a '50s-style pop song with a few lines from the Jimmie Rodgers classic song "Young Love," which were added right at the end of the song.

"I Am, I Am" has kind of a punk feel to it. It was released as an FM single and it got airplay. It sounded great on the radio. Hearing a new song on the airwaves was very, very nice indeed. "Life Goes On" is a guitar riff–driven song and a nice vehicle for jamming. I took the first solo and Brian the second on this toe-tapper. The final song is a short, country-blues acoustic tune played live and sung live, featuring Brian playing harmonica.

Is this AW's last studio recording? It may well be, but time will tell.

Making the record was not always easy, mainly because of Jim Clench's temperament. Jim was very well liked by band members and fans alike, and that makes it harder to understand what happened to Jim in his life to make him so persistently angry and unhappy. One moment he would be great to hang out with and have some laughs with, and then he would be impossible to be around.

In the studio, Jim treated Jeff, our engineer, like shit. He gave him no respect. You don't treat people like that. Many times Jeff told me he was going to punch Jim out or quit the session altogether. It was awful behaviour and totally unnecessary on Jim's part. No amount of talking to him about it made a difference.

The purpose of this book, in part, is to relate what it was really like and what really happened in AW over the years. I want to set the record straight. It's not always easy telling it like it was because fans and friends of the band don't want to read anything negative about a band member, especially Jim. Jim's singing and bass playing have made a considerable contribution to the makeup of AW's sound over the years. His song "Oowatanite" is a classic.

I never explained the reasons for replacing Jim either time. I never aired out our laundry in public. Ever. My replies to certain questions regarding changes in AW's lineup were always vague. "Musical differences," that sort of thing. I got an unfair reputation for being a prick because of the personnel changes made in the band over the years, and folks, I sucked it up. I shut my mouth and took it on the chin. The fact is, I did not want to hurt Jim's feelings or his reputation. Jimmy was my friend. But now, finally, I'm taking this opportunity, no matter how unpleasant it may be for the reader, to share what really happened. It has to be said.

Jim was fired because he was impossible to work with.

"Jimmy was a great guy," recalls Brian. "He'd do anything for you. I looked up to him when I first saw him with the Coven, and we tried to get together a couple of times in bands. It never happened. The first time I got called to join April Wine was in 1977, and he got called to join BTO. Then we went and joined April Wine together. Jimmy's playing never matured as much as that of Myles. What worked for him back in the '60s did not work in the '90s. He clearly could write some great songs, but he stopped writing when the alcohol and tobacco took over, and that was the demise. It was really sad to see it happening and we tried to help him, but he didn't want help. He drove everybody away. There was some demon in him, chasing him, and no one could ever figure out what it was, not even himself, and it got him in the end. We tried. We'd say, 'Jimmy you need help!' And he'd say, 'No, I don't! Who the fuck are you to say something?' Other than an intervention, which none of us were willing or able to do, we just let it go."

Over the years, I took Jim aside and talked to him, one on one, man to man, friend to friend, asking him to please stop with the anger and intimidation. This usually happened in a hotel room on the road somewhere. He was always apologetic and promised he'd stop being difficult. But things never changed. Year after year, Jim and I had these talks. It never helped. It was almost like he wasn't happy unless he was miserable, if that makes any sense. For years, I put up with his BS, determined not to replace him in the band. But it was just a matter of time. He was out.

Brian remembers Jim fondly. "He was fired from the band for the same reason twice. I wasn't there the first time. The overall thought is we miss the good times with the guy. I remember him with the Coven and Richard Cezar and the earlier days with

April Wine. He was happening, and there were those great songs that he would sing. The ending doesn't deserve to be the way it was. If you hated the guy, you wouldn't remember him or talk about him. I always remember him, and he is still talked about by people, so the fun times are remembered. He was an interesting lad. He took life at his own speed. There was something there that happened that really hurt him. He was a good friend; he'd do anything for you."

Sadly, Jim died of lung cancer on November 3, 2010, at the age of 61.

34

Offenbach was a French Canadian band based in Montreal, Quebec. They formed in 1969 and packed it up in 1985, much the same time frame as April Wine's. Breen LeBoeuf joined them on bass and vocals in 1977.

Breen replaced Jim Clench in 2007 and was a member of AW until he left in 2011.

Breen is a cool guy and a fine musician. He worked with Jerry Mercer in a bar cover band called the Buzz Band in the late '80s, so there was a musical relationship there. Breen never got to make a studio record with us, but he is on a few live shows that were recorded for posterity during his time. His first appearance with AW was in February 2007 in Burlington, Vermont.

Brian thought that having a well-known band member from Quebec would boost April Wine's success in *la belle province*. He was right. "We did very well in Quebec because Breen was a bigger star than the rest of us in parts of the province. That had to be expected from what he had done with French bands like Offenbach. Breen did very well. He was dead sober and a real team player. It's too bad he departed because I thought he added a lot to the stage presence. Breen really helped Jerry's perform-ance because they were in the Buzz Band together, so Breen controlled Jerry on stage when Jerry would speed up or slow down whereas Richard, Breen's replacement, and Jerry didn't gel at all because they had different styles in music. Richard's more progressive rock and Jerry was not, whereas with Roy Nichol drumming, it is now more in the style of Richard and the same age range."

With Breen in the band, we were a tight unit. Not that we weren't when Jim was in the band, but as Brian said, Jerry and Breen had a history together, and their reunion on stage was solid musically. Breen is a great singer and has great stage pres-ence. He looks like he's moving even when he's standing still.

At one time in his life, Breen was a big drinker and smoker. He's a recovering alcoholic and makes no bones about it. His nickname, years before I knew him, was "Darts," or so I'm told, because of his habitual use of cigarettes. It kind of sounds like Jim when I put it that way, the booze and cigarettes I mean. But Breen quit drinking and smoking a few decades before he became a member of AW. He was now a clean, mean, rockin' machine.

I nicknamed him "Skittles" because of his love of those packaged candies he consumed on the road. The man made me laugh with his stories, too. I often suggested he write his own book, and I meant it.

On the road, the band rocked and the shows were good. The only thing wrong with the band now was me. Go figure.

My drinking was once again causing me problems. I can make no excuses here that justify it. It was just who I had become. It took a long time to get this fucked up, but I'm a tough, tenacious guy, and I got here through sheer determination. What a sad state of affairs.

I looked like shit. When I see pictures of me from 2007, at the end of my drinking days, I cringe at the way I looked. I looked sore and pained, with squinty eyes that were often streaked the colour of red caviar, my puffy skin the hue of the fish the caviar came out of, and that was on a good day.

My marriage was limping to the finish line, and I was socially shutting down. If we were on a tour bus, the back lounge was my place to be alone, reading, writing, and drinking vodka. Or I hung out in my hotel room where I could sip and sleep. This was the way it was. I often felt weak and languorous, but despite my poor physical condition, I made every show. I sang well enough and I still played guitar with pride, but when the curtains came down, well, then I couldn't wait to be alone again, to hide from people and things and indulge in a bevy or ten. I had no interest in how other people in the band and crew were doing or thinking and absolutely no interest in going for supper with the boys, although I was seldom invited. They knew I'd only say no anyway.

It was around this time that I started working on an idea for a blues record. I started dragging a guitar around with me for the purpose of writing some new tunes, great tunes I hoped. I enjoy the blues when the songs are great. There are a lot of amazing players and singers of the blues out there, but I often don't care for the material all that much. The whole "babe done left me, boo hoo boo hoo" is not my idea of award-winning songwriting. "The Thrill Is Gone," now that's an example of a great blues tune.

The concept and success of the blues project I had in mind depended on my writing quality blues material, and I needed that challenge. That excited me. So I applied my talents as a tunesmith to the task and wrote some blues tunes. It was coming along, and I felt the new songs were quality songs.

Frankly, AW didn't do it for me anymore. There were too many years, too many ups and downs, and too many changes over the decades for me to truly care about what happened to the band anymore. The AW thing was on cruise control. I didn't really need the money, but some others did, so I forged on, detached. Except for the ninety minutes on stage during concerts, my head was somewhere else. The emotional attachment that inspired me almost forty years before back in Nova Scotia was now dull and withering.

My drinking continued to worsen over the months. It was 2008 and I was sixty years old. But I felt older. My health was suffering, and when I looked in a mirror it showed, yet I still ignored my condition. From the time I got up in the morning until it was time for bed at night, I needed a drink. I sipped poison all day long. Vodka in a water bottle was my close companion, my medicine. My undoing.

Radio station Q104 in Halifax was putting on an event called "the Quarter Century Concert," and AW was headlining. The station was also inducting AW members, past and present, into something called "the Rock of the Atlantic Wall of Fame." That was very nice of them to do. I felt honoured. The gig was the next night, and I was scheduled to fly to Halifax in the morning. Eventually, I passed out that night, oblivious to the fact that if I continued to drink alcohol, I would be dead within thirty-six hours.

35

Things come in threes.

I went to rehab for six weeks after my near brush with death in November 2008, as you'll recall I talked about in the prologue. I was back home a few weeks when I was diagnosed with diabetes. Within a week of that life-changing announcement, my wife told me she wanted a divorce. Three *hard* hits and I'm still standing.

While in the hospital near Montreal, I was treated for severe esophageal varices, confined to my bed until I was okay to leave. After breathing recycled forced air for too long, I was finally told I could go outside for some fresh air. A nurse handed me my lighter and the remaining cigarettes I had with me when I was admitted weeks before. I sat in a wheelchair, hooked up to an IV, looking at the cigarettes and lighter for a few moments before handing them back to the nurse. "You can throw them out, please."

From the hospital I was sent to Bellwood Health Services in Toronto. If you're counting, folks, this was my second visit to Bellwood, almost twenty years between visits. This time I was there because of my alcohol abuse, obviously, and my poor physical condition. I was in the right place, and I was going to be there a while.

My stay at Bellwood ran through Christmas. That was tough. I wanted to be home but I couldn't be. I was able to call the kids and wish them a Merry Christmas, and I was thankful for that.

I was "inside" when Obama was inaugurated as president of the United States on January 20, 2009. It was being televised live at a time during the day when we were not permitted to watch TV. I protested adamantly, insisting that this was too historical a moment to miss. They finally agreed and allowed us *misérables* to watch as Barack Obama was sworn in as the first black president of the United States. It was a brilliant moment as far as I was concerned.

Speaking of brilliant moments, I saw the movie *Avatar* the first time I was allowed to leave Bellwood on my own. Day pass in hand, I took a public bus for the first time in years. It was an exhilarating experience being away from Bellwood. I saw *Avatar* on a huge screen with only a few other people present in the theatre. It was absolutely spellbinding and now is one of my all-time favourite films.

My assigned doctor at Bellwood wanted to have my lungs checked while I was there. He knew I had smoked about a pack a day for forty years, and he felt they should X-ray my lungs. He arranged an appointment for me on a Wednesday. I was very nervous for obvious reasons. After all those years of smoking cigarettes, plus the time I spent performing in smoky bars and travelling in smoky tour buses, I had to have done some damage to my lungs. People were dying from occasional second-hand smoke, for heaven's sake. I had every right to be nervous.

I was driven to a nearby facility and had extensive X-rays taken of my upper body from every possible angle. Three Asian guys in white smocks manipulated these robotic-looking machines from behind a large glass window. They took a lot of pictures from every conceivable angle. It was unnerving as hell. I was told the results would take a week to arrive. For a week I had nothing on my mind but what the results would reveal. It was hard to sleep, and I had nightmares about it. A week later, on a Wednesday morning, I was called to the doctor's office.

I sat in a chair in front of his desk as he studied some papers spread out before him. For what seemed like a long time he said nothing. Finally he talked about some of the results and made comments on my progress, but nothing about the chest and lung X-rays. When I couldn't take it anymore I asked him, "So what about the X-rays, Doc? I've been worried about this for a week."

He told me there were small traces of asbestos in my lungs. It wasn't a problem now, but it would be good to check on it from time to time. Asbestos causes lung cancer and pleural mesothelioma. It's a nasty way to go. I can remember Dad using that pink stuff for insulation at home when I was a kid. We were told to use gloves when handling it and not to get it on our bare skin because it would make us itchy. I don't remember us wearing masks.

"Okay, what else?"

"That's it."

"I smoked for forty years and that's it? How is that possible?" I was relieved and incredulous at the same time.

"Genetics. So are you going to start smoking again?"

"No. I got away with it once, at least so far. I'll not tempt fate a second time." I never lit up again.

On the third week of my stay, I was allowed twenty minutes outside in the evenings. There was a small convenience store a block away that we were allowed to visit if we were quick about it. Most bought cigarettes, and some, like me, purchased sweets and other sundry items. Chocolate bars were not permitted at Bellwood, so we had to eat them before returning or smuggle them in. I used to hide a bar or two in my socks, and I got away with it. From time to time, they would come down hard on us and conduct random searches of the rooms. Of course, they found all kinds of shit, including booze and dope.

I did not want to get busted for hiding chocolate bars, so I started a stash on the property outside the main building. I would bury chocolate bars, ends up, like little colourful soldiers standing at attention in the snow, in an area near the front entrance but behind some bushes, out of sight of anyone coming or going. The tops of the bars were hidden about two inches under the snow.

Weather in Toronto can change quickly at times. A warm front with light rain moved into the area overnight towards the end of my stay. A friend came to me giggling and said, "Come take a look at this, Myles." I followed him to a large window that overlooked the front area of the building, and there, sticking out of the snow, were my little chocolate soldiers standing tall and proud for the whole world to see. Busted!

After a month at Bellwood, I was looking and feeling better, but I was still weak and unsteady and I had lost a lot of weight. Regardless, I was fit enough to go home, which was a scary thought. Lisa, understandably, was angry with me, and the brief conversations we had by phone were tense and almost hostile. Did I really want to go home?

With a few days to go before my release, I was told about an extension course I could take that would add two weeks to my stay. One of the counsellors explained to me that the advanced course was a good idea, and it would help me stay out of trouble on the outside.

So I stayed on. It was hard because I really wanted to see family again, regardless of my wife's rancor towards me. Eventually, after six weeks at Bellwood, I was on my way home to Quebec.

When I walked in the door, the reception was mixed. Cary was excited and happy to see me, and Lisa was definitely not. Fair enough.

Home life was plenty stressful, and I tried to keep out of Lisa's way. I knew I had a lot to prove before I could be accepted and trusted again, if at all. The chances of our marriage lasting, regardless of my bad behaviour, was pretty much nil.

In Quebec, there are free government-assisted health clinics called CLSC (*centre local de services communautaires*) throughout the province serving anyone needing basic medical attention. First come, first serve. I went to a CLSC in our area a few weeks after I got home. I was feeling tired all the time, so I decided to get a blood test.

When the nurse checked the result of my blood test she uttered three words a nurse should never say in front of a patient: "Oh my God."

I was told to get my ass to a hospital as soon as possible and have some further tests done. I spent the night at the hospital, the same hospital I'd lived in a few months back when I was admitted for internal bleeding caused by esophageal varices. This time the problem was different. I had type 2 diabetes.

How do you know your marriage is over? Part two.

When I was admitted to the hospital and after initial tests were completed, I was told I would be spending the night. They had to run more tests before I could go home. I called the house to tell Lisa I'd be spending the night and asked if she'd mind dropping off a few things. She suggested I ask someone else as she was busy. I informed her I had already called a few friends, including Brian Greenway, but I couldn't reach anyone. Finally she relented. After arriving at the hospital, she found me on a gurney, wedged in a corner of the emergency ward with chaos all around, the kind of chaos that can only be found in such a place. I looked pitiful, with bandages on the veins on my arms, vulnerable, and forlorn. I was glad to see her.

She gave me a plastic bag of stuff and said, "Here." Then she walked out.

That's how you know your marriage is over. But could you really blame her, folks?

Lisa was in the kitchen the next day when I arrived home from the hospital. She didn't ask what the medical reason was for me being in the hospital or how I was feeling. Nothing. I told her I was diagnosed with diabetes.

There were now two people in the house with diabetes. The prospect of dealing with that reality was too much for her, and all things considered, I do not blame her a bit.

For about a week, Lisa and I avoided each other. It was a difficult time, especially for Cary, who was caught in the middle. There was never mention of my diabetes by either one of us. It was as if it didn't exist. Life was too uncomfortable to continue like this any longer. Enough was enough.

I gave her the out she wanted. I asked if she wanted a divorce. She didn't hesitate to reply. She immediately went to my son's room. I waited until I heard her leave his room before I went to see him. We talked, and then we both sat together on the floor and had a long cry.

36

I was off the road from November 28, 2008, to February 21, 2009.

When we started up again, it took me a while to build up the stamina I needed to work full time.

There were many significant changes in my life at this time. Not drinking was not a hard adjustment for me now that I didn't want to drink anymore. I'd had my last drink back in November 2008, when I was in and out of hospital. I knew it was my last drink. No one believed me and I get that. That was almost ten sober years ago now, but who's counting? It was the same when I quit smoking tobacco. I lost the desire and that was that. I tossed my cigarettes and haven't craved one since.

Lisa moved out. The divorce was horrible. All the clichés and classic shit that happens happened. The consequences linger still and will probably never be fully resolved.

Divorce is traumatic for all involved but especially for the children, and not just mine, I mean everyone's children. Unfortunately, that's just the way it is.

Harriet Sergeant of the *Daily Mail* wrote: "As one man said sadly, divorce 'leaves many fathers on the edge of a bloody great

abyss. Many fall off and are never seen again.'" To try to overcome the emotional damage done during a divorce can be the
biggest challenge a man and his children will ever have in their
lives, but one can never give up hope.

With all these changes in my life coming at me fast and
furious, I needed to focus on positive matters, like my music. I
started back on my blues project again and it was coming along
slowly, but I was in no hurry. The fact that it was working for me
was all that mattered. Blues music is enduring, not some flavour-
of-the month fad. So much of the popular music exists simply
because of trends that go in and out of favour. Case in point:
They just don't write songs like "How Much Is That Doggie in
the Window" anymore.

I wanted to know if I could still write a good tune without
drinking. I was very relieved to find I had no problem. As a matter of fact I found it easier. I had a clear head, and the inspiration for lyrics came from an uncluttered perception of what was
working and what wasn't. I didn't waste any time writing chord
patterns and melodies that I couldn't remember later. There
was a freedom that came with sobriety that illuminated my new
work; it didn't darken it. This was good to know, folks.

April Wine was on the road again full time. With the help
of our friends and agents at Feldman and Associates, George
Elmes and Tom Kemp in particular, the gigs kept rolling in.
The band and its members appeared to be in a good place late
in 2008, when in reality there were problems. Soon there would
be yet another change of personnel in the band, and this change
would shock the fans and confound the remaining band members as well.

Press releases and media announcements stated that Jerry

Mercer retired from April Wine. After thirty-five years drumming for the band and being almost seventy years old, it would certainly make sense. But they had the facts wrong. Jerry Mercer didn't retire, he was fired. Or was he?

Jerry is a "doper" and has been for more than fifty years—let's get that fact out of the way immediately, shall we? How do I know Jerry's a doper? He told me so.

I was no angel. I used and abused drugs and alcohol over the years, and it got to a point where life became unmanageable. I almost died, and finally I cleaned up my act. Brian Greenway abused alcohol for years and recently announced that he quit. "I went on Facebook recently and admitted I had an alcohol problem and it was incredible, the outpouring from people; I had no idea," Brian admits. "They said it's commendable and brave of you to do that, and some said, 'Thank you Brian, I think I have a problem, too. I'm going to take strength from what you're doing and stop.'"

Everyone has their bottom. The smart ones clean up. The lucky ones.

The fact is, chronic users of drugs, in Jerry's case primarily marijuana and hashish, function differently than a straight person. You cannot be a habitual user and smoke dope year after year, literally decades, and be what is traditionally known as normal. That person may establish a state of normalcy that gets them through the day, but their reality is drug induced and, folks, that's not an ideal space to be all the time. (Some of you readers may remember the band that Jerry and Breen played in back in the eighties was called the Buzz Band.)

There are many funny stories about Jerry that have become classics. At the time, I did not always consider his behaviour and perspective were because he was stoned. Now I realize it was likely the dope that made him the way he was.

One time, we were very late going on stage for a concert. Jerry drove himself to the gig while the rest of the band travelled together and arrived at the venue on time. Jerry finally showed up an hour late, and by now the audience was upset. When he walked into the dressing room, our tour manager asked what the hell happened. Jerry said he got lost. Our manager said, "I told you to go straight until you cross a red bridge, make a right, drive one kilometre, and the venue is on the left. Dead simple." Jerry replied, in all seriousness, "I was looking for a redder bridge."

One time at immigration to the States, all he had for identification was a Canadian drum magazine with his picture in it. The immigration agent couldn't stop laughing. "Is this guy serious?" We did not find it fun at all. I was pissed. He was admitted because we vouched for him.

There was always someone in the band or the crew who had at least one Mercer story to tell almost every day. It was remarkable. There was nothing malicious in the telling of Jerry's escapades. We all liked Jerry; he's basically a good guy. It was just that it was all too funny or too unbelievable *not* to share. It was like this for years.

Jerry and I go back a long time. We have shared so many stages over the years, and recorded many albums' worth of material, and we've had many laughs together. We also got in each other's faces over the years, but that's kind of how it goes in a band. There was a lot more rub between Jimmy Clench and Jerry than there ever was between Jerry and me. Everyone in the band had confrontations from time to time with another bandmate.

It's part of being in a rock band. Even the crème de la crème of bandmates have disagreements, like John and Paul, Mick and Keith, and Don and Phil. It's just the nature of the beast.

Unfortunately, Jerry's actions were creating real problems that were no longer funny. I don't want to go deep here, but there comes a point when a person has to clean up all the misinformation that's been written and all the rumours that have circulated for years. You want to know the truth, folks? Well, you came to the right place.

AW was playing a sold-out show in Vancouver, and Jerry did his amazing drum solo as part of the arrangement in "I Like to Rock." When he came out of the solo, instead of playing the segue into "Sign of the Gypsy Queen" as arranged, he went into some Led Zeppelin song that he had played in the Buzz Band years before. The rest of us just stared at him. We couldn't continue. We had to stop the show and regroup. It was unprofessional and extremely embarrassing.

Another night, Jerry played our biggest hit, "Just Between You and Me," with a swing feel. If you're not sure what that means, imagine Brian, Breen, and me playing "Just Between You and Me" and Jerry playing "You Won't Dance with Me" at the same time. If you tried to dance to that you would end up looking like Elaine dancing on an episode of *Seinfeld*.

After the show Jerry denied he was on drugs.

There were other problems, some personal, some musical, and also some company business issues—writing cheques to pay some of AW's bills without informing others—that weren't illegal or anything, but still unacceptable and needed to be addressed. All this resulted in a confrontation with Jerry. I had had enough. I was not alone.

That I *wasn't* indifferent to what was really going on with Jerry may have to do with the fact that I was no longer lubricated to a point where I didn't care about the band enough to take notice and deal with the problems. We were a different band by this time. There was less partying and more diligence regarding the responsibility to take care of business properly and efficiently, our road crew included. They were partying way too hard to be at their best when it was time to work a show. They cooled it. The changes were all good. The fact that half the band didn't drink booze anymore had something to do with it, I think.

And so it was put to Jerry by Brian and me: "No more drugs on the road, please." That request seemed reasonable to me and to the others in the band. I explained to Jerry that we didn't mean he couldn't do drugs ever, that was none of our business, just not when he was working with AW. He was told it was affecting his performances and creating problems in other areas of AW as well. He took great offence. It was like he'd just been told he couldn't hang out with his best friend anymore. I explained to him that he wasn't being attacked but that we needed to discuss the situation. He said he didn't have a problem, but that *I* did. He told Brian to "fuck off" and to "kiss his ass." It did not go well.

It's incredible what some people will say and do to defend themselves. Chronic users will do most anything in order to keep doing whatever it is they're doing, regardless of the consequences. Smokers addicted to tobacco will let it kill them before they'll turn their back on their "best friend." We needed to talk to Jerry again.

"Jerry, no more drugs on the road. What you do on your off time is your business. You have to make the choice. We want you in the band, you are a huge part of April Wine, and we'll miss you and the fans will miss you if you leave. But if you stay, the drugs stay home."

Jerry chose drugs and to leave the band. We couldn't believe it. So was Jerry fired, or did he quit? Either way, the result is the same.

"Jerry was finally let go, a decision that Myles and I agreed on. Jerry thought he was right, and he wasn't," recalls Brian. "It came to a point with me where he told me to fuck off and to kiss his ass. I said, 'Jerry, you apologize and I'll be in your corner.' But he refused and I just washed my hands of it. Jerry is a great guy. He is what he is, I am what I am, Myles is what he is. That's what made us all gel together."

Brian is absolutely correct: We are what we are. Nobody's perfect. As time has passed since Jerry left the band, I think back to all the years we worked together. My favourite memory might be just me and him, locked up in a room together for weeks preparing for *Attitude*, our comeback album and our very first CD ever, back in 1992. I think of the fun we had making records like *Stand Back* and *The Nature of the Beast*. Those were good times. We made history together.

Jerry is an awesome drummer, a powerful drummer. He has more presence and charisma on stage than any drummer I've ever seen. He is, and has always been, totally dedicated to his craft. His forte was not in the studio so much; his strength was on stage where he could do his own thing, and that's why his solos were spectacular.

Jerry is very musical. He was great for figuring out vocal harmonies and intricate guitar parts like the difficult parts on "21st Century Schizoid Man." He could play the piano a bit, and he even played glockenspiel on "Tonite Is a Wonderful Time."

I believe his musical sensibilities were developed in church as a young man. Jerry can also sing, and I understand he sang in a church choir like I did as a youngster.

I miss working with Jerry. As time rolled along, I appreciated his talents more and more. It's funny how we can take so much for granted when times are good. He chose to leave AW and I respect that, I really do, I just don't think it was the best decision, but that's me being selfish, I guess. He's doing things his way and bless him for that.

We still see Jerry when we're performing in his area. He'll show up at a gig from time to time and join us on stage for a tune or two. That's always a thrill, and I look forward to the next time.

37

B lair Mackay joined April Wine as the new drummer in January 2009. I had met Blair at a bar when a friend and I went to see a blues band that was playing there, back when I was living alone and working on writing blues material. Blair seemed like a decent guy. When Jerry left, I thought of him as a replacement because he was the only drummer I knew who lived in our town. Blair is a mercenary, a drummer for hire, the kind of guy with no particular style, good at a number of them.

Breen and Blair were very different players, but the band was tight and we made it work. Life was free of hassles for a change, and the band was on cruise control.

In late 2009, I got a call that some might say was well overdue. The call was from a representative at the Canadian Academy of Recording Arts and Sciences (CARAS), the organization that presents the Juno Awards and the associated inductions into the Canadian Music Hall of Fame each year. (A Juno is the Canadian equivalent of a Grammy in the U.S.) April Wine was going to be inducted into the Canadian Music Hall of Fame in April 2010.

Over the years, AW has received eleven Juno nominations but has never stood in the winner's circle. It was disappointing not winning the first few times we were nominated, but after a while, it kind of felt unfair somehow. So it was a wonderful surprise, and I quickly shared the news with AW members past and present.

To describe the Juno event itself requires understanding what happened exactly and why things went the way they did. It certainly was an evening of mixed emotions. To win this Juno was outstanding and much appreciated, especially at a time in the band's history when it looked like it wasn't going to happen. When AW started out, I was twenty-one years old. By the time we finally got a Juno—and after selling millions of records—I was in my sixties and Jerry Mercer was in his seventies, for heaven's sake. What were they waiting for? Oh, well, better late than never.

Winning made a lot of fans happy because they believed we deserved it. It also validated their support and belief in AW over the years, and I was delighted for them. They deserved this award, too.

The first big decision to be made upon getting the news of our induction was who in AW was going to the Junos and who wasn't. It was a tough call. There were fourteen AW members in total over the forty-one-year history of the band. There was no way we were all going, and the Juno committee made that very clear. I understood completely. That's a lot of rooms, flights, and wives and girlfriends to deal with logistically, not to mention that it would be a very expensive gesture for CARAS. All members, past and present, attending the awards show was not an option offered to us.

Choosing who went and who had to watch it on the telly was difficult, for obvious reasons. Should it be just the original group, which was me, David, Ritchie, and Jim Henman? Maybe just Mercer, Moffet, Lang, and Greenway, because that lineup sold the most records? And then there's the other guys who were also in AW to consider. I knew no matter whom I chose, I would probably upset somebody. After a lot of thought and consideration, I decided to invite the current members of AW.

So I made a choice that seemed most reasonable to me, and I was ready to accept whatever grief was going to come my way because of it.

Part of my rationale when it came to LeBoeuf and Mackay getting a Juno and going to the show was that they were official band members at the time of the induction, just as Brian and I were. Second, they were accomplished professional musicians who had dedicated their entire lives to performing music right here in Canada. Over the years, I saw so many artists win a Juno who didn't deserve it and were never heard from again. I felt that these newer fellows in AW getting a statue was an okay thing.

I was pleased that certain AW members applauded the way I handled the whole situation. The Henmans in particular were gracious. They were respectful of the way I managed things under the circumstances, and I appreciated their kind words and maturity in the matter. It certainly wasn't an easy decision to make.

But not everyone agreed.

"When April Wine was inducted into the Canadian Music Industry [sic] Hall of Fame last week, they did so without veteran drummer Jerry Mercer," wrote Ian Elliot of the *Kingston Whig-Standard* as part of an interview with Jerry.

"Mercer, now 70, said that he and nine other musicians who

had played with the group over its long history had been treated 'shabbily' by Goodwyn, the only remaining original member of the group, because they all deserved to be on stage for the induction, the way they were all on stage with the band at one time or another. 'I feel sorry that it all ended on a bad note, so to speak,' he said yesterday. 'I think everyone should have been there.'"

It all ended on a bad note? Really? I guess he didn't understand the reality of the situation.

Anyway . . .

We have sold more than 20 million records worldwide to date and played for countless numbers of fans over the years, and at the time of this writing, we still headline sold-out shows throughout North America. We owe all this success to our fans. I thought it was only appropriate that a fan present the band with the Hall of Fame award.

I chose Dave Cameron, who as I've mentioned was a big AW fan and supporter. I had met Dave at some AW shows when he was hanging out and giving our crew a helping hand with the gear. I spoke with him a few times and I liked him; he's a cool guy. Dave was a sergeant in the Canadian Armed Forces at the time.

Dave Cameron remembers it well. "Around mid-February 2010, I received a call from Myles Goodwyn. Myles began by saying he wanted a fan to help induct the band into the Hall of Fame at the upcoming Junos. Needless to say, I was in shock and honoured both at the same time . . . but my answer was an absolute 'yes.'"

Besides Dave Cameron presenting in uniform, I also wanted Barry Stock, an ex-roadie/guitar tech/musician, to co-present. Barry is now a member of the internationally successful Canadian rock group Three Days Grace.

I could just picture it. One of our presenters, a serviceman in full military attire, standing toe to toe with a long-haired, hard-core rock musician, both fans of AW and showing respect and appreciation for the years of music.

Unfortunately, CARAS didn't like the idea. First of all, a fan had never presented an award before. Seriously, this is prime-time national television for heaven's sake. And two presenters? We don't think so. I stuck to my guns and, eventually, they agreed to allow Dave and Barry to be presenters on the show. Good for them, and again, thank you, CARAS.

Unfortunately, there was another glitch in the plan. Dave's superiors decided Dave could be on the show but not in uniform. What BS!

"Myles had an idea that I would present the Juno in my CF uniform," Dave Cameron later recalled. "With my being an active service person, he and I discussed this and both felt this would be a great opportunity to pay respect to our Canadian Forces serving in Canada and overseas.

"The next morning, I informed my immediate supervisor of the opportunity that was before me. He told me I needed to get an e-mail or letter from Myles indicating what he was requesting. Myles sent me a very simple, direct, to-the-point e-mail. No room for confusion.

"Approval had to come from National Defense HQ, because a CF member must gain permission prior to appearing on national television.

"I submitted my initial request on a Thursday morning. I remember that because the very next day was a Friday, and on that day, my old boss, a major, called at home after work. He was super curious how I ended up in this unique position. He too was a huge April Wine fan. Mike was over-the-top excited for me. He asked if I would be wearing my uniform during the presentation, and I told him that I hoped so as the request was 'in.'

"So, then we waited. On the morning marking the 14th day after submitting my request, EMI Music had contacted me wanting to book hotels and flights. I told them I would have to get back to them as I had not gained permission at this point in time.

"After my call with EMI, I approached my supervisor to have him check into the status of the request." Dave heard after that there was confusion about what he was actually asking for. Was he asking to attend the Junos or go to the Junos? I found this to be quite odd. The request was clear and concise.

It was recommended to him that he re-submit the request. "I immediately knew this would take too much time. EMI needed an answer right away so I simply pulled the request. I then called Myles and told him the uniform idea would not be able to happen. I told Myles that though I was extremely honoured to be considered for this opportunity, this award was about April Wine and that I would completely understand if he went in another direction seeing that my chance of wearing a uniform was now dead. He totally understood and said he would go back to the guys and figure something out. The very next day, I got another call from Myles. He said to me, 'Dave, I want you there, garb or no garb.' I was thrilled and said I would be honoured to co-present in my civilian clothing, but I was *very* unhappy with the way things were handled by the military. 'I am willing to present, as long as there is zero mention of the military as it relates to me.' Myles agreed and we moved forward."

What a great moment it would have been to show that music

transcends everything, and what a great public relations coup this would have been for our military. I was disappointed but very happy that Dave was there representing the fans.

On a live broadcast like the Junos, everything is scripted to the point of being uncommonly anal. I understand time constraints and format restrictions and so forth, but Brian and I were given two minutes from the time our feet touched the stage to say what we had to say and get off. That's rather tight to thank people for forty-one years of support. I was barely able to read a rather short list of names and Brian had time only to say "thank you" and it was over. Regardless, it was a long-awaited moment for the band, and we are sincerely grateful for the prestigious recognition.

The Junos that year were held in one of my favourite places in the world: St. John's, Newfoundland. It had been years since the city council made the band honorary Newfoundlanders with a ceremony that included being screeched in. We proudly donned our sou'westers, pounded back a shot of screech, and kissed the cod, with genuine pleasure!

Unfortunately, the evening itself was a bit odd. Justin Bieber was in the house and nothing else mattered much.

Recalling that night, Brian Greenway said he felt they were just giving us the award to get rid of us. "So many people had written in about the band being inducted . . . and deservedly so. We had been nominated so many times and never won a Juno. We never went to one, and the record company never sent the band to the Junos. I just felt like a little pretender there. We were walking down the red carpet and nobody gave a shit. The fans weren't there."

I understand what Brian means. Right after walking off

stage with our award in hand, we were led to the press room where about fifty people from the media sat with tape recorders and pads and pens in hand, supposedly doing their job of reporting events live from backstage. We stood on a small platform in front of these curious reporters, and no one asked us a question. No one gave a lick about us just being inducted into the Canadian Music Hall of Fame. Finally, one nice lady asked me a question. She was wonderful to do that. It was a good question, and I didn't rush my reply. Then it was back to silence. So we walked off stage and left the "reporters" to their job of asking Bieber what he had for breakfast.

"It all ended very abruptly because there was the warning of the volcanic ash coming [from the eruption of Grimsvotn, Iceland's most active volcano]," Brian remembers. "Everybody had to split and get to the airport by 3:00 a.m. or we couldn't get out of Newfoundland maybe for days, and other people couldn't get in to Newfoundland for the awards, like Bryan Adams. We just threw shit into suitcases, ran to the airport, and stood in line. I remember standing in this long lineup and Myles had the award. It was the Elite line. We were all musicians . . . we were Elites. There was hardly anyone in the regular line. We stood there for hours, and it was counting down to 3:00 a.m. as we left. As it turned out, nothing ever happened, but it was a precaution. We missed the big parties after the Junos, and god knows what would have happened."

Alex Bilodeau and Jasey-Jay Anderson won gold at the 2010 Winter Olympics in Vancouver. They were also at the airport that evening trying to get a flight off the island. They were going to Montreal, the same as Brian and I were. I could see that the lads were unsure of what to do because of the limited seats available and with so many people needing a seat, so I went over and introduced myself. Then I went to the lady who was handling Brian and me and told her about these two young medalists and asked if she could help them out. Sure enough, somehow she got both of them seats on the only flight to Montreal that night.

With that milestone behind us and a shiny Juno—a glass human figure wrapped in a spiralling musical staff—on the mantelpiece, it was back to touring and business as usual for April Wine.

38

After the induction into the Canadian Music Hall of Fame, April Wine went back on the road, but there were still a few more changes to occur in the band to bring us up to date.

First, Breen left the band to, as they say, milk the Quebec scene, and that was a good choice for him. Breen needed to be the boss of his destiny, and AW was not a perfect fit for him after all. I hear he's doing very well these days in the Quebec market, which is great, as he's the real deal. Breen's departure was amicable. He even suggested a replacement bass player by the name of Richard Lanthier. It was a fine suggestion, and Richard became the new bass player in AW.

Richard lives in the Laurentians north of Montreal. His background is in progressive rock, and he was playing in a Yes tribute band before joining AW. But Richard can rock hard, folks, pounding on a set of round-wound bass strings with a pick in hand, cranked through a classic Ampeg that's growling and spewing snot. Nothing like it!

I'm not a technical person, and when I need help with my Mac or my iPhone, stuff like that, I can call Richard. Richard's also great with research, and I'll take advantage of his generous nature and ask for help when I'm stumped. The <u>other</u> guys in the band know this tech-media shit in and out, too. I hear them talking another language when we're all together, when all I can do with the technology I have at my disposal amounts to about 20 percent of its capability. A waste, I know, but I'm very old school with no burning desire to learn new tricks. Even when I buy a car, I never know what half the buttons do. Anyway, Richard's a cool guy, and Brian and I are lucky to have him in the band.

AW was close to being the band it is today, but not quite. Fate would soon intervene and force one more necessary change.

Blair Mackay had gone against group policy twice during his stint in AW. He formed a band with Brian to do gigs when AW was off the road. That was definitely a no-no. AW is not to be watered down under any circumstances. This is not a new rule— it's been around since day one. When I heard about Brian and Blair forming a band together, no matter what the group was about or its purpose, it was against band rules, and I put my foot down and said, "Guys, that's not cool!"

Brian and Blair agreed and apologized, promising it wouldn't happen again. And that was that, until about a year after Breen left the band when, by sheer happenstance, I was in a town close to where I live and spotted a poster that looked, at first glance, like an AW poster. I took a closer look and realized it was a poster of a band with pictures of Brian, Blair, Breen, and some other guy. This poster featured the faces of three quarters of the AW band as we had existed only twelve months earlier. It was like John, Paul, Ringo, and Larry.

And to be more accurate, the pictures were right off the AW website. It was a blatant attempt to cash in on AW's name. I was irked, and my 100 percent fine-cotton Stanfields twisted into a tight knot.

AW had a gig a few days later in Cobourg, Ontario. That night, I spoke to Brian and Blair about the poster. They attempted to make it seem like there was nothing to it. Nothing had been planned or thought out, it was just a jam. I might not be the brightest light in the room, folks, but I'm no dimwit either. Of course it was planned out, and they had every intention of doing more gigs. I mean, if you form a group with three out of four AW members, past and present, and give the band a name, have band rehearsals, book gigs, and make posters using pictures lifted off the AW website, I'm thinking it was deliberate and thought out. They apologized, promising once more that it wouldn't happen again.

I drove home the next day, and I soon got a message from Brian informing me he was not doing the gig with Blair and Breen. He was out of the band. The fact that Brian was part of all of this nonsense at all, after the last time and the promises, really hurt. Brian knows me well enough to know I would not be pleased. I guess that's why he never brought it up to me. But Brian and I have a long history together, and that's a strong bond. I don't want things between him and me to ever end on a bad note.

Blair had to go. As far as I'm concerned, he got what he deserved.

With a big tour in Western Canada in less than two weeks, I needed a drummer immediately. I had someone in mind.

I had first heard Roy "Nip" Nichol play about three years before all this Blair nonsense at a party given by Indie Guitars in Cornwall, Ontario. I endorse Indie Guitars and even have a

Myles Goodwyn Model. It was a Halloween party, and friend and ex-Winer Steve Segal and I went to check it out. A local cover band called Sam Hill was hired for the gig. The players in Sam Hill were excellent, with great playing and vocal work. Nip's drumming and singing caught my attention, and I made a mental note to self: Remember this guy. So when Blair got the boot several years later and I needed a drummer, I called my friend Mark Owen, the owner of Indie Guitars, and he gave me Roy's contact information. Mark also said Roy was a hell of a nice man. I liked that. One thing led to the next, and voila, he's now drumming for April Wine.

Nip's joining AW was the subject of a report by Kathleen Hay of *Choose Cornwall*: "The invitation came officially last week via Myles Goodwyn, the band's leader and front man. Nichol had been approached by him on the pretense of auditioning for April Wine's warm-up group and met with the lead singer March 23 in Montreal for a jam session.

"'I was under the impression he was scouting out a drummer for their opening act,' explained Nichol. 'He'd asked me to learn four April Wine songs, and then come to his place last Friday.

"'At the end of the evening, he told me I had the job if I wanted it.'

"The drummer didn't have to think twice and immediately agreed."

Roy is a great rock drummer. His style is hard hitting, more like Jerry's style than our last drummer, and it's a welcome change. AW really does shine when there's a powerful backbeat and a heavy foot. Nip lives in Cornwall, Ontario, where he is also a recording engineer, which is cool for when we want to make history. Nip and Richard not only forge a solid rhythm section but also add background vocals to the mix, and that is so much a part of the AW sound. Nip, in particular, is an excellent singer. The fans took to the "dynamic duo" immediately, which is important in the legacy that is AW. Perhaps we'll get to record a new CD together before the band packs it in. I hope so. Meanwhile, we continue to tour, taking the winters off these days but travelling all over Canada and the States the rest of the year.

Life is good.

Epilogue

Nova Scotia is calling me. I'm a Maritimer, and I can't deny that I want to come home to "Canada's Ocean Playground."

Since I left Halifax forty-seven years ago, I have lived in the Montreal area, with the exception of several years in the Bahamas during the 1980s. The St. Lawrence River cannot replace the Atlantic Ocean, with its majestic beauty and power that has washed the coastlines of the Maritime provinces for an eternity. I have every intention of returning when I finally retire, and that time is getting closer.

After my divorce from wife number two, I was a bachelor and I acted accordingly. Lady friends of mine from coast to coast comforted me. It was a selfish period in my life, and I took advantage of their willingness to give without any concern about the consequences for them. I'm not proud of that. At the time I was only looking for company and nothing more. It was a lonely time nevertheless.

We all know it is very difficult to find the right life partner. Impossible even. That person who is the perfect fit, a soulmate, a best friend and consummate lover. I often wondered if I would ever be lucky enough to one day meet that right person. I honestly didn't think I would. I am not a young man anymore, and I didn't have the luxury of years of time ahead of me to take advantage of. I'll never marry again; it is not necessary, and besides, why jinx a good thing? After my second, and last, divorce, I was advised not to look too hard for that special person and to be patient. I was told the time would come when I was least expecting it. They were right.

AW had a gig on June 6, 2010, at the Bear Claw Casino on White Bear Lake, Saskatchewan, two hours south of Regina. Translation: in the middle of fucking nowhere.

The casino is native owned and operated and is located on the White Bear First Nations. The casino is quite nice and they treated us well. The only odd thing about the gig was that security was unnecessarily extreme. We couldn't even go down the hall to squirt without a uniformed person standing outside the toilet door.

The stage was outdoors in a field, and there were about five hundred people in attendance. There was a roped-off area for the audience for security reasons, and it started about a hundred feet or so in front of the stage.

During the show, I could not take my eyes off a beautiful, smiling face in the front row. This woman distracted me the whole time. Before the last song of the night, I waved my guitar tech aside and pointed out this lovely person and asked him to go to her right after the show and invite her backstage.

When the band finished the last song, I immediately went over to the tech and told him I'd go down front myself. I walked off the stage and went right to the front line of the crowd and motioned her to come to where I was standing. She made her way to me, smiling that gorgeous smile of hers. I couldn't help but notice that she had a lovely body to go with the lovely smile. Schwing! I asked her if she'd like to come backstage with me. She said, "Yes!" And as they say, folks, the rest is history!

The beautiful lady's name is Kim Nyles. Her mother is of Nakota descent and her dad is Polish.

That encounter was six years ago, and we are very happy together and enjoying our good fortune because of that chance meeting in the middle of Fucking Nowhere, Saskatchewan.

I still have the house in the Montreal area, and recently I acquired a place in Nova Scotia so Kim and I can spend our summers near the ocean. We have a townhouse in the Dominican to escape the Canadian winters.

Besides the ocean drawing me back to the east coast, I have friends and family here. It is brilliant being near them these days after so many years living in other parts of the world. Life here on the east coast is laid back and good for the soul. We both love it here. But, hey, what's not to love?

In a few weeks, I'll be going into the studio to finally finish my bluesy CD titled *Myles Goodwyn and Friends of the Blues*. It just needs to be mixed and mastered. I really like how it turned out thus far. I managed to write a collection of quality blues songs after all, and I was fortunate that the blues guys I contacted about contributing their talents to the project were all on board. A partial list of the players on the CD are David Wilcox, Amos Garrett, Jack de Keyzer, Rick Derringer, Kenny "Blues Boss" Wayne, Frank Marino, and Garrett Mason. It will be released in 2016.

In 2014, I started a non-profit organization with my friend

Dr. Stan Van Duyse. It's called Soleful Caring—Shoes for the Homeless. Dr. Stan and I both have diabetes. He's been diabetic much longer than I have, and of course, being a doctor, he understands the disease and the complications that can occur if it is not treated properly. We talked about the importance of protecting our feet and how difficult it must be for homeless men and woman to do so without proper footwear. Dr. Stan stresses that all human beings living on the streets need to look after their feet in order to survive, not just people with diabetes. It is a basic human requirement. "I think it's very important to get good shoes on all of the homeless," he said in an interview. "But I certainly think that diabetics should be prioritized."

I thought about these discussions Stan and I had until, finally, a few years later, I decided to try to do something to help collect and distribute gently worn boots and shoes to the homeless in Canada.

This is what I had to say about the motivation for starting up Soleful Caring: "I have a sensitivity regarding proper footwear and the importance of protecting my feet that is both physical and emotional. Physically, being a diabetic, it is very important to protect my feet from cuts and sores and other problems that can occur if the feet are not properly protected and extra care taken in looking after them. Those of us with diabetes risk losing our toes, feet, and even our legs, due to complications caused by neglecting proper care of our feet. Being homeless, whether or not a diabetic, is a challenge. We can help.

"The emotional connection for me goes back to my youth. I was brought up in a family that was financially challenged and wearing worn-out shoes was a fact of life. I used to put cardboard in my shoes to keep the small nails from digging into my feet.

Even to this day, if I see someone wearing shoes or boots that are 'beat up' and worn down on the heels, it touches my heart in a deep, dark, and sad place.

"I also had an uncle who died homeless on the streets of Montreal many years ago. He was from Nova Scotia.

"I've been very fortunate in my life, folks. I have what I need for myself and my family. Soleful Caring gives me the opportunity to give back. I hope that you will join me in helping those in need of proper footwear this year and in the years to follow. Be well."

Soleful Caring has partnered with Shelter Nova Scotia, Value Village, the Canadian Diabetes Association, and most recently, the National Recycling Organization of Canada in collecting and donating pairs of gently worn shoes and boots to thousands of homeless persons from coast to coast. If you wish to learn more about our organization and how you can help, please go to our website at solefulcaring.com.

As I was writing this book, I stayed true to course and told the truth, the whole truth, and nothing but the truth, as I know it, so help me. Writing my memoir was not easy at times, and I'm sure you can understand and appreciate that. Personal faults are especially difficult to expose, at the risk of leaving oneself vulnerable for easy criticism—I get enough as it is—but I felt it was important to be completely honest, regardless.

I tried my damnedest not to be vengeful when finding the right words to describe or explain people and situations, although there were a few moments when it would have given me great personal pleasure to do so. But the high road prevailed.

Now that it's all been said and documented in these pages, it's mission accomplished. I can rest easy knowing that family, friends, and fans will understand the way it really was. It certainly was a rocky journey at times filled with excitement, laughter, pain, and sorrow, but that's life and I mostly appreciate it for what it has been.

I have regrets, of course. I wish I had been more moderate in my lifestyle choices. The abuse of booze and drugs over the years has left marks unwelcome later in life. Physically and emotionally.

Although, at the time, I rationalized my reasons for including Breen LeBoeuf and Blair Mackay in the list of AW band members to get a Canadian Music Hall of Fame award, I wish I hadn't, to be honest. Both left the band shortly after for reasons I've already explained in these pages. How was I to know their time in AW would be short-lived? Oh, well. Live and learn.

I have the reputation of being a cheap, selfish, self-serving so-and-so, or so I've been told. That kind of goes with the territory, folks, especially when you wear all the hats that I do in this band. I'm an easy target. I'm used to it. The fact is, I'm a generous person. How generous? Well, I'll tell you, but you might want to take a seat for this.

From the time AW got back together in the early '90s, and for years after, I paid each member in the band equally. So when Breen, Blair, and Steve Segal joined the band, they received the same money I did. I had logged twenty-five years in this band, and yet, when we performed live, the new guys got the very same pay I got, right from day one. And an equal share of the merchandise! Yes, I know! Does that sound like a cheap, selfish person to you? I was generous to a fault and I realize that now, but what's done is done. People who don't know me should shush with the detrimental, baleful comments.

To be clear, I never shared a nickel of my hard-earned writing, producing, or publishing royalties, or any other income derived from my personal livelihood, with other members. I'm not *that* generous.

Looking back, I most regret the time I didn't give to my children when they were young. I was away from home so much during my career that I missed out on the important day-to-day stuff that really defines a family. Even when I wasn't touring, I was unreasonably unavailable because I was always writing new material or in a recording studio or just doing my own thing. I could have managed my personal time better back in those days, but I didn't. I was selfish, and now those opportunities have long passed us all by.

I love my children deeply, and it hurts to think about the catastrophic impact that my two divorces had on them. "What if?" is a question that should be ignored as it serves no good purpose and has no relevance anymore, but still, it haunts me and it always will, I suppose.

These days life is real good. I have my health, although managing my diabetes is a constant challenge, especially when touring, yet I can't complain. A few years ago, I announced that I was retiring. I was finding the travel too much. After almost fifty years in the band and the effects of diabetes, I was getting tired.

We held auditions to find someone to replace me, but the other guys in the band didn't think there was a single person who auditioned who could do the job well enough. As much as I wanted to retire, I had to agree. Finding a replacement proved to be a lot more difficult than we thought it would be. So I compromised and agreed to stay on for a few more years at a reduced touring schedule. They're cool with that arrangement, more or less, and for me, it's ideal. I get to have my cake and eat it, too. The fans were happy to hear I was sticking it out a while longer, albeit doing fewer concert dates during the year.

I'm busy creating, on my own terms finally. I have my blues project and my charity, and they are wonderful, satisfying adventures for me to explore.

My first novel, *Elvis and Tiger*, is nearly finished. The Myles Goodwyn Band will be going into the recording studio this year. AW might even do another CD. We'll see. Yes, indeed, times are good, folks.

Finally, I have the love of a good woman, and I'm a very lucky guy to have her in my life. I appreciate her every day I wake up in this world.

I spend time with my children when they have time for their old man. Of course they are no longer children, and their lives are full. My daughter made me a grandfather for the first time in 2014. Our times together, at this time in my life, are precious, and I'll take what I can get.

The world these days presents a very different reality from when I was their ages, and I worry, as parents do, about the fate of the world, the planet they inherited, and their future.

I'm not a religious man, but I'm still trying to mature spiritually. I want to learn patience. To accept the changes my body's going through at this time in my life. As stated, in part, in the Serenity Prayer, I want to learn to accept the things I cannot change, and have the courage to change the things I can and the wisdom to know the difference.

To quote Mark Twain: "Twenty years from now you will be more disappointed by the things you didn't do than by the ones you did do. So throw off the bowlines. Sail away from the safe harbour. Catch the trade winds in sails. Explore. Dream. Discover."

Be well.

Acknowledgements

When I decided to write this book, I knew I would need some help. As it turned out, I needed lots of help. I was up for the challenge and the fun of writing the story of my journey through life thus far, but I was not prepared—nor did I have the experience—to gather outside material, conduct interviews, and piece all the related information together to form a book. In my opinion, no one knows the Canadian music business better than Mr. Martin Melhuish, and so I was delighted when Marty accepted my invitation to help me put this book together. During the time it took to finish the project, we became great friends, and that's a very cool bonus. Thanks, Marty.

Thanks to all at HarperCollins, in particular Jim Gifford, who helped me understand how to manoeuvre through the trials and tribulations of writing this memoir. He was always patient and encouraging during the process. My appreciation is considerable. Also a special thanks to Patricia MacDonald, Noelle Zitzer, Alison Woodbury, and Michael Millar for their expertise.

And mostly, a big thanks to my friends and fans, and the fans of April Wine. Without your years of support, this book would not have been possible.